Welcome to the Wired World

We are all great abbreviators. None of us has the wit to know the whole truth, the time to tell it if we believed we did, or an audience so gullible as to accept it.

Aldous Huxley, *Brave New World*, 1932

Always be ready to accept the naked truth about yourself and others; and you'll get far in life by doing right and being good. Failure to grow and prosper is often caused by an inability to face the truth or sheer ignorance on behalf of individuals involved. However, remember that most people want to do well and be successful. It is very rare for people to deliberately set out to become a failure or cause damage to others. If people are given reasons to feel secure and appreciated, and provided with opportunities to grow and learn, then people will prosper and we will have a better world. In my experience this is true at all levels in our lives – whether professional or personal.

Anne Leer, 1999

The new networked economy

Welcome to the Wired World

Anne Leer

To my most important teachers – Michelle, Marte and Per.
They gave me the ability to believe in people's good nature and
the courage to face the world with honesty and openness.

PEARSON EDUCATION LIMITED

Head Office
Edinburgh Gate
Harlow CM20 2JE
Tel: +44 (0)1279 623 623
Fax: +44 (0)1279 431 059

London Office:
128 Long Acre, London WC2E 9AN
Tel: +44 (0)207 447 2000
Fax: +44 (0)207 240 5771
www.business-minds.com

First published in Great Britain in 2000

© Anne Leer 2000

The right of Anne Leer to be identified as author
of this work has been asserted by her in accordance
with the Copyright, Designs and Patents Act 1988.

ISBN 0 273 63560 3

British Library Cataloguing in Publication Data
A CIP catalogue record for this book can be obtained from the British Library.

All rights reserved; no part of this publication may be reproduced, stored
in a retrieval system, or transmitted in any form or by any means, electronic,
mechanical, photocopying, recording, or otherwise without either the prior
written permission of the Publishers and the author. This book may not be lent,
resold, hired out or otherwise disposed of by way of trade in any form
of binding or cover other than that in which it is published, without the
prior consent of the Publishers.

10 9 8 7 6 5 4 3

Typeset by Pantek Arts, Maidstone, Kent
Printed and bound in Great Britain by Biddles Ltd, Guildford and Kings Lynn.

The Publishers' policy is to use paper manufactured from sustainable forests.

Contents

Foreword ■ **ix**
Acknowledgements ■ **xi**
Introduction ■ **xiii**

1 Visions of the Wired World
The shrinking planet ■ **1**
Imagining the future ■ **3**
Market drivers and key agents of change ■ **6**
Hype versus reality – guru talk and those great ideas ■ **7**

2 The Global Information Infrastructure
Emerging global systems ■ **11**
The rise of the Global Information Infrastructure (GII) ■ **17**

3 Technology
The development of media and
communications technologies – from Gutenberg to Gates ■ **27**
Innovation and the rate of change ■ **32**
Managing technological investments ■ **36**

4 The market
The search for a market and the challenge of sizing it ■ **39**
The meaning of convergence ■ **45**
The new evolving market structure ■ **47**
Redefining the market ■ **48**

5 Content
What content, which customer? ■ **51**
The trouble with information assets ■ **53**
The intellectual property system ■ **56**
Copyright ■ **58**

6 Electronic commerce

Defining electronic commerce ■ **74**
Trends in, and the value of, e-markets ■ **75**
Information transactions – tangible versus intangible assets ■ **76**
The challenge of security ■ **78**
Cryptography and the role of encryption technology ■ **79**
Transactional systems for network commerce ■ **83**
Possible future developments ■ **93**

7 The networked economy

Towards the Knowledge Age ■ **96**
Human capital and knowledge management ■ **97**
Barriers to be resolved ■ **102**
Conditions for market efficiency and potential risk ■ **105**
Projections of future developments ■ **107**

8 Wired organizations

Challenges and strategic responses of key players ■ **109**
Publishers in a mixed media environment ■ **112**
Digital television ■ **123**
Transforming advertising ■ **126**
Value creation and changing business models ■ **129**

9 Public services

Reinventing government ■ **139**
Lifelong learning and the rapid transformation of the education sector ■ **141**
Global overview of ICT initiatives in education ■ **145**
The call for public- and private-sector partnerships ■ **150**

10 People

The individual citizen and the Wired World ■ **155**
The opportunities and impact of teleworking ■ **159**
Net addiction and other cyberspace side-effects ■ **164**
The digital divide ■ **166**
The Global Information Society versus information city states ■ **168**

Appendices

1 Chapter 1 of the Bangemann Report
*Europe and the global information society:
Recommendations to the European Council, 26 May 1994* ■ **170**

2 Speech of US Vice President Al Gore at the International
Telecommunication Union's first World Telecommunications Development
Conference, Buenos Aires, March 1994 ■ **180**

3 Speech of US Vice President Al Gore, 15th International
ITU Conference, 12 October 1998 ■ **192**

Select bibliography and further reading ■ **203**

Glossary ■ **207**

Index ■ **217**

Foreword

The long-heralded global village is upon us. The arrival of digital communication networks is having a profound impact upon societies around the world, forever changing the way we do business and live our lives. Yet we have scarcely begun to exploit what today's communication technology is capable of, let alone plan for future developments, which will bring new discoveries and intelligent technology far beyond our current imagination.

The development of wireless communications is racing ahead and will eventually supersede and replace the fixed communication networks some time into the 21st century. It is starting now, with cellular networks, mobile phones and pagers, wearable computing devices, wristwatch communicators, etc.

During the coming decade, more and more people, business executives and journalists will be carrying communication devices that permit direct two-way communication with their homes or offices, via the most convenient satellite. These will provide voice, data, video and Internet facilities as well as satellite TV links. Imagine what this means for business as well as personal communications.

Consider the opportunity this brings to further democracy and freedom. No government or organisation will be able to conceal, at least for very long, evidence of crimes or atrocities. The existence of widely accessible information channels, operating in real time and across all frontiers, will be a powerful influence encouraging civilised behaviour. If you are arranging a massacre, it will be useless to shoot the cameraperson who has so inconveniently appeared on the scene. His or her picture will already be safe in the studio 5000 kilometres away; and those images may hang you.

Technology is exciting and provides us with endless opportunities to break new boundaries and achieve new accomplishments. However, technology itself is merely a tool and a vehicle for development. Man is still the master. It is up to the human race to determine the purpose and the outcome of its use. The same technology can of course be used for both good and bad purposes. Anne Leer calls this the challenging paradox of technological invention – with technology we can destroy or create, waste or preserve, lose or win. The choice is ours.

Modern warfare is based on communication technology, but so is the fight for peace and prosperity. Those who control the access to communication technology and the content of global media can exercise a new kind of electronic cultural imperialism which has the potential to eradicate local culture, change national identity and destroy much that is good. Yet the same media and communication technology is also making it possible to preserve for future generations the customs, performing arts and ceremonies of our time, in a way that was not possible in the past.

Of course, there are a great many present-day customs, which should not be preserved, except as a warning to future generations: slavery, torture, racial and religious persecution, treatment of women as chattels, mutilation of children because of ancient superstition, cruelty to animals – the list is endless and no country can proclaim total innocence. I wish I could claim that improved communications capabilities would inevitably lead to peace, but the matter is not as simple as that. Such an aspiration requires the use of far more uniquely human qualities such as empathy, tolerance, understanding. Nevertheless, good communications of every type, and at all levels, are essential if we are ever to establish peace on this planet.

As the century which saw the birth of both electronics and optronics draws to a close, it would seem that virtually everything we would wish to do in the field of communications is now technically possible. The only limitations are financial, legal, or political. In time, I am sure, most of these will disappear, leaving us with only the limitations of our own morality. There will always be those who seek to abuse any technology for their own ends but I can only hope that they will remain, as throughout history, in the minority. In any event, the surest answer to such profiteers is for society to remove the need on which they depend for their survival.

The next millennium will be, I am sure, even more amazing than the last. Never before in our history have we been able to enjoy such a tremendous amount of a simple human freedom – choice. We are now faced with the responsibility of discernment. As we begin to learn how to cope with massive amounts of information and rapidly changing technology we also understand that it is not the information itself nor technology that determines our future; only the use we can make of it.

Sir Arthur C Clarke
Columbo, September 1999

Acknowledgements

Books are never created by the author alone – and this book is certainly no exception. Many people past and present have influenced and shaped this work. I am indebted to them all for helping me develop and communicate my thoughts and perspectives, enabling me to make a little more sense out of our complicated and fascinating world. In particular, I am deeply affected and touched by the outstanding works of Heidi and Alvin Toffler, and honoured to have them contribute to my books. If you haven't yet read their books, go buy them all!

This book would not have been written had it not been for the positive encouragement and generosity of my friends, and the support of colleagues working in the media and publishing industry around the world. Special thanks to my colleagues at Oxford University Press, and to John Dale at the BBC, whose professional insights I greatly appreciate.

I would also like to extend my gratitude to Pradeep Jethi, Elizabeth Truran and Martin Drewe for their patience and enthusiastic support and to the rest of the publishing team at Pearson Education who have made this book possible. I could not wish for a better publisher.

To all of you who have given me input and inspirations along the way, thank you!

Introduction

'Pick up virtually any magazine or newspaper these days and you will be told, by advertising or editorial, that the electronic future is here. This is a future in which the world will run on digital communication networks, fibre-optic cables and satellites, in which your home will become an "interactive information/entertainment centre", your office a filling station on the "electronic highway" – and everything from your bank to your back-ache will be processed through a computer' (Brian Murphy, *The World Wired Up*, Comedia, 1983).

These words were written back in 1983, but, in fact, this statement rings just as true today as it did then. Evidently, delivering the promises of the much-heralded 'information society' takes a long time. Contrary to popular opinion, learning how to utilize progress takes time. The cheerleaders and promoters of the Wired World have called for our immediate response to the information revolution for well over three decades now. If it is a revolution, it must be the longest-running one in history.

Perhaps the sense of urgency is misguided and what we are witnessing is a deep evolutionary shift that takes considerable effort and time to assimilate and respond appropriately to. Rather than the quick and instant fix of a well-understood revolution, what we are faced with is a rapidly changing technology-dependent environment that requires us to deal with change at all levels in our lives. What we need is a much more organic and holistic approach if we are to survive in a changing environment that we

What is urgent is that we develop strategies for change to avoid being drawn into business-blind technology-driven actions.

no longer can control or understand by ourselves and where most of our trusted models of thinking and managing seem to break down or be totally inadequate. What is urgent is that we develop strategies for change to avoid being drawn into business-blind technology-driven actions.

By now, nobody should dispute the essential importance of taking part in the development of the Global Information Society and that we need to truly welcome the Wired World. Our nations' competitiveness depends on our involvement and skill in shaping the new networked economy. However, many organizations are rushing into action for the wrong reasons and without clear objectives, driven by a sense of panic and fear of being left behind. It may be good to get on to the learning curve earlier rather than later, but it can also prove to be very expensive: 'Experience is a good teacher, but she sends in terrific bills' (Minna Antrim, *Collins Dictionary of Quotations*, Collins, 1995).

Managers often feel pressured to be seen to be doing something in the digital domain and, consequently, allow their organizations to dip a toe into experimental waters and set up a few web sites, and invest in multimedia and information and communication technology without any clear business strategy driving such decisions. Active research, experimentation and pilot projects are essential activities if any organization is to be competitive in a changing market. However, more often, the toe-dipping or half-hearted investments in information and communications technology is something managers do rather reluctantly, with no real enthusiasm for what is new, and without any long-term commitment to such research and development. Toe-dipping in digital waters can be a welcome escape strategy, designed to make management and shareholders alike feel comfortable, rather than entrepreneurial. It can lull managers into an operational sleep mode where they believe they can carry on more or less as before and where no one will force them to face up to any major decisions about digital opportunities. Hiding behind rather meaningless web sites – which merely serve as a poor screen version of the annual report or the product catalogues – is only going to benefit the competition and bar a company's access to future growth.

Toe-dipping in digital waters can be a welcome escape strategy, designed to make management and shareholders alike feel comfortable, rather than entrepreneurial.

Experimentation that does not have full management backing and funding usually fails and, by doing so, gives research and development into digital applications a bad reputation as the experience becomes 'lots of expenditure for nothing'. The need to get properly involved is urgent for those who want to be competitive or who want to be in the driving seat for developments. Organizations and individuals that haven't already done so should really go for a deep dive into those digital waters and submerge themselves in all the new opportunities flooding everyone's way. But, a word of warning: don't go diving before you know how to swim and don't set sail before you know how to navigate. Read some books first and listen and learn from other people and organizations in the marketplace.

Another sad indication of leadership failure is the common observation that management will leave crucial decisions in information and communication technology investment that will fundamentally affect the entire business to their IT departments or outside consultancy firms. IT professionals are, by definition, technology oriented and, as wonderful and capable as they may be, they are not qualified to run the company and should not be expected, or allowed, to make the decisions that belong with senior management. In many organizations, the new business processes have sneaked in the wrong way, via IT departments. Perhaps in some cases it could be said, 'Oh well, better that way than no way at all'. However, it is a very expensive lesson for many organizations that have to suffer the cost of bad investments. For instance, consider how poorly many companies run their intranets and web sites. The implementation of information and communication technology needs to be driven by the overall business strategy and integrated with business processes.

What is really urgent is that we invest resources in the understanding of change and develop strategies to take advantage of these changes. Haste, combined with short-term vision and fragmented thinking, is a widespread contemporary disease. Instead, we need to focus more clearly on what exactly it is we want to achieve, not allow technological events and shifting market pressures to dictate our direction. Throwing huge sums of money at anything with the words 'digital' or 'Internet' on it will save neither the world nor corporate profits.

> **Throwing huge sums of money at anything with the words 'digital' or 'Internet' on it will save neither the world nor corporate profits.**

Buying a multimedia PC in order to improve your child's education will not guarantee educational success or turn your child into a high achiever. Merely owning a piece of technology does not deliver instant results. Technology is, at its best, a means to an end, not the end itself. Technology delivers tools designed with a particular purpose in mind, but the purpose is defined by human intelligence and ambition, not technology. Technology itself is dead. It only comes alive when there is human intervention. The interesting challenge is to apply and extend all the various tools technology is providing us with. To reap the benefits of technology, we need to know what we want to achieve, understand the applications of various technologies, find the appropriate tools and learn to master them.

Results will depend on how the technology is being used, the content and support available and who the individual user is. That is, the individual user's skills and capacity for interaction with available content and tools are critical factors for success. The most significant dependent variables on the chart of success are not of a technological but a human nature. Whether your child will benefit from using a multimedia PC or the Internet will depend much more on the quality of the learning environment and on the content than on the technology and mechanics of operating the PC.

Similarly, providing all your employees with Internet connections will not guarantee the company a secure future or deliver any instant results beyond a significantly larger telephone bill. Investing in a Global System for Mobile (GSM) phone may make you more available and give you that ego-boosting feeling of being very well connected, but it will not make you instantly more productive. Even the cutting edge of digital telecommunications will not change your ability to generate economic value – only you can do that.

Enough of technological scepticism. It is happening – the 'electronic future', the Wired World, is here, at least in terms of technical achievements. Information technology has invaded our environment and its influence will continue to spread, probably without us even noticing. Think of how we take the TV, fax, mobile phone or e-mail for granted. The most significant change often happens almost without us paying any attention to it. It is a fact that digital communication networks will cover the globe before long and bring significant changes to most aspects of society.

It doesn't take the artist long to buy the paint, but it takes considerable knowledge, talent and a very long time to master the art of using it.

If you are aware of the past and have taken the opportunity to learn about history, you will know that the concept of the information society is not a new one. Throughout history, wise political leaders, philosophers and writers have seen the importance of intellectual creations and information as fundamental to the acquisition of power, economic growth and social benefits.

In all parts of our society, people are talking of transformation and the need to master the processes of change. However, there seems to be much confusion as to exactly what the scope, value and implications of these changes are beyond those in the short term. Furthermore, the rate of change is typically exaggerated, as the quotation at the start of this introduction clearly demonstrates. It doesn't take the artist long to buy the paint, but it takes considerable knowledge, talent and a very long time to master the art of using it.

So, how far have we come, what impacts have digital technologies had on our society, and how much really has changed? What are the key strategic issues that we need to tackle in the new networked economy? And what are the challenges and options for governments, businesses and people as we move deeper into our Wired World? This book sets out to seek some answers, but I believe I will only succeed in scratching the surface of all these complicated topics and hopefully give you some inspiration to help you find your own answers. This book has been published as a companion volume to my book *Masters of the Wired World*, which brings together contributions from 42 leading voices from different parts of the globe representing industry, government and people. You may find it useful to refer to that book to enrich your reading of this book with a journey through real-life examples and a whole range of fascinating perspectives on our new civilization in the making.

1

Visions of the Wired World

The shrinking planet

At the turn of the century, the business world is under immense pressure to change and adapt appropriately and quickly enough to secure competitiveness and future growth. Organizations across the board feel the impact of increased competition, globalization and digitization. To survive and prosper, individuals and organizations alike will have to master constant change and growing complexity. The mapping of power across our planet is being redrawn and the race is on to win the market shares of the new networked economy. To win, organizations will need to reinvent and create their business models in line with fast-changing market demands. To manage the supply chain, they will need to put in place highly effective processes to grow and exploit human capital.

As advances in technology leap ahead the world is becoming smaller, but, paradoxically, at the same time, the world is also becoming larger – smaller in terms of time and geographical distance and communications; larger in terms of market reach and competition, scalability and complexity of operations, product/service offering and economic impact. This trend is also reflected in the combination of proliferation and consolidation of market operators. There is a growing number of successful individuals and small enterprises working alongside each other or together, with a decreasing number of very large, multinational corporations – global giants that keep getting bigger as they continue to expand through mergers and acquisitions.

One of the reasons for the growing success of individual and small enterprises is the fact that it is easier for them to master change as they do not have the same burden of legacy problems and rigidity that large organizations have. The essential properties of resilience and velocity – which determine the ability to adapt to

> **The essential properties of resilience and velocity are more often demonstrated by smaller organizations than large ones.**

fast-changing environments – are more often demonstrated by smaller organizations than large ones. Just as vital are the abilities to innovate, create and learn, which also seem to be more difficult the larger organizations become. Easier for small to be beautiful, the challenge is for the large to learn the art of being beautiful, too. Unless they do, I fear we face a grim future in terms of quality of life in the Wired World. The supplies of meaningful content and high-value services, as well as cultural diversity, are at risk if the main corporate stakeholders fail to facilitate creativity and the development of human capital.

> **The supplies of meaningful content and high-value services, as well as cultural diversity, are at risk if the main corporate stakeholders fail to facilitate creativity and the development of human capital.**

A manufacturing company based in Wales can finance its operations in the United States, run production in remote parts of China, assemble in Denmark and ship from Germany. The customer can purchase goods and services in cyberspace and the point of consumption and the place of residence may be irrelevant or even impossible to determine. Fundamental concepts of commerce and politics no longer seem to work properly as traditional borders have shifted or even disappeared.

There is a mismatch between, on the one hand, our conventional commercial and political road maps and traffic rules and, on the other, the changing landscape of the Wired World and the way in which the new networked economy is actually working. We need to look beyond geographical borders, national jurisdictions, legal domains and markets of the past to be effective tomorrow. We need to learn to think in new ways and expand our vocabulary to account for the new phenomena. Just think how inadequate the term 'country of origin' has become in a trading reality where goods are produced in global operations – 'world of origin' would be more accurate, but legally meaningless.

The application of communication networks and digital technologies has changed the constraints of time and space, shifted geographical and industrial borders, and reduced the importance of physical location. Time, location and national jurisdictions still matter, and will continue to do so. These concepts will not be eradicated by the digital network revolution, as some have suggested. What's happening is change, not obliteration.

Computer technology is all around and has transformed our lives – the way we do business, conduct scientific research, provide education, practise medicine, create art, how we run the country, preserve our history, travel from one place to another, function at home, communicate with one another and

Time, location and national jurisdictions still matter, and will continue to do so. These concepts will not be eradicated by the digital network revolution.

so on. Business correspondence that used to take days to deliver is now instantly communicated via fax or e-mail. Newsworthy events from around the world are transmitted live into our homes as and when they happen. Scientists publish and discuss their research on global networks. Children do their homework on PCs, using the Internet to access all kinds of information. Doctors supervise operations remotely via telemedicine networks, no longer always having to be physically present in the operating theatre. People can stay in touch and access global networks from anywhere in the world using digital mobile phones. Supermarkets and other retailers operating across national borders accumulate detailed records of individual customers' shopping patterns – who buys what, when, and where.

Imagining the future

The Global Information Society is like an island that is barely visible on the horizon, still some distance ahead. We can see it from our current standpoint, but only through today's spectacles. Our experience of the past and what we know today restricts our vision. The success of our journey will largely depend on the ability to adapt, our willingness to change and sail into unfamiliar waters. As we sail further towards this island of tomorrow, we discover more and more details and begin to understand the complexities of the new.

One difficulty with describing the current state of the Global Information Society is that people have different views of the world. It is very hard to get the main operators in the marketplace and the policy makers and regulators in governments to agree and share a common perspective on what the Global Information Society is all about.

It gets even more difficult to establish some kind of consensus about expectations of future developments, particularly with respect to technology. Even the inventors themselves often fail to understand the market potential and functionality of their own inventions. For instance, Alexander Graham Bell who invented the telephone didn't see its communication potential and suggested it should be used for transmitting concerts.

History demonstrates that 'the future' is a moving target. People's concepts of the future change with experience and exposure to new technologies. The future is never what it used to be. Forecasts of the future rarely stand the test of time and can never be accurate, as decision parameters will and do change. We cannot usefully measure the unknown.

Nevertheless, speculating about and planning the future is an important activity. In fact, we have the power to shape the future with decisions and actions we make, both as individuals and organizations. Gazing into that crystal ball, attempting to visualize what the future will bring and what role we will play, is essential in order to move forward. We need a concept of the future, to be able to define our objectives and set our course in the right direction. Without any vision of the future, we would not be able to stimulate developments or motivate those who will bring progress and deliver results.

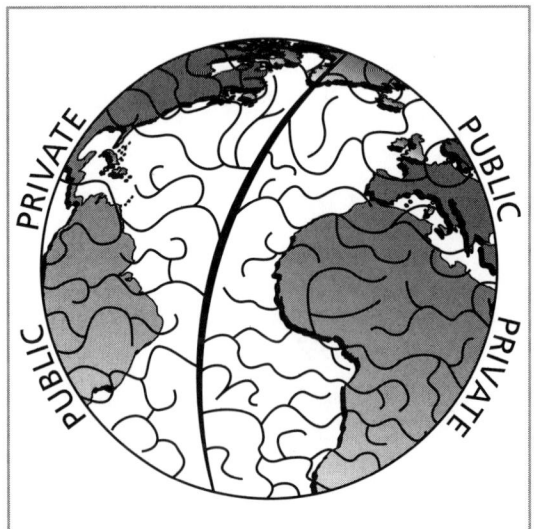

Figure 1.1: the political vision of the Global Information Society – a digital nervous system for public and private sectors

Our visions of the future will drive us in a certain direction and influence the choices we make about where we want to be tomorrow. That is why it is important to examine what the future vision of the Global Information Society is and what expectations will follow.

There seem to be three main visions driving the development of the Global Information Society, which are the:

- political vision (see Figure 1.1);
- commercial vision (see Figure 1.2);
- social vision (see Figure 1.3).

The political vision of the future

The predominant political vision of the Global Information Society identifies it as the key to prosperity – that is, to a society that optimizes the use of digital technologies to secure growth by means of an interconnected world where organizations and individuals live more happily networked ever after. The political vision can be referred to as an electronic or digital nervous system for government, education, healthcare, culture and commerce.

The commercial vision of the future

The commercial vision of the Global Information Society is that of a global marketplace consisting of numerous electronic shopping malls. The dominant players advocating this concept come from the entertainment, communication and information industries. Telecommunications, software, media and electronics companies are all investing heavily in what they see as a new market for their products and services. They will want to charge in a variety of different ways for network access, content and other services. This vision is of the Global Information Society as the ultimate global marketplace where all consumers can be reached individually, via their network connections – a marketer's dream come true! Sellers of all kinds of goods and services can finally capture us all as they know precisely when we are where, who we are, what we buy and what we do.

Figure 1.2: the commercial vision of the Global Information Society – e-commerce heaven of a global marketplace with electronic shopping malls

The social vision of the future

There is a third vision of the Global Information Society, which is that of a social phenomenon – a virtual village green with open networks for individuals to communicate and share ideas on an informal basis. This vision is strongly held by many Internet users, who will want to preserve the use of the Internet as a place to access free information and learn, a place for scientists and academics to exchange and develop knowledge.

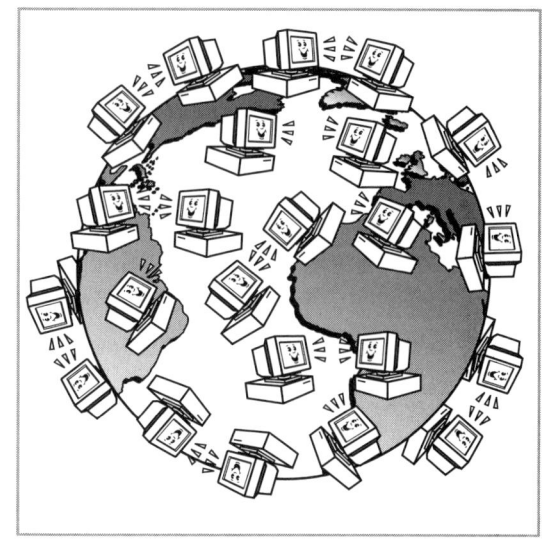

Figure 1.3: the social vision of the Global Information Society – a virtual village green

> **It will be increasingly important to separate the economics of constructing the public and the private sectors of the Global Information Society.**

These different visions are not mutually exclusive and the development of the Global Information Society should be able to accommodate all three. However, it will be increasingly important to separate the economics of constructing the public and the private sectors of the Global Information Society, including, for instance, the cost of maintaining the social value of the Internet and the cost of funding continued access to education and cultural heritage.

Market drivers and key agents of change

Visions of the future are important agents of change, motivating people and organizations to make decisions that will ultimately have an impact on future realities. For instance, because powerful corporations and governments across the world believe in their visions of a Wired World, considerable investment and effort is made to turn those visions and promises into reality.

There are other equally important market drivers and agents of change, such as technological drivers, political drivers and socio-economic drivers. Together, these market drivers all influence the structuring and the content of the new networked economy and determine the distribution of investment across the various building blocks required for the Global Information Infrastructure (GII).

Most of us are familiar with the technological drivers – the development of computer technology, multimedia and digital networks, resulting in a proliferation of new distribution channels, media delivery platforms and communication devices.

The socio-economic drivers stem from a range of fundamental social and economy-based changes taking place across society – changes in demographics, market structures, consumer behaviour, people's lifestyles and the ways organizations operate. The growing demand for access to knowledge and more effective education is a significant driver. The fact that governments across the world have defined education and the GII as essential keys to wealth creation and competitiveness has made it a strong political driver for change throughout the public and private sectors. The world needs to tackle the growing problems of illiteracy and innumeracy and find ways of raising educational standards.

Hype versus reality – guru talk and those great ideas

Listening to our political leaders deliver their grand visions of the Global Information Society, it is easy to get carried away, believing that getting wired is the all-important answer to 'everything' – the stairway to heaven, or at least the new world to come.

There is a lot of hype about the Global Information Society generated by political leaders as well as so-called corporate visionaries and 'experts' in the field. We are being told that, soon, every office, every home, every school, every hospital – as well as every individual, business and government in the world – will be connected to the GII! There will be instant access to everything from anywhere for everyone via the GII. The GII will be the ultimate one-stop shop. The GII will provide us with entertainment, education, work, healthcare, financial services, love and friendship and all kinds of information. The GII will penetrate every aspect of society and will bring fundamental change to the way we work and live our lives.

A senior manager at IBM told delegates at a conference in London to expect Transmission Control Protocol/Internet Protocol (TCP/IP) Internet connection in their fridges before long: 'Wouldn't it be great if the fridge could call you at work or in your car to let you know you were out of milk and tell you to buy some on the way home?'(John Patrick of IBM, speaking at the World Internet Conference in June 1996). Better still, the fridge could call the on-line home shopping service direct and make sure you never ran out of milk.

I am not sure I feel comfortable with the idea of letting my fridge do my shopping. What if something went wrong here and my fridge ordered 100 bottles of milk instead of the one I wanted? Would I have to pay? Who would be liable for my fridge's behaviour and shopping activities? Would it be the shop, the network operator, the on-line shopping service, the network service provider, the retailer who sold me the fridge, the software company that made the program, the manufacturer of the fridge, the manufacturer of the computer terminal that makes the fridge interactive, my credit card company, my bank – or me? I think I feel safer with the milkman, who still delivers to my doorstep.

Nicholas Negroponte of the MIT Medialab is excited about what he calls 'body area networks' and the idea of 'wearable computers', which take the form of a multipurpose wristwatch that also includes a phone, pager, television, radio and computer, the computing power for which is housed in the heel of the wearer's shoe! He talks about digital technology being woven into the fabric of our lives, and quite literally too.

At the Conservative Party conference on 'The Challenge of Cyberspace' in July 1996, MP David Shaw announced that 'The Internet may well be the biggest thing to happen to mankind since the Creation'. GII prophets rave about how we are now about to experience the biggest upheaval since the Industrial Revolution and the GII will have even more impact than the invention of the printing press. All this hype is then amplified by the media, fee-hungry management consultants and conference organizers. Reports are often biased and media coverage is frequently deliberately aimed at stirring up excitement to stimulate investment. It is not easy being on the receiving end of all this information, trying to make head or tail of it. Seeing through the hype in search of the reality is quite a challenge, but of course essential in order to be able to make informed decisions. Although there is a lot to be excited about, many of the expectations created by these promises will probably never be met. That is unfortunate, as it takes a long time to recover from failed expectations. Wrong decisions will no doubt be made and investments will fail as a result.

It is hard to know when to stop listening to the prophets and corporate gurus. We rely on them to highlight the issues at stake, provoke our thinking, bring us new ideas and enthuse us. However, we shouldn't let them seduce us without any questioning or thought on our part. The challenge is to distinguish between hype and reality, learn to skim off the froth. Managers need to ensure that their organizations have a feasible vision of the near future and a clear understanding of what they want to be and what kind of business they want to operate in the new environment. Corporate vision is a key driver and motivator, enabling the required individual and organizational changes to happen. Managers with no vision or with visions well past their sell-by date constitute a major risk to the very organizations they have been employed to ensure survive and prosper.

The definition of a guru may be someone who has gone too far and, to some extent, lost touch with reality. Being in love with their own thoughts and inventions, our gurus, self-appointed or elected, frequently cross the line between visions and hallucination. Although individuals who are referred to as gurus are often exciting visionaries and great stimulators, it can prove dangerous to rely on their visions. Organizations need to have sound visions of reality to drive forward successfully. Be especially aware of the gurus or heroes who claim to have the ultimate answers – nobody has all the answers alone. The best we can try for is to collaboratively arrive at some answers and constantly work on the right questions to ask. What's more, what seems the right answer today could be terribly wrong next year. For instance, consider the fascinating U-turn made by Bill Gates and Microsoft in the early 1990s with respect to the company's strategic response to the Internet and Netscape. At first, Microsoft ignored network developments and insisted on its PC-centric vision of the Wired World. It understandably stuck with the business it knew and, at first, rejected the idea of an Internet-embracing strategy. Visiting sales representatives proclaimed, 'The Net is dead'. However, as the phenomenal growth and popularity of the Internet escalated in parallel with the stock evaluation of Internet-based businesses, Microsoft was forced to retract and re-evaluate its initial approach. It then surprised the market by swiftly adopting a strategy that seemingly centred on the power of networks. The same sales representatives now travelled the world equipped with the opposite soundbite answer – 'The Net is the bet'! At the time of writing, Bill Gates is preoccupied with the much talked about 'digital nervous system' of our new economy – a metaphor used by many before him, including myself. However, he may be too late to win the battle for dominance in the market for network software. Many of Gates' competitors defined their network visions long before him and are well on the way to supplying what the new market demands. However, Gates has the capacity to invest whatever it takes to catch up and, so far, Microsoft has demonstrated its ability to learn and change as it gains market knowledge.

> **Managers need to dispose of their Darwinistic approach to business development . . . if they want their organizations to flourish.**

What organizations need to do to succeed is learn to let go of old-style control measures and the management insistence on possessing all the facts and all the answers. Managers need to dispose of their Darwinistic approach to business development and bring out their green fingers if they want their organizations to flourish in the new networked economy. All types of organizations and individuals will need to adapt an open learning attitude and a willingness to change as new knowledge is manifested if they want to survive in the Wired World.

Gurus always simplify the real world to suit their particular ideas, which they will not relinquish or willingly change. Change, though, is something we all should be better at. The business model that worked so well yesterday will not necessarily work tomorrow (as will be explained in subsequent chapters). Always question the gospel preached by the corporate gurus, whether the theme is the 're-engineering revolution', 'total quality control', the 'learning organization', 'going global', 'being digital', 'change management', 'digital nervous systems', 'organizational velocity' or any other fashionable soundbites.

Our language is littered with banal metaphors and fashionable buzzwords. We talk of the 'Information Superhighway', 'digital revolutions', 'global access', 'killer applications', 'one-stop shopping', 'teleworking', 'multimedia entertainment', 'web lifestyle' and so on. All this playing around with language is symptomatic of a changing society and, to some extent, we need this tabloid-speak to explore what we do not yet understand. Linguists tell us that when our language changes, behavioural change soon follows.

2

The Global Information Infrastructure

Emerging global systems

> Is it a fact . . . that, by means of electricity, the world of matter has become a great nerve, vibrating thousands of miles in a breathless point of time? Rather, the round globe is a vast head, a brain, instinct with intelligence! Or, shall we say, it is itself a thought, nothing but a thought, and no longer the substance which we deemed it!
>
> Nathaniel Hawthorne
> *The House of the Seven Gables* (Bantam, 1982)

Nathaniel Hawthorne's reflections on the invention of electricity seem to fit even better with the invention of the Global Information Infrastructure. I can't help wondering what he would have written had he been alive today.

People perceive the Global Information Society in different ways, use different words and interpret developments according to their respective standpoints and level of understanding. However, it is still possible to establish an overview that outlines the base technologies and the application domains that will be the backbone of this society. That said, such an overview will need to be revised continually and is not meant to be taken as either complete or static. One certain maxim of today is that things will change tomorrow. Many assume, but nobody knows in specific terms how, the market and society will evolve. We are moving through a major process of transformation and many of the key parts needed to form the infrastructure and content of the emerging Global Information Society are currently in the mould.

As far as emerging global systems for the GII are concerned, there are four basic architectures:

- fixed and wireless telecommunications (including satellite);
- cable television;
- digital television;
- the Internet (including Intercast, a system for providing interactive television services using existing analogue TV signals launched on 20 June 1996 and backed by the Intercast Industry Group, established on 23 October 1995).

Unfortunately, a lot of people confuse the Internet with the GII (also popularly referred to as the Information Superhighway). The Internet is an essential part of the process of developing the communication networks that make up the GII. The Internet provides conceptual models and references for usability and functionality in terms of shaping the GII. However, the Internet in its present form is a transitory phenomenon. Communications activities and electronic commerce will gradually be transferred from the Internet of yesterday to the high-performance networks and platforms of tomorrow, which will be able to offer the broadband capability of future GII services. We will probably still call it the Internet and users will not be aware of the technological transformations happening behind their screens.

It is important from both economic and political perspectives to distinguish between the Internet as a social phenomenon and the construction of the interconnected global networks that will be the economic backbone of future commerce.

It is important to distinguish between the Internet as a social phenomenon and the construction of the interconnected global networks that will be the economic backbone of future commerce.

The history of the Internet is well covered by other publications (for a detailed history see, for instance, Ed Krol, *The Whole Internet*, O'Reilly & Associates Inc, 1994). However, it is useful to consider the historic connections in order to understand how the Internet is constructed and why the Internet, at least in technological terms, may be limited to playing a intermediate role in the construction of the GII.

The Internet has existed since 1978. The father of the Internet is the US Defense Department. The origin of the Internet was the need for a closed, decentralized communications network that could facilitate military communication, even after nuclear attacks. The US Defense Department's network, called ARPAnet, was connected to a number of other radio and satellite networks, and the Internet was born. The network was specifically designed to require a minimum of information from users. Throughout the 1980s, network developers within the academic sector (in the United States, Britain and Scandinavia) developed the Internet concept for use as a communications and information tool for science and research purposes. The National Science Foundation (NSF), a US government agency, commissioned the setting up of NSFNET in the late 1980s. JANET was set up in Britain and UNINETT in Norway. These Internet networks and others that followed were based on the Internet Protocol and technology developed by ARPAnet.

According to the International Telecommunication Union (ITU), by early 1999, the Internet, as a network of networks, had grown to comprise some 217 million users. There were 43.5 million Internet host computers, over 70 per cent of which were located in English-speaking countries (see Figure 2.1). The registration of Internet domain names had exceeded 2 million and the Internet data traffic was doubling every 100 days.

One particularly fast-growing segment of the Internet is the World Wide Web (WWW). It has set up its own WWW consortium, attracting a range of commercial interests. Estimates vary immensely, but many agree that close to 1 billion people will be connected to the Internet by the year 2000 (see Figure 2.2).

The Internet is a formation of thousands of interconnecting, open networks. The development of the infrastructure has happened in a bottom-up fashion. It gives individual users the opportunity to 'surf' between myriad different applications, search for information and use services provided by an increasing number of networks. It also gives individual users the power to interact with others and become information providers themselves by putting information on the networks.

There is a sharp contrast between the way in which the Internet has been constructed and the way in which telecommunications, cable and broadcasting networks have been set up. The latter were formed in a hierarchical top-down fashion, with massive capital investment.

It is primarily the telecommunications industry that is developing the global broadband network that will provide the essential building blocks for the GII, although there is fierce competition from new communications service operators and providers resulting from the deregulation and privatization of the industry. The telecommunications industry owns and controls much of the global fibre-

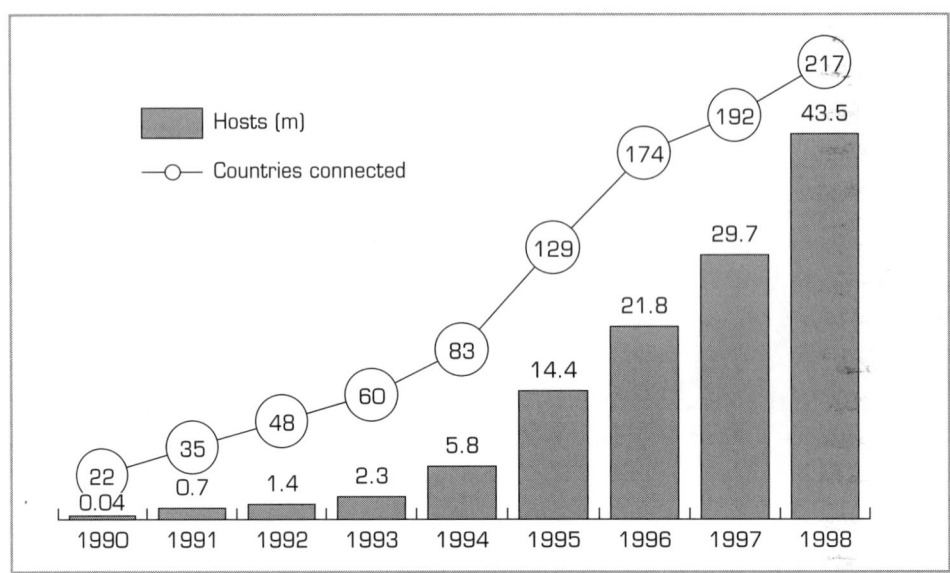

Figure 2.1a: Internet hosts worldwide (millions)

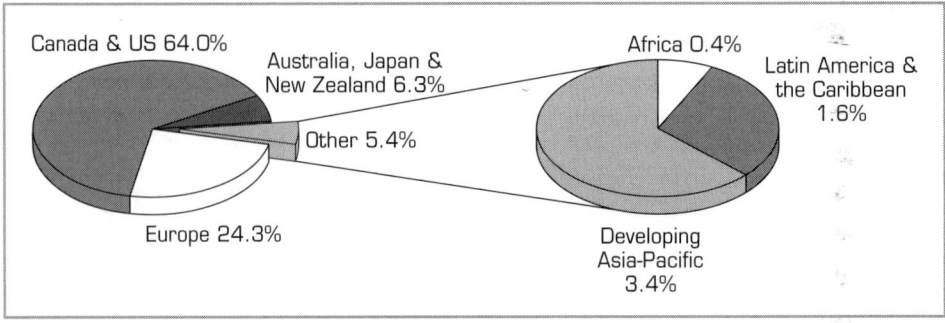

Figure 2.1b: distribution of Internet hosts, January 1999

Notes: In Figure 2.1a, data refer to January of the following year. A new method was used to calculate Internet hosts from January 1998 onwards. Data were adjusted, based on the new methodology, from January 1995.
Source: Network Wizards

optic capacity that has become available in the last decade. It will understandably want to keep control of it in the future and want to charge for it. Any computer company, content or service provider or other organization wanting to capitalize on the GII should not base expansion and development plans on the assumption that access is going to be open and bandwidths free – this may not be the case.

The telecommunications companies are well positioned to capture future growth in GII markets. Today they derive around 80 per cent of their total revenues

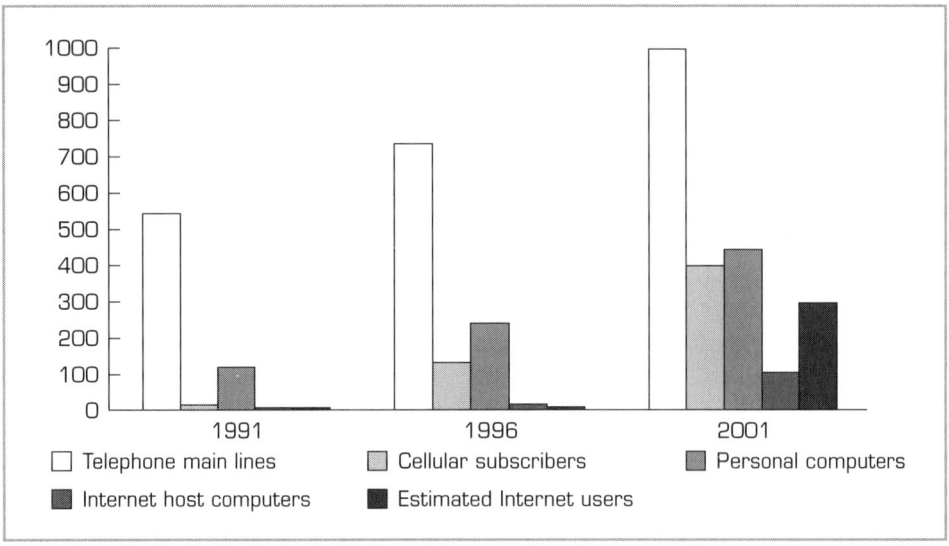

Figure 2.2: Millennium networks
Source: ITU

worldwide (around $600 billion a year) from voice telephony services. However, the voice telephony business is declining and the old incumbent telecommunications companies are in the midst of seeing their business totally transformed. The industry is expecting the decline of voice revenues and portfolio services to continue and it is clearly looking to the GII and value-added services to generate revenues in future. For instance, Cable & Wireless' forecast shows a very sharp decline in voice revenues: by 2001 down to 50 per cent, within ten years down to 30 per cent. So, in other words, somewhere between 50 and 70 per cent of the estimated $3 trillion market in convergence has to come from new entrants, either in competition or in co-operation with the traditional telephone companies (statement from Denis Gilhooly, Senior Adviser, the World Bank Group).

The cable television networks will also provide a platform for the GII. Many cable TV companies are offering telephony services, Internet access, Web TV and interactive TV services through 'set top boxes' with built-in decoders. The industry is struggling with the high costs of telecommunications lines and satellite television providing the programming. Cable television is limited to physical cable penetration and also suffers from legal constraints, which makes it hard for the industry to move towards GII markets. The cable television industry is clearly conquest territory at the moment for telephone companies as well as other key players set on acquiring a major stake in the GII.

> **The divisions between current global systems are likely to change or even disappear over the next couple of decades as the digitization of communication networks continues.**

The other interesting development, in terms of global systems, is the emergence of direct satellite television, particularly in the United States. For instance, Denis Gilhooly states that GM Hughes Networks signed up over 400,000 subscribers within the first 9 months of starting up its operations. The divisions between current global systems are likely to change or even disappear over the next couple of decades as the digitization of communication networks continues. Telephony, broadcasting, cable and satellite technologies will eventually come together and gel, forming the GII of the future.

Intercast is another transitory system using the basic idea of teletext television services such as Oracle or Ceefax. The data is sent piggybacking (during the vertical blank interval, VBI) on the standard analogue video signal (NTSC or PAL). Intercast is also broadcasting World Wide Web pages and viewers can, in that way, have limited access to the Internet. However, if the user wants to click on links and use the Web in a normal interactive fashion, they will need an account with an Internet service provider and a modem.

Intercast was launched on 20 June 1996 and is backed by the Intercast Industry Group (IIG). Companies already providing services include CNN, NBC, WHBG Educational Foundation, Time Warner and QVC shopping channel. Other members of the group so far include Viacom, America Online, Intel, Asymetrix, Netscape, Gateway 2000 and Packard Bell.

Intercast is a good example of how the installed base of analogue television sets is being used to gradually introduce new interactive services that will only be fully in play once digital technology and fibre-optics have replaced today's analogue systems and coaxial cables, a process that will take several years. However, digital television has experienced rapid growth since the first commercial digital television channels were launched in 1997/1998 in different parts of the world. The cost of a new digital television set or set top box/decoder is a major deterrent to uptake in the market. Digital television sets are available, but so far they are significantly more expensive than conventional ana-

> **We shall see many interim solutions arriving in the market over the next decade that will try to make use of the existing networks and installed platforms, while waiting for this gradual replacement by new fully broadband-capable technology.**

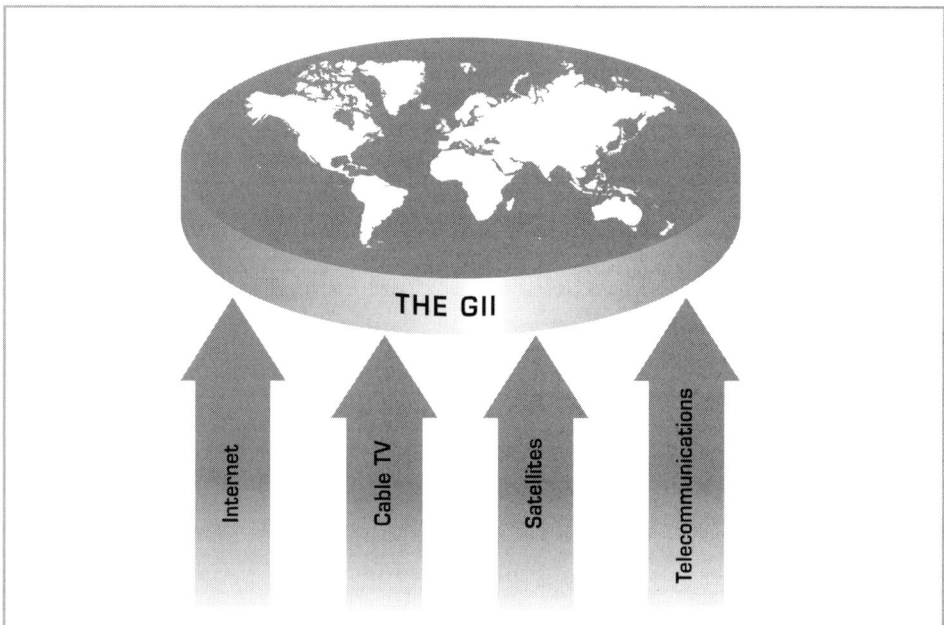

Figure 2.3: the Global Information Infrastructure

logue ones. Most people who switch to digital television do so by subscribing to cable or satellite services, which provide them with set top boxes that work with their old analogue television sets by decoding the digital signals from their cable/satellite dish or terrestrial aerial. The competition in the TV market is fierce and many of the cable and satellite TV providers subsidise the cost of the set top box and satellite dish, offering them at a discount or even free to users in order to win the battle to sign up digital television subscribers.

We shall see many interim solutions arriving in the market over the next decade that will try to make use of the existing networks and installed platforms, while waiting for this gradual replacement by new fully broadband-capable technology.

The rise of the Global Information Infrastructure (GII)

During the period 1993–96, governments around the world announced plans to develop 'national information infrastructures' and the idea was quickly extended, giving rise to the 'Global Information Infrastructure' (see Figure 2.3). Al Gore, Vice President of the United States, firmly established the concept of the GII with his speech at the ITU's first World Telecommunications Development Conference in Buenos Aires in March 1994 (there is a copy of this historic speech in the appendices).

The year 1993 was significant in the history of the GII. Government initiatives in the United States, Europe, Singapore and Japan sparked off debate worldwide on the use of information and communication technologies, and the implications for economic and social change. These initiatives have become important milestones in the process of building the Global Information Society.

In the United States, President Clinton announced an 'Agenda for Action' for the creation of a national information infrastructure. He set up the White House Information Infrastructure Task Force to work with Congress and the private sector to develop comprehensive telecommunications and information policies aimed at articulating and implementing the Administration's vision for the National Information Infrastructure (NII).

In Europe, President Delors of the European Commission presented the 'White Paper on Growth, Competitiveness and Employment', calling for action to establish a European infrastructure. As a response to this paper, the Bangemann Report recommended a course of action towards a European Information Society.

Japan's Ministry of Posts and Telecommunications (MPT) announced the development of 'a new information communication structure', and NTT, the main Japanese telecommunications carrier, launched a 25-year programme entitled 'OFL-21' (Optical Fibre Loop for the twenty-first century), which aims to build a broadband network that will reach every business, school and home by the year 2015.

The US Information Superhighway: the US NII 'Agenda for Action' and the US GII 'Agenda for Co-operation'

Clinton and Gore put much of the emphasis of their 1992 presidential campaign on the importance of building 'Information Superhighways' and a 'twenty-first-century infrastructure'. They stressed the importance of developing a National Information Infrastructure, saying it was fundamental to economic growth in the position paper of the Clinton Campaign (1992). Clinton called for a new economic policy that would include an information infrastructure strategy:

In the new economy, infrastructure means information as well as transportation. More than half the US workforce is employed in information-intensive industries, yet we have no national strategy to create a national information network. Just as the

interstate highway system in the 1950s spurred two decades of economic growth, we need a door-to-door fiber-optics system by the year 2015 to link every home, every lab, every classroom, every business in America.

('The Economy', Bill Clinton's presidential campaign speech, Wharton School of Business, University of Pennsylvania Philadelphia, 16 April 1992)

Having won the election, President Clinton and Vice President Gore could move on to implement their ideas and make sure that the development of an advanced National Information Infrastructure became a top US priority. In September 1993, the Clinton Administration launched 'The National Information Infrastructure: Agenda for Action':

A major goal of the NII is to give our citizens access to a broad range of information and information services. Using innovative telecommunications and information technologies, the NII – through a partnership of business, labour, academe, consumers and all levels of government – will help the United States achieve a broad range of economic and social goals.

(speech by Larry Irving, Head of National Telecommunications and Information Administration, US Department of Commerce – 'Constructing the National Information Infrastructure: Ensuring that all Americans get connected', at the Vermont Telecommunications Forum, Winooski Park, Vermont, 20 March 1995)

The White House set up the Information Infrastructure Task Force (IITF) (chaired by Ronald H. Brown, then US Secretary of Commerce) to 'articulate and implement the Administration's vision for the NII'. All the key agencies concerned with telecommunications and information policy are represented on the IITF, which operates under the White House Office of Science and Technology Policy and the National Economic Council. A high-level advisory council for the IITF was also established, to function initially for two years. The advisory council consists of a broad range of experts from the private sector, academe, state and local governments, and public interest groups.

The IITF has so far set up three committees with a number of focused working groups.

- The Telecommunications Policy Committee (chaired by Larry Irving, Head of National Telecommunications and Information Administration of the US Department of Commerce) will 'formulate a consistent position on key telecommunications issues'. The Committee has a Working Group on Universal Service, which will 'work to ensure that all Americans have access to and can enjoy the benefits of the NII'.

- The Information Policy Committee (chaired by Sally Katzen, Head of the Office of Information and Regulatory Affairs at the Office of Management and Budget, OMBI) is dealing with 'critical information policy issues that must be addressed if the NII is to be fully deployed and utilized'. The Committee has three working groups:

    - Working Group on Intellectual Property Rights, which is focusing on 'protecting copyrights and other IPRs in an electronic world';

    - Working Group on Privacy, which is dealing with 'Administration policies to protect individual privacy despite the rapid increase in the collection, storage and dissemination of personal data in electronic form';

    - Working Group on Government Information, which 'focuses on ways to promote dissemination of government data in electronic form'.

- The Applications Committee (chaired by Arati Prabhakar, Director of the National Institute of Standards and Technology) is 'co-ordinating the Administration's efforts to develop, demonstrate and promote applications in information technology in manufacturing, education, healthcare, government services, libraries and other areas'. The Committee has a Working Group on Government Information Technology Services (GITS), which co-ordinates 'efforts to improve the application of information technology by federal agencies'.

Everyone involved in this work soon realized that it would be impossible to limit the NII to national borders and that the development of the information infrastructure is a global issue of international concern. The Clinton Administration responded by extending the plans for the NII to include the GII. This was the background for Al Gore's famous speech at the ITU conference in Buenos Aires in March 1994, where he presented the 'US' Agenda for Co-operation'. This was further elaborated on and issued in a press release at the G7 summit meeting in Brussels on 27 February 1995.

Everyone involved in this work soon realized that it would be impossible to limit the NII to national borders.

Vice President Gore called on every nation to establish an ambitious agenda to build the GII, using the following five principles as the foundation:

- encouraging private-sector investment;
- promoting competition;
- providing open access to the network for all information providers and users;

- creating a flexible regulatory environment that can keep pace with rapid technological and market changes;
- ensuring universal service.

'The purpose of this GII "Agenda for Co-operation" is to amplify these five principles and to identify the steps the United States, in concert with other nations, can take to make the vision of the GII a reality. We hope that it will also serve as the basis for engaging other governments in a consultative, constructive, and co-operative process that will ensure the development of the GII for the mutual benefit of all countries.

'By interconnecting local, national, regional and global networks, the GII can increase economic growth, create jobs, and improve infrastructures. Taken as a whole, this worldwide "network of networks" will create a global information marketplace, encouraging broad-based social discourse within and among all countries' ('The Global Information Infrastructure: Agenda for Co-operation', report by Ronald H. Brown, US Secretary of Commerce, Version 1.0).

The European approach

The US 'Agenda for Action on the National Information Infrastructure', announced in September 1993 by Vice President Gore and the Clinton Administration, provoked a widespread debate in Europe. In December 1993, the European Council accepted the European Commission's 'White Paper on growth, competitiveness and employment – The challenges and way forward into the 21st century'. This White Paper proposed an action plan based on five priorities:

- stimulate the use of information technologies via strategic projects with a European dimension;
- provide basic trans-European services, such as ISDN and broadband;
- create an appropriate regulatory framework to address issues such as privacy, security and intellectual property;
- develop training on new technologies;
- improve industrial and technological performance.

The strategic projects address generic services such as interactive video, access to information and electronic mail, and other priority applications such as teleworking, teletraining, telemedicine and the linking of European administrations.

The investment required for these projects is estimated to be B Euro 150 over the next ten years. The money is expected to come mainly from the private sector.

Financial support from national and community authorities is limited to research and development support, feasibility studies, loan guarantees and interest subsidies.

In underlining the importance of an appropriate regulatory framework, the White Paper indicates five areas for possible action:

- end distortions of competition;
- guarantee a universal service;
- speed up standardization;
- protect privacy and ensure the security of information and communication systems;
- extend intellectual property law.

The European Council set up two high-level groups to follow up the acceptance of the White Paper. The first, chaired by Commissioner Christophersen, dealt with the financing possibilities of these networks. The second, chaired by Commissioner Bangemann, formulated a concrete action plan to realize the potential of the Global Information Society in Europe. The Bangemann group analyzed potential markets and how an infrastructure could work, and identified key issues concerning policy and regulatory frameworks. Both groups presented their reports at the EU summit in Corfu, Greece, at the end of June 1994 (there is an extract from the Bangemann Report in the appendices).

The Bangemann Report quickly became a source of inspiration and a point of reference for governments and organizations inside and outside Europe. It pulled people together across public and private sectors and gave them something important to talk about. The Bangemann Report, together with Al Gore's historic speech at the ITU's first World Telecommunications Development Conference in Buenos Aires in March 1994, the US 'Agenda for Action on the National Information Infrastructure' and the GII 'Agenda for Co-operation' that followed, were fundamental political documents that came to play a key role worldwide. These initiatives acted as a great stimulus on both sides of the Atlantic.

Initiatives in Asia

Singapore has become a textbook example of a high-tech success story – how a small nation has exploited information and communications technologies to achieve economic growth, political control and a high degree of automation throughout the public and private sectors. The government in Singapore published a report in March 1992 entitled 'Information Technology 2000: A Vision of an Intelligent Island', which describes how the information infrastructure will be used to turn Singapore into an 'Intelligent Island' with a complete information network in place by the year 2000.

In Korea, the development of an information infrastructure is regarded as essential to maintain international competitiveness. There is a three-stage plan in operation that aims to 'complete a Super-High-Speed Information Network by the year 2015'. This will be a broadband network, 'capable of transmitting multimedia information, voice, images and data at ultra-high speeds'.

Japan has taken a strong lead in promoting the Global Information Society in Asia, working closely with other Asian countries to develop a Pan-Asian Information Infrastructure (AII). The Japanese Ministry of Posts and Telecommunications also recognizes that the creation of an efficient information infrastructure is a global enterprise and therefore has established communication and collaboration with countries around the world, including the United States and the European Commission.

To the Japanese government, the information infrastructure represents a chance to use information and know-how instead of material production in order effectively to solve the problems confronting the country. Japan aims to lay fibre-optic cables to every household in the nation by the year 2015 (the same target date as that set by the Clinton Administration for the NII in the United States). The fibre-optic technology will enable interactive, broadband transmissions of enormous amounts of data. The scale of the information industry will expand and countless new businesses are expected to be created once the fibre-optical network is in use: 'Assuming that the network is in place by 2010, we estimate that the information-communication industry will represent a $12 trillion market and will have created 2.4 million more jobs' (Ichiya Nakamura, Directory Posts and Telecommunications International, 'Development of the Info-Communication Infrastructure in Japan', paper presented at the International Publishers Association's Copyright Congress, Torino 23–25 May 1994).

> **Japan aims to lay fibre-optic cables to every household in the nation by the year 2015 (the same target date as that set by the Clinton Administration for the NII in the United States).**

In 1993 Japan set up a major project in the Kansal area, where the objective is to research the technical feasibility and cost-effectiveness of an integrated information-broadcasting network, find out what applications are needed and investigate regulatory requirements, including copyright issues. The project has a budget of $98 million and initially involves the fibre-optical cabling of 300 households. More than 100 private-sector companies are participating in the project, from telecommunications carriers, broadcasters and hardware manufacturers to trading companies and banks. Network trials started in 1994.

The MPT expects the development of fibre-optical networks and applications, and the multimedia industry, to grow rapidly and it is taking strategic action to facilitate the distribution of software that these businesses will generate.

The developing world

The developing world consists of 77 per cent of the world's population, 58 per cent of its land mass and less than 5 per cent of its gross national product. There are, on average, only about 55 television sets and 28 telephones per thousand people, concentrated in urban areas, in developing countries (UNDP, 'Human Development Report', 1993). In India, for example, there is less than one computer per thousand people. There are more telephones in the City of London than there are in the whole of Africa.

The developing world is not homogeneous and there are extreme variations in levels of development, forms of government, receptivity to other cultures and acceptance of high-tech innovations. The infrastructure for delivering information technology, products and services is poor with, for example, problems of power supply, lack of trained personnel, obsolete technology, equipment being unable to cope with extreme weather conditions and so on.

There is also a fear of dependence on suppliers of technology and other countries, and that the information products produced outside their respective cultures may corrupt their own values and traditions, spreading dangerous, radical ideas. These fears can be a barrier to the acceptance of the latest technologies. However, many leaders in the developing world recognize the advantages of information technologies and understand the need to maintain positive international relations in order to secure access to them.

In the process of developing the Global Information Society, provision must be made for developing countries. Access needs to be made possible on a worldwide basis if there is to be a truly global infrastructure. It should not matter if people are poor, physically disabled, have a low IQ or whatever, IT has the potential to bring benefits to almost everybody. It is crucial for us to include as much of the world as possible in our global interconnected village (Ashok Bhojwani, 'Information Strategies for the World: A Response from the Developing World', paper presented at the International Publishers Association's Copyright Congress, Torino 23–25 May 1994).

> **Access needs to be made possible on a worldwide basis if there is to be a truly global infrastructure. It is crucial for us to include as much of the world as possible in our global interconnected village.**

The optimistic view is that the GII will reduce the gap between North and South, between rich and poor, by providing developing countries with GII access and thereby creating new opportunities for economic growth. The optimists also believe that developing countries can leapfrog their way to developments that take advantage of the GII because, unlike developed countries, they start with a clean slate, without any pre-existing infrastructure. Unlike the developed nations, they do not have to resolve an existing legacy of industrial and legal structures. They can avoid the risk of being delayed, for example, by regulatory frameworks.

The pessimistic view is that the GII will do exactly the opposite and further widen the gap between the wealthy and the poor. Commercial interests in the developed parts of the world are expanding into new growth markets as their existing markets reach saturation. The pessimists claim that the rich will dominate the poor and that access to the GII will be restricted to those who can afford it. They fear that the winners to benefit from the GII will be the competitive nations of this world, not the starving ones.

> **The pessimists claim that the rich will dominate the poor and that access to the GII will be restricted to those who can afford it.**

One thing is clear, the GII is here to stay and will continue to grow as the backbone of the world economy. A major step forward was taken in 1998 with the implementation of the World Trade Organization's (WTO) Basic Telecommunication Agreement and the approval of several other important international agreements on standards and communication services, including the commercial Internet Protocol.

The GII is evolving all the time, with the rapid advancement of technology and new inventions. It is important to understand the evolution of media and communication technologies – and the impact the changes involved have on human history and civilization.

3 Technology

All the new ways of living our lives and conducting business have come about as a result of technological invention, but the Wired World of today is a very young child of human history. By recent estimates, our planet is over 4000 million years old and the first human beings walked the Earth approximately 300,000 years ago. Yet most technological developments have taken place and evolved during the course of only the past 500 years of human history, and computer technology in particular in just the past 100 years or so. However, it does not follow from this that people were not creative or did not value information and knowledge before the advent of modern technology.

The development of media and communications technologies – from Gutenberg to Gates

In technical terms, the history of electronic media and communications technology started with the inventions of the printing press and the telegraph. The telegraph was patented in 1837 in England by the British physicist Sir Charles Wheatstone and in the US by the American inventor Samuel F. B. Morse, both of whom had discovered the communication capabilities of electricity (Morse tried unsuccessfully to secure patents in Europe and there were many legal disputes over the claims of ownership of the telegraph invention. There were several scientists and engineers in different corners of the world who contributed to the development of the telegraph). The first telegraph line in the US was commissioned by the US Congress, which gave Morse $30,000 to set

The history of electronic media and communications technology started with the inventions of the printing press and the telegraph.

up a line between Washington DC and Baltimore. His first successful demonstration was when he sent the message 'What hath God wrought!' on 24 May 1844.

Tom Standage has written a fascinating book entitled *The Victorian Internet* (Weidenfeld & Nicolson, 1998) in which he tells the story of the development of the telegraph and what he refers to as the first Internet:

Over the course of a few years in the middle of Queen Victoria's reign, a new communication technology annihilated distance and shrank the world faster and further than ever before. A worldwide communications network whose cables spanned continents and oceans, it revolutionized business practice and gave rise to new forms of crime. Romances blossomed over the wires. Secret codes were devised by some, and cracked by others. The benefits of the networks were relentlessly hyped by its advocates, and dismissed by the sceptics. Governments and regulators tried and failed to control the new medium, and attitudes to everything from news-gathering to diplomacy had to be completely rethought. Meanwhile, out on the wires, a technological subculture with its own customs and vocabulary was establishing itself. Does it all sound familiar?

Standage has dug through historical records for us, reminding us that the promise of the Networked World is not at all new and exclusive to our moment in history. People have been here before us. In 1871 a statue was erected in New York as a tribute to Morse, and the telegraph was praised for 'uniting the peoples of the world, promoting world peace, and revolutionizing commerce'. The telegraph was referred to as 'the greatest instrument of power over earth which the ages of human history have revealed'. It was said at the time that 'The highway girdling the earth is found in the telegraph wire'. So these are the roots of many current Internet buzz-words – it is somewhat comforting to learn that the Information Superhighway stems beyond Al Gore, who is widely reputed to have coined the phrase.

The Networked World is not at all new and exclusive to our moment in history. People have been here before us.

Yet the telegraph is a relatively new invention compared to the very first major technological breakthrough in media and communications technology – the printing press. Gutenberg printed the first publication in 1442 on his new printing press, 395 years before the telegraph was invented. As a consequence, 'mass printing' became a market reality by 1445.

The inventions of the printing press and telegraph have nothing in common in terms of technology. However, they are strongly connected in that each provided a cornerstone for the later development of electronic media and communications technology. Together, these two separate events were to lay down the foundations for three major media industries: print publishing, telephony and broadcasting. These

Gutenberg printed the first publication in 1442 on his new printing press, 395 years before the telegraph was invented.

technologies evolved as separate disciplines for over two centuries before converging, towards the end of the 1970s, in a mixed media and communications industry.

Today, print is being challenged as the dominant media for distributing information. Communications technology has developed from simply the telegraph to include the radio, telephone, photography, film and television, and, most significant of all, has been the arrival of the computer and digital technologies, bringing fundamental changes to the media and communications industry (see Figure 3.1).

The last decade has seen several technical breakthroughs that are causing an upheaval in the media and communications industries, particularly advances in semiconductors, video, cable and satellite technology – that is, digital video, fibreoptics, broadband transmission, Asymmetric Digital Subscriber Line (ADSL), Asynchronous Transfer Modes (ATMs), high-speed cables, modems, and a range of satellite equipment, among others. The ways in which we produce and distribute media content today would have seemed like science fiction to someone living only ten years ago.

Although the different media have developed in separate traditions, they have from the very start been strongly influenced by each other. As Marshall and Eric McLuhan put it in *Laws of the Media* (University of Toronto Press, 1988) 'The content of any new medium is an older medium.' The first print publishers were influenced by pre-print media – professional

1445	Print
1835	Camera
1837	Telegraph
1843	Facsimile
1876	Telephone
1895	Film
1905	Radio
1925	Television
1956	Magnetic videotape
1965	Computers
1975	Videodisc
1978	VCR
1982	Audio Compact Disc
1985	CD-ROM
1985	Digital video
1986	CDI
1987	DVI
1996	DVD-Video, DVD-ROM, DVD-RAM

Figure 3.1: key milestones in the development of media technology

communicators, such as storytellers, messengers, preachers, teachers, entertainers. These ancient forms are now coming back in the shape of intelligent agents and other mediating characters in multimedia publishing.

The printing press is significant for an appreciation of how the media have evolved as an industry. The printing press permitted the development of mass print publishing, which constituted the first major change of a medium of communication into a complex business operation. Print publishing – in particular newspaper publishing – had a substantial influence on television. Although the influence is still there, it has diminished over the years as television has developed into a major media industry in its own right. For the past decade or two, it has been more popular to study the impact of television on newspapers than vice versa.

Today, print is still the most widespread, established and distributed medium. The professionals of the printing press developed a tradition that provided the frame of reference for broadcasters when they arrived on the scene half a century later.

The first radio broadcasters copied the recipes of the newspaper format – a blend of news, reports and commentaries, sports and entertainment. In fact, entertainment was the chosen market application for the first radio broadcast and also the first television broadcast. And entertainment has continued to be the most important application for broadcasting – the exception being during World War II when radio and film were used by the Nazis to control and direct the nation and by the British and their allies to inform and provide moral support to their people.

Today, print is still the most widespread, established and distributed medium.

In the course of the evolution of the media industry over centuries, every time a new medium was invented, it was first rejected, then seen as a threat to the existing media. People thought the telephone was a stupid idea and were not impressed when, in March 1876, Alexander Graham Bell reported the world's first successful telephone call: 'Mr Watson, come here, I want you.' Who would use such a silly contraption?

In the course of the evolution of the media industry over centuries, every time a new medium was invented, it was first rejected, then seen as a threat to the existing media.

The British filmmaker Lord Puttnam reminds us that 'It took the movie business 20 years to develop into anything approaching a serious medium in its own right. For those first two decades it was busily dismissed as much ado about nothing, a gimmick, even just a new source of depravity – just as some of the more inflated claims about the current communications revolution are dismissed today.'

Even when writing was first introduced in Egypt during the fourth century BC, it was rejected. The story goes that one day King Thamus of Egypt had a visit from Theuth, who presented him with some writing, saying, 'Here is an accomplishment, my lord the King, that will improve both the wisdom and the memory of the Egyptians.' However, King Thamus reputedly replied, 'Theuth, my paragon of inventors, the discoverer of an art is not the best judge of the good or harm which will accrue to those who practise it. So it is in this; you, who are the father of writing, have out of fondness for your offspring, attributed to it quite the opposite of its real function. Those who acquire it will cease to exercise their memory and become forgetful; they will rely on writing to bring things to their remembrance by external signs instead of their own internal resources. What you have discovered is a receipt for recollection, not for memory. And as for wisdom, your pupils will have the reputation for it without the reality: they will receive a quantity of information without proper instruction, and in consequence be thought very knowledgeable when they are for the most part ignorant. And because they are filled with the conceit of wisdom instead of real wisdom they will be a burden to society' (Plato, *Phaedrus*, quoted by Neil Postman in *Technopoly*, Vintage Books, 1993).

> **Even when writing was first introduced in Egypt during the fourth century BC, it was rejected.**

King Thamus was right, but he was also terribly wrong. Technology is a two-edged sword. In our day, Neil Postman, a frequent commentator on the state of our information society, is warning us about the one-eyed prophets who see only what new technologies can do and are incapable of imagining what they will undo: 'It is a mistake to suppose that any technological innovation has a one-sided effect. Every technology is both a burden and a blessing; not either/or, but this-and-that.'

Those who thought television would be the end of the cinema, and that computers would kill the book, have been proved wrong. When Nicholas Negroponte predicts the end of the peer-reviewed scientific journal in printed form, because the on-line electronic journal will replace it, he sounds like yet another one-eyed prophet (interview with Nicholas Negroponte, Joia Shillingford, *Financial Times, IT Review*, 6 March 1996).

> **Those who thought television would be the end of the cinema, and that computers would kill the book, have been proved wrong.**

Indeed, it is not a question of either/or, but a question of choice and combinations. Just as you would select the appropriate means of transport to go to different places – you don't take the jumbo jet to go to the local post office, you walk; and you don't drive the car across a lake, you take a boat – you will select and combine different media for different purposes according to convenience, functionality and availability.

To successfully exploit the opportunities of today, it helps to acquire an understanding of how media and communications systems have developed in the past.

Ignorance of history feeds the arrogance of today.

It seems that, when it comes to our history, we always fail the 'being humble enough' test. Ignorance of history feeds the arrogance of today. We are often too busy and consumed by the new to appreciate the old. However, history also tells us time and again that people were wrong to be so quick to dismiss the new. Progress has always depended on a process of continuous innovation.

Innovation and the rate of change

> Progress, man's distinctive mark alone,
> Not God's, and not the beasts'; God is, they are,
> Man partly is and wholly hopes to be.
>
> Robert Browning, 'Death in the Desert'

The invention of writing enabled man to record, share and archive useful information for future generations. The next major breakthrough in the development of human knowledge came with the invention of moveable type and the printing press. Alvin Toffler once pointed out (in *Future Shock*, Macmillan, 1991) that, prior to Gutenberg, only 11 chemical elements were known. The twelfth chemical element to be discovered, antimony, was found around the same time as Gutenberg was working on his press. The eleventh chemical element, arsenic, had been discovered 200 years earlier.

With the power of computer technology and scientific tools, the rate at which discoveries are made is accelerating all the time.

Had discoveries continued at this same rate, we would have by now added two or three more elements to the periodic table since Gutenberg. Instead, in the 450 after his time, some 70 elements were discovered. Also, since 1900, we have been isolating the remaining elements not at a rate of one every two centuries, but of one every three years. Today, with the power of computer technology and scientific tools, the rate at which discoveries are made is accelerating all the time.

The use of technology has always been a catalyst for social and economic change. Technology is all about creating and mastering tools to enable our progress. However, in the past, it used to take a lot longer for new technology to find its way to the marketplace. For example, the first patent for a typewriter was issued in England in 1714, but typewriters did not become commercially available until the 1870s. The first patent for a fax machine was issued in 1843 to a British clockmaker called Alexander Bain who invented a basic prototype for sending images electronically. However, the first commercial facsimile system was introduced by Abbé Caselli 22 years later in 1865 on a line between Paris and Lyon, and it was not until the 1980s that the fax machine really became a market success. Sales of fax machines exploded in 1986 and today fax machines are vital pieces of equipment in every modern office and many homes.

Technological innovation is commonly divided into three main phases: invention, exploitation and diffusion. In the case of the typewriter and the fax machine, there was a considerable delay between the first stage (original concept and proven invention), the second stage (exploitation of the idea) and the final stage (market uptake).

The cost of this delay, in terms of lost economic and social benefits, can only be speculated on. It was no doubt a significant loss of opportunity and it is a textbook example of why it is important to manage all three phases of the innovation process in order to reduce time-lag between the various stages of development so as to achieve success and encourage further innovations.

One technological invention invariably leads to another. Technology feeds on itself. Much effort over the past 50 to 60 years has been devoted to improving technological innovation and what has been termed the 'innovation loop' (see Figure 3.2).

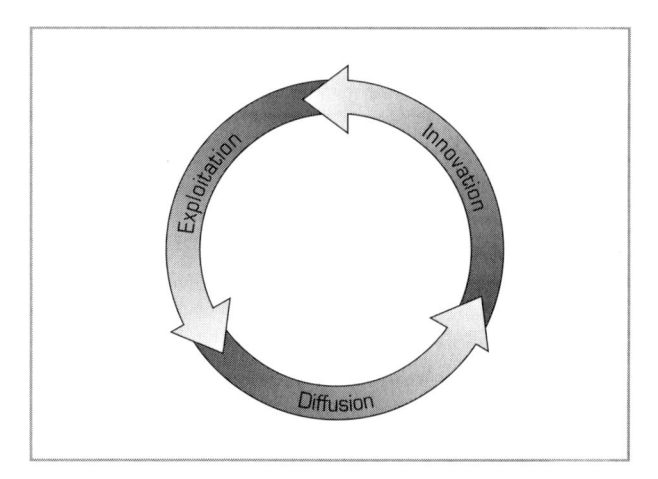

Figure 3.2: the innovation loop

A good indicator of significant change is when people take the technology for granted and are able to do what they want without wasting a thought on the technology they are using. The success of communications technology can be measured by ease of use (degree of seamlessness) and the functionality it provides. In other words, technologies that seem invisible to the user are often the ones that have the strongest impact.

The explosion of tools, gadgets and 'killer applications'

The convergence and marrying together of computing, media and communications technologies has resulted in a phenomenal development of new applications and electronic appliances. New software, tools and gadgets appear almost daily in the marketplace. People are being bombarded with an ever-growing range of products and choice. It has probably never been a more interesting time to be a consumer. Prices continue to fall while the quality of functionality improves. Customers are getting used to having more for less.

It has probably never been a more interesting time to be a consumer. Prices continue to fall while the quality of functionality improves. Customers are getting used to having more for less.

The flip side, however, is that this impressive explosion of rapid product development also causes much frustration for individual consumers and business organizations alike because of the short lifespan of many purchases of technology. As soon as the product is bought, it seems, another and better version is launched. This is good news for suppliers and creates a buoyant market in software and electronics items.

Certain nations and industry players dominate the trade. For instance, in the US, the Department of Commerce estimated that computing and communications now generates 25–40 per cent of US real economic growth. Not surprising perhaps considering the amount of software exported and the growing trade imbalance between the US and other OECD countries. The figures clearly demonstrate the great lead and competitive advantage the US has achieved over other nations (see Figure 3.3).

The competition in the market is fierce and for every winner in the information and communications technology business there are many casualties. The nature of the industry is rapid change and the pressure is constantly on to come up with

By segment, US and rest of the world

- Application solutions 49.6%
- US
- System level 21.7%
- US
- Application tools 28.7%
- US

By region

- Rest of Asia 12.4%
- Rest of World 1.7%
- Japan 11.4%
- Other Western Europe 2.8%
- Italy 2.8%
- France 4.9%
- UK 5.7%
- Germany 8.6%
- US 46.2%

Worldwide market = $109.3 billion

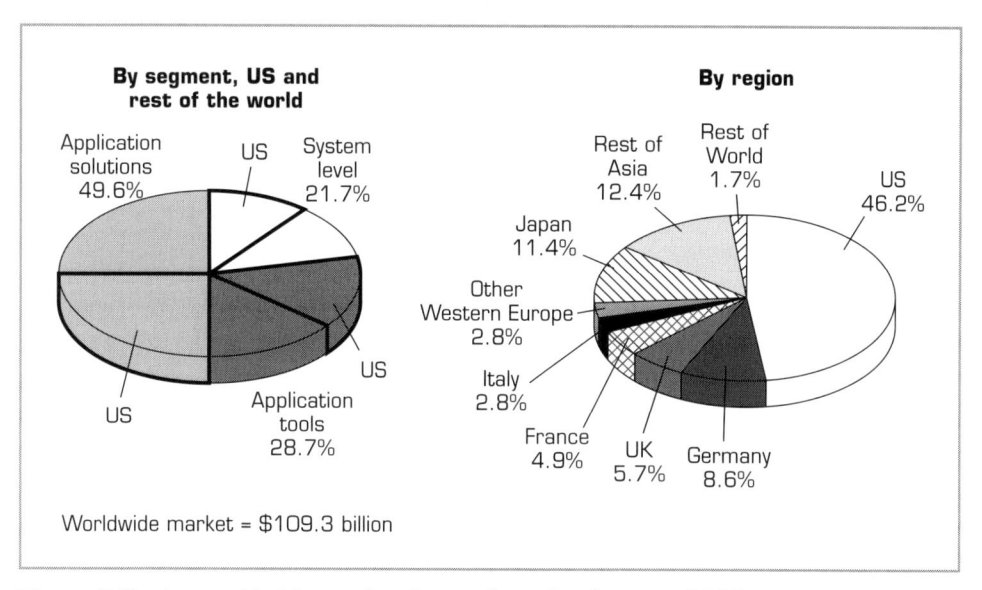

Figure 3.3: the worldwide market for packaged software, 1996

Source: IDC, quoted in *US Industry and Trade Outlook 1998*, US Department of Commerce, in OECD: 'Measuring Electronic Commerce: International Trade in Software', DSTI/ICCP/IE(98)3, 1998.

new, innovative products and winning gadgets. The range of products is endless – from personal organizers, mobile phone wristwatches, satellite tracking, car tracking, intelligent agents, talking Web navigators that recognize your voice, to wearable computers and interactive virtual pets.

For many inventors, the ultimate dream, and golden egg, is to come up with a so-called 'killer application'. Randall Hancock of Mainspring has spent much time studying the killer app. phenomenon and says 'the elusive killer app. has become the mythical Holy Grail pursued by all' (in *Masters of the Wired World*, Anne Leer (ed.), Financial Times Management, 1999). He has traced and described the development of killer applications from the telephone, radio, TV and typewriter to the word processor, spreadsheet, fax, cash point, e-mail and the Internet. To help us define the term 'killer application', Hancock offers this statement: 'It is much more useful to think of killer apps as bundles of functionalities or capabilities, delivered at an attractive price, which meet specific underlying needs better than anything else.' This is an excellent approach to killer applications and, indeed, to product and service innovation, because it demands a focus on the users' needs and market demands. So much technology is being developed with no real understanding of what people actually need and want.

Managing technological investments

Many of us feel caught in an avalanche of technological inventions and struggle to understand the impact of change on individual circumstances – on business, society and our lives. It is quite understandable that managers often give up trying to fathom the consequences of such rapid change, let alone keeping up to date with developments.

The combination of information overload and the sense of being overwhelmed by so much change is a dangerous managerial bug that can render managers ineffective and unfit to lead. Otherwise intelligent individuals in boardrooms across the corporate world are resisting involving themselves and their organizations in the major change processes required by the arrival of the Wired World. Successful leaders of the past can be seen withdrawing their corporate presence from the cutting edge and risking the survival of their businesses by doing so. Often, the justification given for ignoring change in this manner is that it is futile to invest resources in something that is going to change so quickly anyway.

Knowing when to invest in what is a major challenge.

We all recognize the problem. Should we buy now or wait for the next, even better, model that is always just around the corner? This will be familiar to anybody who has ever considered buying a new car, computer, television set, camera or any other kind of technological invention. Knowing when to invest in what is a major challenge for individual consumers and corporations alike. Will it be all right to purchase an analogue television set or should I wait for the digital sets? Should the company wait for the fibre-optic cable networks or invest in Asynchronous Transfer Mode technology?

Those who bought into Philips (Compact Disc-Interactive, CD-I) technology will have learnt the painful lesson of making an unwise investment. CD-I was a market failure right from the start – and many people tried for years to tell Philips this. This is a classic example of what happens when the perception of the market is completely technology-oriented. It is a story of how a brilliant inventor comes to make some fatal misjudgements about the market because the company refuses to see the limitations of its own 'marvellous' invention. Philips tried so hard to create a market for a product that wouldn't last or would be only short-lived. There was something better around – for instance, CD-ROM, multimedia PC software, interactive television and digital video.

The irony is that the people at Philips knew that all along: the company was also busy inventing and developing the better technology, and still is. CD-I was a product that was not wanted or needed by publishers or their customers. Philips made the mistake of embarking on a game it did not have the skills or resources to understand – namely publishing. It strayed away from its core competence and insisted, for a very long time, that its vision of the CD-I market was real and not a figment of its imagination. Philips stopped listening to the market and refused to walk away from a bad investment until it got so bad it had no choice. The company had to admit failure and, in August 1996, it pulled the curtain down on CD-I. What about those million or so customers who bought CD-I drives and software? Philips will look after them for a while and then those customers will simply get over it and buy something else exciting and interesting, maybe even from Philips!

> **There is no escape from digital change.**

There is no escape from digital change. There are only two options: take part or retire. Assuming we all want to take part, we will not be allowed a lot of thinking time. Seductive marketers are staring us in the face, opportunities keep pounding on our doors and the pace of events demands action. We live in exciting, complicated times. The art of planning and timing one's actions has become all important. Nobody wants to miss the boat and everybody wants to be a winner. As so often in business, timing will be a major factor in determining who the winners will be: 'He who seizes the right moment, is the right man' (Goethe, *Faust*).

Although there are plenty of exaggerated perspectives on the meaning of this particular momentum in history, many political and industrial leaders agree that the development of the networked economy is bringing about fundamental and irreversible changes to society. It is a matter of fact that there is considerable commercial and political interest in how to take advantage of the new opportunities of digital technology, multimedia and networked communications. There is a race on between corporations, industrial sectors, countries and governments – each stakeholder investing substantial amounts of energy and resources, mostly technology-oriented, hoping to gain competitive advantage by judging the market correctly and picking the right road to success.

The Global Information Infrastructure envisaged by Vice President Al Gore in the United States and the Global Information Society promoted by the European Commission do not yet exist. However, the construction of them is well under way and, before long, many of these political promises and plans will be delivered. How and when the market potential of the GII will be realized depends on four main factors: political action, international co-operation, commercial investment and creative innovation.

Some will say that the infrastructure is already in place. They are right – in terms of basic technology. Hardware – such as network wiring, computers, cables, switches, satellites and so on – are available. We have at least a multinational, if not a global, infrastructure in place, based on the existing telecommunications and cable networks, accessible via telephones, television sets and computers. However, substantial developments in technology are still needed to achieve common standards, interoperability between platforms and functional access to open systems.

One thing is certain: there will not be just one broadband network or one type of appliance and interface to connect to the GII. There will be a multitude of interconnected networks and many electronic devices for access and usage. Anyone hoping to master the market will have to deal with not just one infrastructure, but many – and not just one delivery platform either, but several. The new market reality means multiple distribution channels and mixes of products and services.

Anyone hoping to master the market will have to deal with not just one infrastructure, but many – and not just one delivery platform either, but several.

There will be a range of choices for customers – some would say too much choice. The computer industry and the consumer electronics industry are already engaged in fierce competition and will no doubt bombard the market with an ever-growing range of electronic devices and software. In addition to the familiar telephone, television and personal computer, there will be game terminals, network computer terminals, set top boxes, digital video disc players, network radios, infra-red remote controls, cellular handsets, pocket computers, smart cards/electronic wallets and other hand-held devices and products yet to be invented.

It will be exciting to see whether these new products will actually succeed in the market and add some value to customers or be simply passing fads and gadgets. Sceptics are warning us that it will all simply lead to electronic overkill. The digital gold rush that is driving huge investments in information and media technologies could be deceptive. Is there really a market out there? How will the consumer respond? That is the multi-million-dollar question.

4

The market

The arrival of the new networked economy, fuelled by so much technological progress, has had a profound impact on market structures and environment. Market operators are facing a host of new demands and rules. There are new demands for products and services and new rules of price performance and competition. Opportunities are plentiful for those who embrace the change and brave the new uncharted territories. Forget the question of survival of the fittest, what counts now is the survival of the quickest and the wisest. The new winning game belongs to the fastest and most skilful drivers, those who are adept and flexible enough to respond to constant change and a string of surprises, those who have their integrity, focus and core values intact regardless of being subject to permanent turbulence and volatile market forces.

> **Forget the question of survival of the fittest, what counts now is the survival of the quickest and the wisest.**

The search for a market and the challenge of sizing it

Does the 'new market' exist? If it does, what is it, where is it and what are the entry options? What does the competition look like and what are the market demands? What's my competitive advantage and where do I want to be on the value curve?

Organizations across the board are groping in the dark and running into problems when it comes to defining and sizing up the markets. It is a real struggle to identify, scope and assess the value of the new market opportunities. It doesn't seem to matter whether you are a dominant player or a new market entrant, the challenge of sizing the market is equally frustrating. Traditional sources and methods of market analysis and forecasting fall short in the markets of the Wired World as they are based on the old map of distinct business sectors and cultures. Research methods and market intelligence have been developed differently for a range of industrial sectors that are now converging. Reputable market research companies publish reports that do not take the impact of convergence into account. Consequently, many organizations relying on such sources are basing their strategies on flawed data. Typical market reports are often distorted and quite inaccurate as they distinguish between categories that now overlap, and apply benchmarking figures and industry-by-industry indexes in a manner that no longer makes sense. Important variables are missed out and information is duplicated.

Traditional sources and methods of market analysis and forecasting fall short in the markets of the Wired World.

This does not stop people using whatever figures they can lay their hands on, however. It is hard to distinguish between the real and the phoney charts. The numerous attempts at estimating what this market is worth make very amusing reading indeed. There are huge discrepancies between different sets of figures, despite the fact that all the reports claim to measure and forecast the same thing, and they are published by reputable companies. Figures vary, but all the charts seem to have one feature in common – the curve plotting 'market value' rises steeply and consistently, as if it were designed to smell of gold! Worldwide estimates of the GII market range between $500 billion and $3 trillion. In the United States alone, people are talking 'conservative figures' when they estimate the market to be $400 billion.

It is interesting to study how analysts arrive at such staggering forecasts. One technique is to base the forecast on accumulated annual expenditure figures from all industrial sectors that can be defined as players in the GII or 'digital industries'. Varying estimates of new business to be generated directly from GII products and services are then added, and the whole is totalled up. This is of course a flawed method, but it is better than some wild guesses, such as those based, for instance, on the entire existing telephony subscriber base, or all PC owners being instantly converted to paying GII subscribers. It is better because using actual expenditure figures tells us something about what customers (where) are willing and able to pay for (see Figure 4.1).

Another technique – widely used for sizing the market for publishing products, on-line services and network traffic – is to base the forecast on the size of the

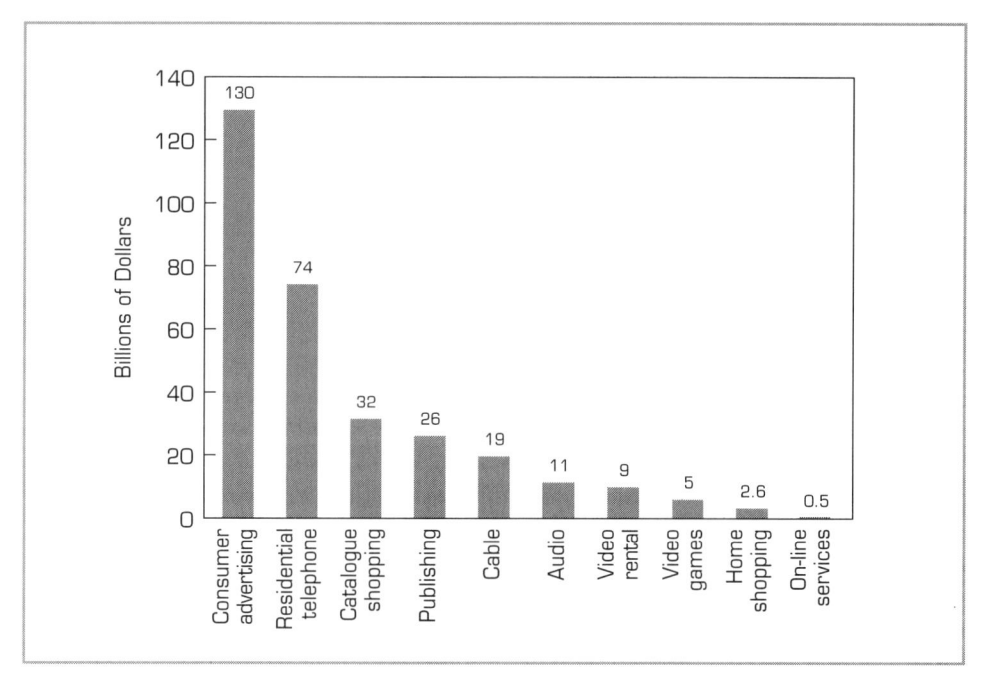

Figure 4.1: the $300 billion market in converging industries
Source: Gemini Consulting, 1995.

Bar chart values (Billions of Dollars): Consumer advertising 130; Residential telephone 74; Catalogue shopping 32; Publishing 26; Cable 19; Audio 11; Video rental 9; Video games 5; Home shopping 2.6; On-line services 0.5.

installed base, be it the number of Internet host connections, telephone or cable subscribers, or PCs and CD-ROM drives shipped, operating software packages sold and so on (see Figure 4.2).

We should be cautious about reading too much into charts such as these. We need to look beyond simplistic summaries of hardware sales and expenditure figures if we want to estimate demands for electronic commerce over GII networks. Some of the most popular products and services available today have been created without the expectation of a distribution base equal to a share of some installed hardware base or population of network subscribers. A better recipe for success may simply be to go for it, and focus investment on making something the consumer wants.

The fact that most adults have access to a box of matches does not prove there is a market for cigarettes. The tobacco industry relies on far more sophisticated methods for managing market demand for cigarettes and sizing up the market. Investments are based on psychological knowledge of consumer behaviour as well as tangible facts and hard figures. Demographic data, consumer group

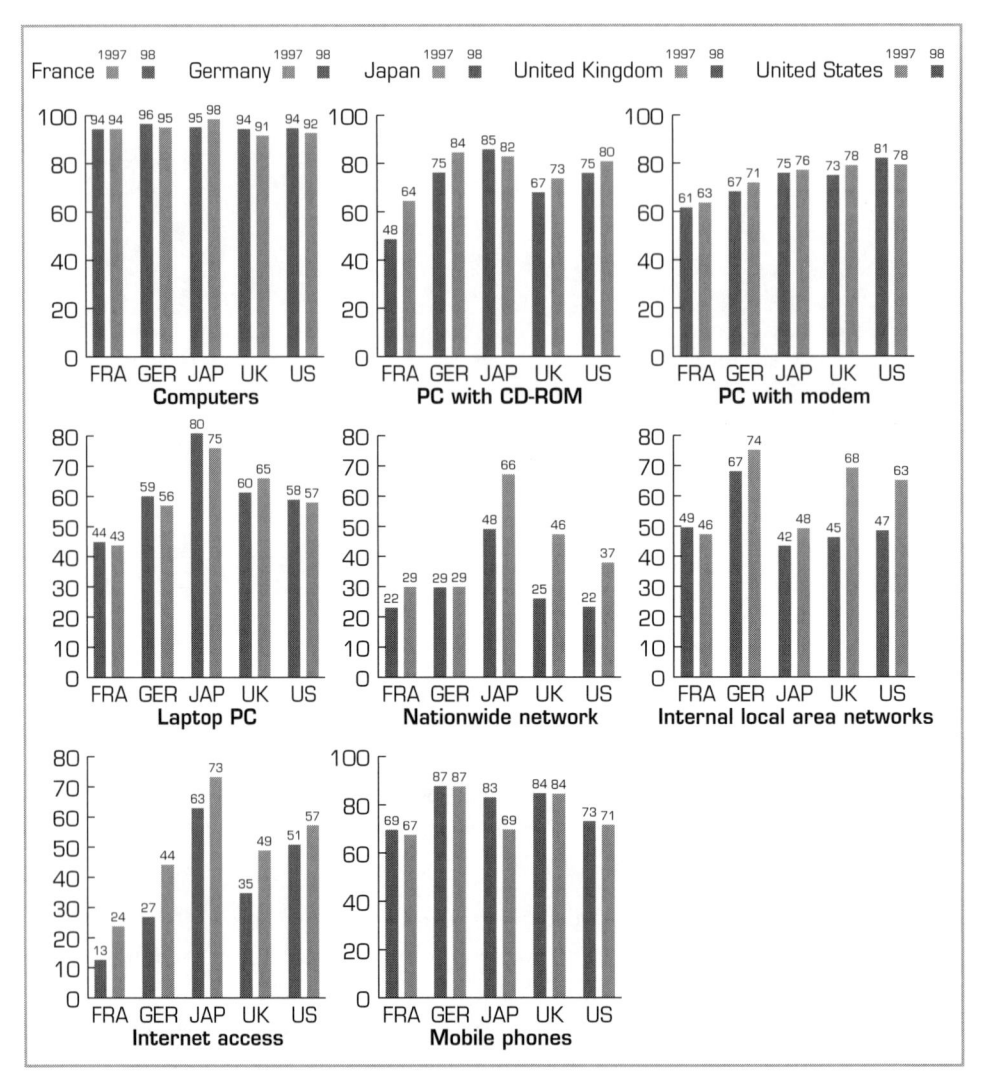

Figure 4.2: penetration of multimedia/communication technolgy
Source: DTI/Spectrum, 'Moving into the information age: An international benchmarking study', DTI, 1998

surveys, detailed analysis of what attracts people to smoking and why they continue are all important tools in this process. The health risks linked to tobacco, people's attitudes to smoking, the impact of regulatory frameworks, such as legal constraints with regard to advertising and liability risks, are also significant factors that are taken into account.

The penetration of so-called multimedia PCs is interesting if you happen to be manufacturing or retailing PCs, CD-ROM drives, sound cards or other components for such multimedia PCs. It is also of interest to those who have already produced software programs for this particular platform. For all others, however, the penetration of a particular consumer appliance should be of less interest.

Although it is important to know that there is an installed base of *x* number of *y* systems out there, it would be wrong to automatically translate this into a market for GII products and services. The critical factor that will determine the success of a new product or service is not the technology it will run on, but the functionality and attractiveness it can offer the individual consumer (see Figure 4.3). When it comes to electronic devices, computer software and the media industry, consumers are used to rapid change and increasing choice. They will quickly discard the useless and change over if something better comes along.

Consumers are used to rapid change and increasing choice. They will quickly discard the useless and change over if something better comes along.

"IT'S MY TURN TO BE INTERACTIVE

Figure 4.3: customers demand interactivity applications

The market

When organizations are considering which platform to build products and services around, and when consumers are considering what to buy, the critical question should be whether or not that particular technology can do the job. Ask yourself, is it good enough? Will it serve your purpose and for how long? Don't ask if this is the ultimate solution – there will always seem to be something better in the pipeline. If you don't take the first step, you'll never get started.

Technology is only a small part of what is needed in order to deliver the promises of the Global Information Society. The challenge really begins with the task of understanding how people and organizations will want to use the technology. What kinds of products and services will add value and be of interest to the market? Who are the customers and where is the market?

This line of questioning leads us into the post-technology stage, where we will have to focus on understanding the user and the content, rather than the container and the context (see Figure 4.4). The user is the one who will ultimately pass judgement on the value of being connected to the GII and who should be directing the show. The user does not care about technology. The nuts and bolts should be invisible to the user. The user should not have to care about whether it is the PC, network terminal, television, telephone or other device that is used to access the GII. The user is interested in the content and how the content meets their expectations and requirements for what they want to do.

The user does not care about technology.

Content is a much more difficult and resource-intensive part of the process of constructing the GII than technology is. We have only just begun to play with the new opportunities. The best is yet to come. It was Ernest Hemingway who once said, 'A great story is like an iceberg. One-eighth is above the surface; the other seven-eighths is below.' Today we are looking at the very tip of the iceberg,

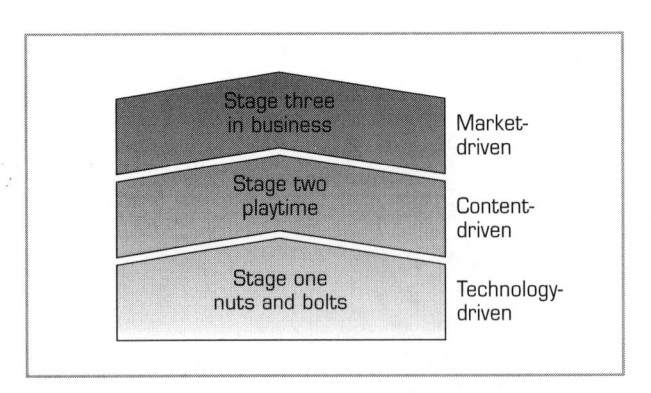

Figure 4.4: three main phases in the process of constructing the Global Information Market

Stage three in business — Market-driven
Stage two playtime — Content-driven
Stage one nuts and bolts — Technology-driven

mostly ignorant of what lies underneath and beyond the physical infrastructure of the Wired World. Most investments have so far been driven by technology and the need to control and manage the nuts and bolts. Many organizations are moving rapidly into the next stage, driven by the need for content.

Together with early adopters in the market they are busy experimenting and playing around with content in many shapes and forms. This activity will not only provide greater knowledge of what new applications can offer, but hopefully also result in better understanding of what the market really wants. It is when this avalanche of early experiments matures into a number of sustainable products and services driven by market demand that organizations reach the third stage and we can call it real business. Innovation will always continue and people will have to make up their minds and place their bets as new achievements are announced and new products emerge. Organizations will continue to invest and more players will enter the market. Inevitably, there will be several shake-outs, reducing the number of players and the noise in the marketplace. There will be expensive lessons and lost bets, but there will also be exciting results and plenty of winners.

The British filmmaker Lord Puttnam has pointed out that 'the CD-ROMs now on the market are digital equivalents of those rather aimless, almost embarrassing, flickering silent movies from before the First World War' (speaking at a seminar on the Global Information Society facilitated by the Oxford-Templeton Forum for Leaders of Industry and Government, at Templeton College, Oxford University, 13 May 1996). We have a long way to go before we realize the potential of a connected society, which, to a large extent, will depend on the ability to identify customer demand and deliver useful content. Few will claim to have reached the third stage yet. Many are between the first and the second stage, looking to content as the critical issue. The US GII 'Agenda for Co-operation' points out:

The GII extends beyond hardware and software; it is also a system of applications, activities, and relationships. There is the information itself, whatever its purpose or form, e.g., video programming, scientific or business databases, images, sound recordings, library archives, or other media. There are also standards, interfaces, and transmission codes that facilitate interoperability between networks and ensure the privacy and security of the information carried over them, as well as the security and reliability of the networks themselves. Most importantly, the GII includes the people involved in the creation and use of information, development of applications and services, construction of the facilities, and training necessary to realize the potential of the GII. These individuals are primarily in the private sector, and include vendors, operators, service providers, and users.

The meaning of convergence

The concept of 'convergence' is frequently used to describe the development of the Global Information Society. Unfortunately, the term is often applied carelessly as a crude blanket label, giving people a false impression that the entire world is about to converge into one – one technology, one market, one business, one type of customer, one form of government, one model for education, and so on. That is, of course, not the case, and we need to pay a lot more attention to precisely what the so-called process of convergence means.

Convergence is taking place in a number of areas at various levels – in science and technology, industrial sectors, the marketplace, the legal and regulatory domain, education and research, and politics. We need to distinguish between these different areas of convergence in order to see how they interrelate and to understand the changes taking place around us. The process of convergence started with previously separate technologies coming closer together as a direct consequence of the advances made in microchip and computer technology. The most profound changes will probably take place as a result of the process of technological convergence of the previously separate telecommunications, cable, information, publishing and mass media industries. These industrial sectors are now often referred to as 'the converging industries'. Borders that once separated them are increasingly being blurred. In the past we had different types of networks for the delivery of mail, print, telephony, radio, television and data services. These networks are regulated differently and usually by separate authorities. In a digital world, these services can be combined and offered over the same transmission and delivery system. In the words of the US GII 'Agenda for Co-operation':

Multiple networks composed of different transmission media, such as fiber-optic cable, coaxial cable, satellites, radio, and copper wire, will carry a broad range of telecommunications and information services and information technology applications into homes, businesses, schools, and hospitals. These networks will form the basis of evolving national and global information infrastructures, in turn creating a seamless web uniting the world in the emergent Information Age. The result will be a new information marketplace, providing opportunities and challenges for individuals, industry, and governments.

The convergence of technologies is causing fundamental changes to occur in the structures of traditional industries. New business models require new market positions. Collaboration across industrial and cultural borders is required to succeed in the new environment. The strategic response of many companies is one of growth by means of acquisitions and/or strategic alliances as part of a process of vertical or horizontal integration.

The new evolving market structure

The growth of strategic alliances and the degree of vertical and horizontal integration in the marketplace have fundamentally changed the structure of the market. It no longer makes sense to apply the traditional distinctions between industrial sectors. Telecommunications carriers are now also broadcasters, cable operators are telephony providers, film companies are generating more revenue from selling merchandise than they do from films, libraries have become publishers, software developers are offering banking services, consumer electronics companies are running film studios and publishing all kinds of media content, and so on.

The emerging market structure can be split up into six layers representing the key business areas or reshuffled industrial sectors (see Figure 4.5). These consist of the following.

Layer 1: broadband network

Telephony, satellite, cable and broadcasting companies owning and developing the physical communications network. Companies manufacturing microchips, security technology and network control systems will provide the 'engine power', the security and quality control systems needed to operate the network. Standards organizations and industry regulators will ensure that standards and regulations are followed.

Layer 2: electronic appliances and components

Companies providing consumer electronics, PCs, hardware-based user interfaces (from smart cards to set top boxes).

Layer 3: operating software

Computer and software companies providing network and PC operating systems.

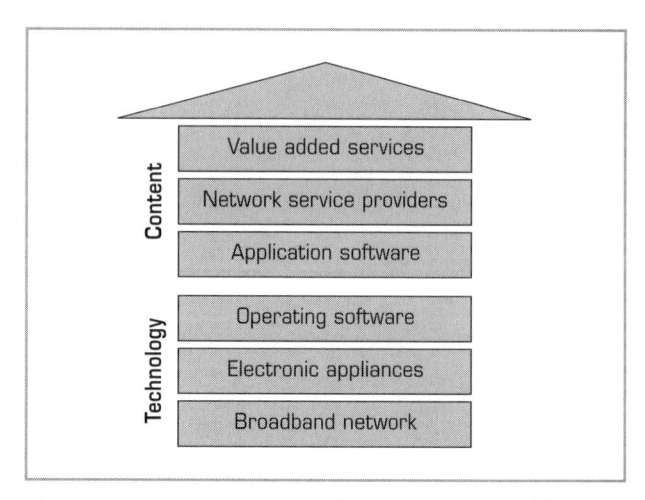

Figure 4.5: the emerging Global Information Market structure

Layer 4: applications software
Companies developing and publishing computer programs to make the various applications work, including user interfaces.

Layer 5: network service providers
Companies providing network access to a range of facilities, such as the Internet, interactive television, cable and satellite.

Layer 6: value-added information services
Government administrations and public services, including education and national health. Companies providing on-line services within various sectors, for instance:

- banking and financial services;
- healthcare;
- business and professional services;
- academic and scientific research;
- libraries and archives;
- education;
- mass media;
- entertainment and culture;
- home shopping.

Also, companies offering support services:

- advertising and marketing agencies;
- consultancy.

Key players in the marketplace are searching for optimum business models, busy trying to pick the winning positioning combination in this market structure. Many of them are moving up towards the value-added services. Take the telecommunication companies: all the larger ones have expanded into new products and services, growing out from their original base in the technology domain and right through to the top layer in the content domain.

Redefining the market

Most organizations will have to redefine their markets. Market dynamics are changing and the market can no longer be reached efficiently by relying on the traditional way of segmenting it (see Figure 4.6). Boundaries between once very different markets are becoming increasingly blurred.

There is a process of convergence going on that makes it necessary for many companies to review their marketing strategies. The old map of the market does not reflect the changed landscape. By investigating the degree of change and redrawing the map according to the findings, companies find a world of new marketing challenges and opportunities. Old, outdated market definitions are thrown away.

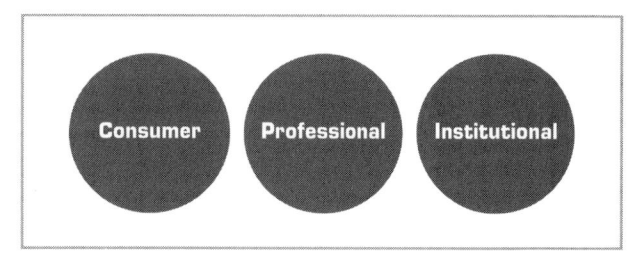

Figure 4.6: a traditional way of segmenting the market

New ways of re-segmenting the market are applied (see Figure 4.7), which has enormous implications for the organizational structures of companies and how they manage their operations. Many companies find they have to reorganize themselves completely in order to operate competitively and match the changing landscape of the market.

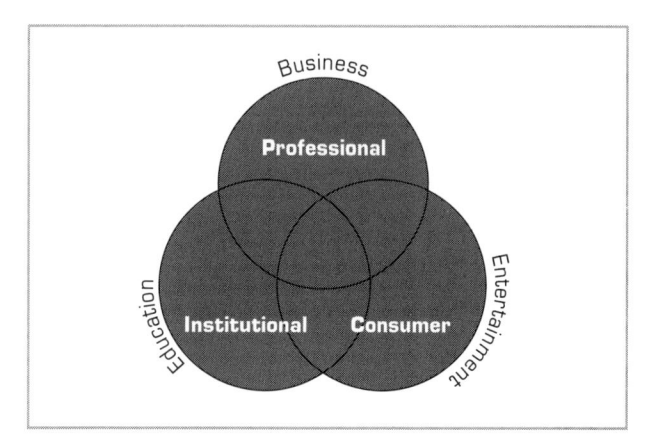

Figure 4.7: the new, resegmented market

The market

5 Content

We are standing at the very start of the 'content race' – today's equivalent of the great Gold Rush – and many hopeful would-be GII players have become serious content gamblers. There is a growing sense of panic among those who have invested the most in the technology as they realize that technology alone is useless – the GII needs content. 'Content' is another of the buzzwords associated with the Global Information Society.

Market studies and government papers covering electronic commerce and the so-called 'content industries' are currently circulating throughout political and commercial camps. There are even suggestions that a new 'digital industry' is emerging. This terminology is symptomatic of the evolutionary change that is taking place within the different market sectors, but words such as 'content' and 'digital' do little to explain the nature of that change. These all-embracing labels are so broad they become meaningless for the purpose of defining the specifics of the new networked economy.

Many prominent speakers at business conferences around the world frequently proclaim 'content is king!' and the audience applauds, recognizing that the mere physical shape of the GII leaves little to be excited about – we need something to fill our magic box with. As we enter the next century, many of us will have access to an estimated 500 television channels. What are we going to fill them up with? The lyrics from that Bruce Springsteen song come to mind: '50 channels on TV and nothing on'.

Content may be the lifeblood of the GII, but, unlike human blood, there isn't a universal 'type O' that is suitable for all. There is no type O donor among the content owners, capable of pumping out generic content acceptable across the

GII. The fact that the term 'content' is being used as a blanket label for some omni-potential bag of magic demonstrates a lack of understanding for what content means in relation to the needs of specific user groups connected to the GII. Content only becomes meaningful the moment an individual customer makes use of it.

What content, which customer?

It was the technology-oriented players – the telecommunications and software industries – that started using the term 'content' some time in 1993/94, and, unfortunately, it seems to have stuck. Authors, publishers and producers now find themselves renamed as 'content providers' and government officials talk about 'the content industries'. Now there is a pressing need for differentiation between different kinds of content and refinement of activities, products and services within the GII. We suffer from the fact that the development of the Global Information Society originates from technology. Consequently, we have inherited an outlook that is coloured by technical capability, rather than commercial and social benefits (see Figure 5.1). We need to shift our perspective in such a way that we can focus clearly on the main driver of this development. It is not the content that is king, but the customer (see Figure 5.2). We should place customers at the centre of our focus, not technology, not content. Content

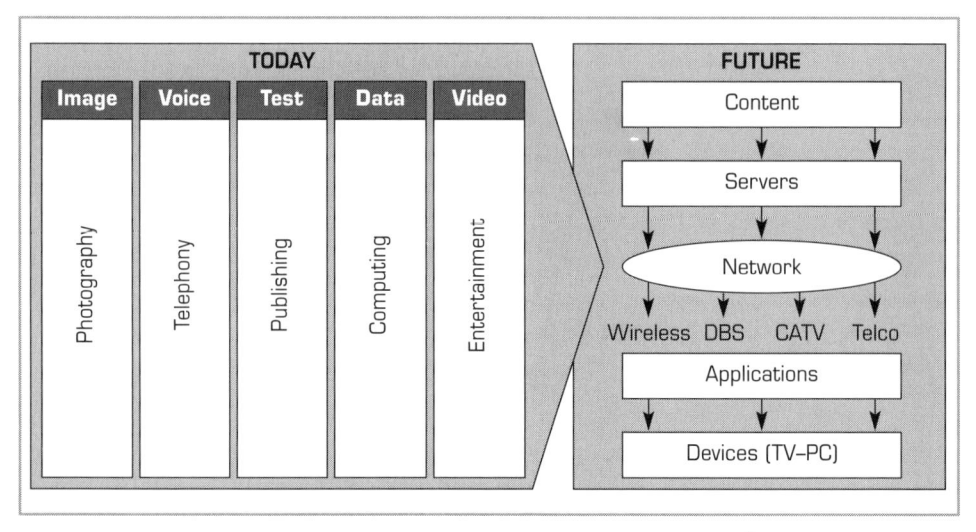

Figure 5.1: a technology-oriented view of the market
Source: Jagdish Sheth, Emory University

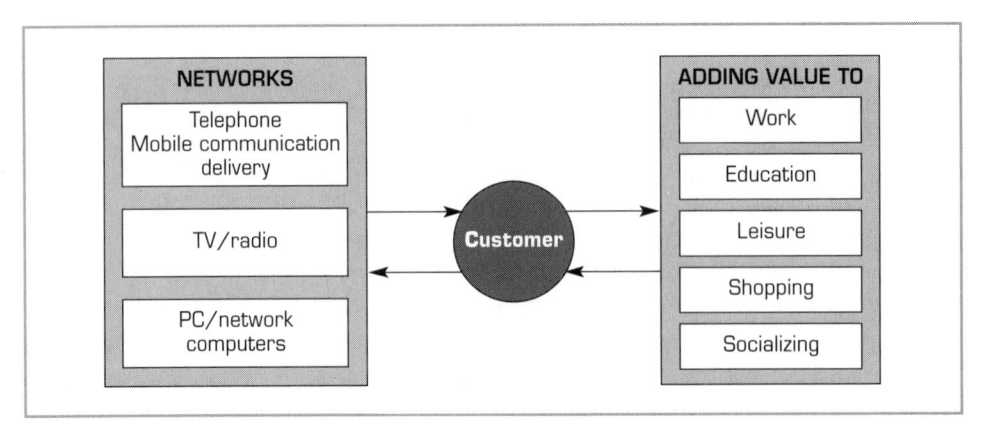

Figure 5.2: a customer-oriented view of the market

only becomes meaningful when there is interaction and contact with users. It is the understanding of customers' needs and market demands that will drive the development of this market.

Who the customer is will, of course, depend on what type of business you represent and what you have to offer. There is a lot of confusion regarding markets, caused by convergence and the perceived digital melting pot of the GII. Many organizations are suffering from a serious identity crisis. It is a classic problem – how to grow and prosper beyond what you are and do now. We often forget who we are when we let ourselves be seduced by prospects we cannot attain. Success in one area often makes organizations overconfident and arrogant. Just because a company has been immensely successful as a telephony provider, it does not follow that it can replicate this success in the business of broadcasting or publishing. Companies frequently forget who they are and what their competitive advantage is. They lose sight of what their core competences are and neglect their own assets in an attempt to capitalize on what they do not yet control or even comprehend. They embark on overambitious and omnipotential growth strategies, and these bring more failures than successes.

> **The challenge of exploiting the business opportunities of the GII is that no one company can do it alone.**

The challenge of exploiting the business opportunities of the GII is that no one company can do it alone. We need to collaborate and reach outside our own comfort zone and core areas of expertise. Even the richest and most dominant players – such as, for instance, the telecommunications giants or media/software companies of the likes of Time Warner, Microsoft, the BBC or Bertelsmann –

will have to let go of the degree of control they have enjoyed in the past and enter into a multitude of collaborations and strategic partnerships to enable them to deliver products and services within the GII.

The networks of the GII will be used as another set of marketing channels for trading all kinds of assets. Manufacturers of goods and retailers from a wide range of industries are already using the Internet as a new form of catalogue shopping, allowing consumers to window-shop via their PC or television screens and place orders for goods to be paid for and delivered by traditional means. However, increasingly the main economic activity over these global networks will be the trading of information and media assets.

> The networks of the GII will be used as another set of marketing channels for trading all kinds of assets.

An 'information asset' can be defined as any tradeable media commodity of commercial value in any medium or combinations of media formats (text, pictures, sound, moving images). The term 'information' is, in this context, used in its broadest sense for the purpose of understanding the transactional process for trading all kinds of information and media assets on international digital networks. Many basic mechanisms and procedures involved in such information transactions can be applied generically, regardless of what type of information asset is being exchanged.

However, special attention and focus is given to information assets that can be defined as intellectual properties – in particular, assets protected by copyright and related rights. This is necessary, because it is in the area of protected information and intellectual property rights that the problems for transactional systems and global information exchange accumulate, posing many challenges in terms of achieving competitiveness and growth in the information market.

The trouble with information assets

Most economists are not very fond of information assets. They are harder to understand and differ from other commodities in many respects. Information assets are different from other commodities because:

- information is of an intangible nature;
- information is considered a public good and a political instrument of democracy;
- information cannot be owned;

- information is vulnerable and subject to human communication skills;
- information is expressed in tangible forms that are exclusively protected.

The degree of tangibility required to make a value assessment is often hard to define. Also, information assets usually fit rather poorly with established economic models. For instance, consider this dilemma. If I have some information I know will be of value to you, I will have to tell you about it. However, once I have told you about it, you already know, so you may not need to buy my information any more.

The 'information asset owner' often depends on marketing resources to persuade the market that what they have is worth purchasing and they need to know exactly how and how much to disseminate for free to ensure that customers will want to come back and buy some more.

Information is one of the main pillars of democracy and the right of public access to information is a fundamental principle in all democratic nations. Indeed, it is defined and cemented at the international level in the 1946 United Nations' Universal Declaration of Human Rights.

Another challenge for the information market is that information cannot legally be owned. It follows that what cannot be owned cannot be stolen — that is, the concept of theft cannot be applied to something that cannot be owned. Thus, although there are intellectual property rights attached to defined categories of information and these rights are owned by the rights-holder, the information itself cannot be owned in legal terms.

Information is generated and received by individuals and will, consequently, be subject to various sets of communication criteria in order to gain value. This is also the case with intelligent computing, where the terms of communicating information will, to a large extent, have been pre-defined by the human beings who designed the programs. This makes information vulnerable and dependent on individual human skills at both the producer and the consumer ends of the chain. For instance, information is only as good as its source. A journalist may have misjudged a report or a film may fail at the box office because it was not interpreted and received in the way intended. It is often hard to establish the real value of information until the transaction has taken place and the information has been consumed.

The final characteristic distinguishing information assets from other commodities is the 'monopoly rights' that may be attached to these assets when the expression of the information appears in tangible forms defined as intellectual properties that have been granted exclusive legal protection.

The economic value of information increases according to the degree of tangibility that can be defined and attached to the information. There are other dynamic factors – such as brands, the credibility of the information provider, the nature of the content, and market demand – that influence and determine the economic value of information assets.

The economic value of information increases according to the degree of tangibility that can be defined and attached to the information.

The intellectual property system is a fundamental economic strategy enabling industries as well as individual authors and information providers to secure the value of their core assets. However, intellectual property rights are not the only means of protecting the value of information assets. Commercial enterprises are continuously looking for new ways of protecting the value of information assets in the struggle to achieve competitive advantage. This can be achieved by, for instance, strategic marketing techniques such as brand building, the creation of 'hybrid products' that have a modular product design with interlinking features and add-on functions, bundling and packaging of products and services, lock-in measures, proprietary technology or process solutions, and more (see Figure 5.3).

Global networks such as those available via the Internet, including the World Wide Web, open up many new opportunities for marketing information assets. The way in which information is presented, distributed, sold and used in the networked environment is different from that found in the traditional marketplace. For instance, consider the role of publishing. With electronic access to complicated databases, almost anybody will be able to put together new editorial products, create information assets and sell them to the market. The process of publishing is changing, and electronic publishing requires new kinds of authorship and new ways of publishing.

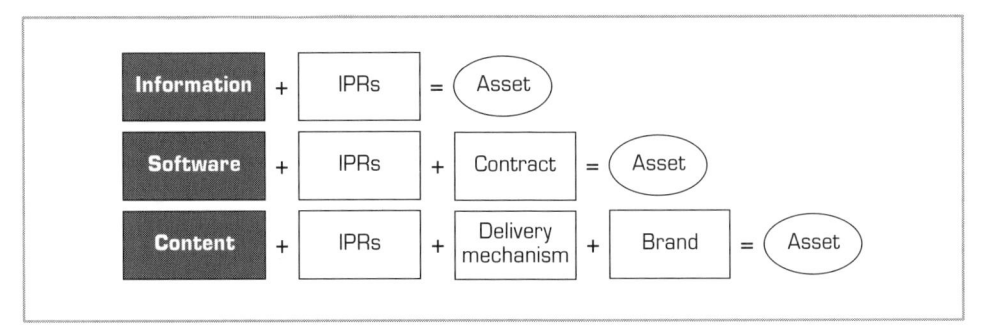

Figure 5.3: the aggregate nature of information assets

The intellectual property system

Intellectual property rights represent fundamental trade mechanisms, facilitating a protected commercial exchange of information assets. The trading of intellectual property commodities – information assets – is becoming more and more significant in the world economy. For instance, in the European Union, copyright and related rights alone account for 5 per cent of the gross domestic product (Directorate for Science, Technology and Industry, 'Towards realisation of the information society,' discussion paper, OECD, March 1995).

With electronic access to complicated databases, almost anybody will be able to put together new editorial products, create information assets and sell them to the market.

'Intellectual property' has been defined as 'works of the mind' in 'tangible form' – for instance, literary and artistic works, photographs, films, video, music on records, tapes or discs, architectural drawings, industrial designs and patterns, computer software and database programs. The 'tangible' versus the 'intangible' is a central issue of debate on intellectual property as both are required in order for an intellectual property to succeed in the market.

The history of the 'intellectual property system' began with the Industrial Revolution, which created a need to protect commercial exploitation of intellectual property, such as new industrial inventions. Patents were the first form of legal protection to be conceptualized in English law. 'Copyright' came much later.

John Gibbons (*Intellectual Property Rights in an Age of Electronics and Information*, Robert E. Krieger Publishing Company, 1986) defines the intellectual property system as follows:

> **. . . it is useful to conceive of the (intellectual property) system as a set of incentives and rewards designed to affect the behaviour of individuals or organized groups engaged in creative or inventive activities (see Figure 5.4). This system is divided into five interrelated parts:**

1 policy goals that it seeks to accomplish;

2 property rights that provide incentives and rewards;

3 operating rules;

4 mechanisms by which policy goals are achieved;

5 a realm of people and activities that the system is designed to influence.

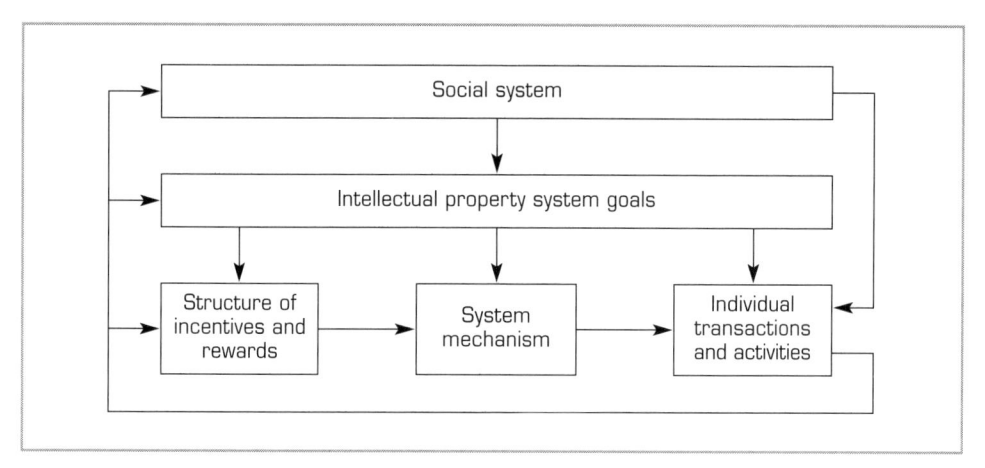

Figure 5.4: the intellectual property system
Source: Office of Technology Assessment, US Administration

In other words, the intellectual property system exists in order to protect, enforce and develop 'intellectual property rights'. The system is concerned with three different levels of activity, balancing social, economic and political interests:

- policy;
- principles;
- rules.

The system consequently consists of a number of laws, policy and trade agreements, as well as relationships between interested parties, tradition and practice, on both national and international levels. It includes the legal and political structure of patents, copyright, trade secrecy, contract and competition law.

It is increasingly difficult to maintain the traditional distinctions between the various components of the intellectual property rights system. This is true, for example, on a functional level between patent and copyright, and on a policy level between the World Intellectual Property Organization (WIPO) and the World Trade Organization (WTO, formerly GATT). This shifting of borders is particularly interesting to observe in the areas of computer software, databases and electronic publishing where owners of new forms of intellectual property have to 'choose' categories and lobby for measures of protection of different types.

Copyright

The origin of copyright

England was the first country in the world to develop 'copyright legislation', and served as a model for the development of copyright in other countries. The term 'copyright' was coined in fifteenth-century England after William Caxton introduced the printing press in 1477, although the term has not been noted as being in use until much later in register books in the 1670s.

Bookbinders, printers and booksellers were organized in the Stationers' Company, which succeeded in lobbying for the very first exclusive copyright and was granted a royal charter in 1557. The charter limited almost all printing to the members of the Stationers' Company and gave it the power to identify and destroy unlawful books found anywhere in the kingdom. This historic origin of copyright is often forgotten, but it is important to remember it because it demonstrates the fact that, from the very start, there has been an intimate relationship between copyright legislation, market conditions and the political environment. The stationers' desire for a market monopoly on print and publishing coincided with the political desire to control the output of the press: '. . . the stationers immediately proved to be a valuable ally of the government in its campaign to suppress dissent by controlling the output of the press (which, indeed, had been Mary [Tudor's] motive in granting the royal charter' (L. Ray Patterson and Stanley W. Lindberg, *The Nature of Copyright*, University of Georgia Press, 1991).

There has always been an intimate relationship between copyright legislation, market conditions and the political environment.

At first, the protection of copyright was given to the stationers – or, in modern terms, the publishers. As Gavin McFarlane reports (*A Practical Introduction to Copyright*, Waterlow Publishers, 1989):

The call for effective protection in statutory form, when it came, did not emanate from authors, a body which has historically been disinterested in acting for its own interest. It arrived eventually when commercial men moved in to develop writers' works in saleable form, which came about with the invention of printing. Naturally the state swiftly came to appreciate the political and economic significance of the new invention, and at an early stage the king assumed the monopoly of granting licences to print.

Copyright in the early days was not an 'author's right', nor, indeed, a 'user's right', nor was it a political tool to stimulate progress in society, which is the intent of modern copyright law. The first copyright was clearly limited to two functions – the stationers' economic right of market monopoly and the government's right to full censorship of the press.

What has become known as the 'stationers' copyright' lasted for nearly two centuries and has had a strong influence on successive laws, including the current copyright law, which also reflects the origin of copyright and its legal heritage. Copyright legislation has been developed and revised as a consequence of changes that have taken place both in the marketplace and in the political environment. The historic developments in the West during the rise of Protestantism, the Reformation and the Age of Enlightenment had a profound impact on politics, trade, commerce and society as a whole. Consequently, the issue of copyright was also affected by them.

After almost 200 years of the stationers' copyright monopoly, coupled with censorship and central control of the press, protest and frustration had accumulated. It is important to remember the political environment of these times, which had a strong progressive movement favouring knowledge and learning in a free, competitive society – a movement that clearly was contradictory to the copyright policy of the time. The major objection was against the power of the Stationers' Company and the fact that it abused its monopoly status by charging artificially high prices. This objection finally resulted in the stationers losing the public legal protection in 1694.

For some time after this, the stationers petitioned Parliament to reinstate the censorship laws and revive their public legal protection, but, when they failed, they changed their strategy and started to use the authors as an excuse to bring back copyright. This worked and brought about the copyright law often referred to as the first in 'modern' copyright history – the Statute of Anne, passed in England in 1709, which came into force in 1710.

Although the Statute of Anne was the world's first statutory copyright legislation, it is dangerous to mark this as its beginning as the preceding two centuries of the stationers' copyright contain important influences and valuable lessons for the intellectual property system of today. Thus the Statute of Anne marks the second step in the evolution of copyright and introduces the use of copyright as a trade-regulation concept. It also introduces the concept of 'author's right' and of copyright as a political device for the public good by stimulating the creation of works and encouraging learning. Indeed, the full title of the Statute reads 'An act for the encouragement of learning, by vesting the copies of printed books in the authors or purchasers of such copies, during the times therein mentioned'.

In the United States, the Statute of Anne was, in effect, imported into US copyright law and served in full as the model of the first National Copyright Act in 1790, which was later revised several times. American copyright tradition is coloured by the fact that the initiators had the experience of the authoritarian politics, tyranny of censorship and religious fanaticism of fourteenth to seventeenth-century England fresh in their minds. In fact, copyright law is directly connected to the First Amendment of the US Constitution, Section 8. Article I of the constitution authorizes Congress to grant exclusive ownership rights of writings and inventions for a limited period of time. The purpose was twofold:

- to foster the progress of science and the useful arts;
- to encourage the creation and dissemination of information and knowledge to the public.

Copyright in the international environment

Europe has had a different copyright tradition and direction from that of the United States, although this is less obvious today. Continental European copyright law – particularly in France – has focused very strongly on the moral rights of the author, or, *droit d'auteur*. Anglo-American copyright law has, until more recently, not included 'moral rights' to the same degree, but, rather, focused on the 'economic rights'.

As intellectual property is traded and used extensively across national borders today, it has been necessary to establish both bilateral and multilateral agreements on an international level. The first and single most important international convention in this respect is the Berne Convention. The international issues of copyright used to be almost exclusively controlled by the United Nations (UN) via the Berne Convention administered by the World Intellectual Property Organization and the Universal Copyright Convention administered by the United Nations' Educational, Scientific and Cultural Organisation (UNESCO), both set up under the UN. However, today the international picture is much more complicated and includes many other important actors. As intellectual property has grown to become a large proportion of nations' gross national products, almost every major intergovernmental agency is now dealing with issues concerning copyright. This includes, for instance, the EU, WTO, OECD, UNCTAD, COE, EFTA and several others.

As intellectual property has grown to become a large proportion of nations' gross national products, almost every major intergovernmental agency is now dealing with issues concerning copyright.

The Berne Convention
The Berne Union was established in 1886. The initiative came originally from the International Literary and Artistic Association, which had proposed a draft and eventually succeeded in getting the Swiss government to call an international meeting. As of 1999, a total of 140 countries have joined the Berne Union, and adhered to the Berne Convention and its various protocols. The Berne Convention offers the highest level of international copyright protection and also serves as a model for national legislation in many countries. The Convention has been revised many times and there are several additional protocols to the original 1886 text – for example, the protocol concerning computer software.

The Universal Copyright Convention
The Universal Copyright Convention (UCC) was set up in 1952, primarily to offer registration and administration of copyright and a lower level of protection than the Berne Convention in order to attract a wider range of member states. It included, for instance, the United States, the then Soviet Union, China and some developing countries, that were not members of the Berne Convention at the time. However, today, most nations are members of the Berne Union, including the United States, which joined in 1989, and enjoy a great deal of legal protection.

Other legal protection
There are four EC directives dealing with copyright:

- Software Directive – Council Directive 91/250;
- Rental and Lending Directive – Council Directive 92/100;
- Satellite and Cable Directive – Council Directive 93/83/EE;
- Database Directive – Council Directive 95/464.

Legislation in the mould
There are, at the time of writing, several pieces of proposed legislation on the table at both national and international levels that aim to respond to the impact of new technology on intellectual property rights and protect information assets. The EU Database Directive of 1995 has had a significant impact on the process of national legislation concerning information as it introduces a *sui generis* right (that is, not an intellectual property right) whereby the 'manufacturer' of a database will be able to prevent unauthorized acts of 'extraction or re-utilization' of

Consideration	Copyright	Patent	Trade secrecy	Contract law
Duration	50, 75 or 100 yrs	17 years	Until disclosed	As agreed
Enforceable	Worldwide*	Nationwide	State-by-state	Worldwide*
Acquired by	Act of creation	Application	Agreement	Agreement
Lost by	Improper notice	Legal challenge	Disclosure	Expiry or breach
Cost to obtain	Trivial	Significant	Trivial	Low
Cost to maintain	Trivial	Trivial	Significant	Low
Cost to defend	Moderate	Moderate	Significant	Moderate
Protects/prevents:				
Ideas and designs	No	Yes	Yes	Yes
Copying	Yes	Yes	No	Yes
Use	No	Yes	No	Yes
Independent invention	No	Yes	No	No
Distribution	Yes	Yes	Yes	Yes
Material must be:				
Unique	No	Yes	No	No
Novel	No	Yes	No	No
Used in business	No	No	Yes	No
Not generally known	No	Yes	Yes	No
Remedies available:				
Injunction	Yes	Yes	Yes	Yes
Statutory damages	Yes	No	No	No
Attorney's fees	Yes	Yes	No	No
Suitable for:				
Retail sales	Yes	Yes	No	No
Licensed use	Yes	Yes	Yes	Yes
Subject matter covered	Works of authorship	1. Machines 2. Articles of manufacture 3. Processes 4. Compositions of matter	Valuable business information	Anything
	* with exceptions			* with exceptions

Table 5.1: overview of legal protections

Source: Ernest E. Keet, *Preventing Piracy,* 1985

that collection for a period of 15 years. According to Article 6 of this new directive, in respect of databases, the following acts will be protected:

- the temporary and permanent reproduction of the database by any means and in any form, in whole or in part;
- the translation, adaptation, arrangement and any other alteration of the database;
- the reproduction of the results of any of the acts listed in the first two points;
- any form of distribution to the public, including the rental, of the database or copies thereof;
- any communication, display or performance of the database to the public.

The intention of the Directive is to provide legal protection of databases that may not be covered under copyright laws, and thereby to encourage investment and growth in the European information market. However, opponents claim that the Directive will create legal uncertainty concerning what types of databases are protected under which laws. In many EU member states, databases are defined as compilations of works that are covered by both national copyright laws and the Berne Convention. Opponents in the US market see the Directive as an attempt to protect and favour European industry, and question whether it is in breach of the General Agreement on Tariffs and Trade (GATT) agreement on Trade-Related aspects of Intellectual Property Rights (TRIPS).

The publishing industry is well aware of its need for, and dependency on, statutory protection. It is also lobbying for the inclusion of a 'new' right: the 'publisher's right', justified on the basis of the increasing amount of creative effort that the publisher contributes to the process of publishing. In fact, much material is authored and created by the publisher's own staff. The layout and typeface of a book have long been the debate of copyright claims, but there is much more than these aspects to the publisher's role in creating works in electronic multimedia publishing.

> **The publishing industry is lobbying for the inclusion of a 'new' right: the 'publisher's right', justified on the basis of the increasing amount of creative effort that the publisher contributes.**

Two other important documents released in 1995 will also have a significant impact on the development of policy and regulatory frameworks for the GII. They are:

- the *White Paper on Intellectual Property and the Global Information Infrastructure* (US Department of Commerce, July 1995);
- the *Green Paper on Intellectual Property and the Global Information Society* (European Commission, August 1995).

Copyright as a trade mechanism

It is widely recognized and agreed that copyright is the most appropriate set of intellectual property rights for multimedia and information assets in digital form. Much effort has been invested at both national and international levels over the past few years to develop copyright law to accommodate the impact of digital technology. However, although copyright law is reasonably up to date and has been harmonized on an international level, the interpretation, administration and practice of the laws vary tremendously depending on cultural traditions, national domain and individual perceptions. This causes enormous practical problems when industry and commerce attempt to establish services and create activities that require a global administration of intellectual property rights.

> **Copyright is the most appropriate set of intellectual property rights for multimedia and information assets in digital form.**

If a group of leading representatives of industry, authors and publishers, legal experts and those in the government and educational fields could come together to discuss the critical issues currently facing them, copyright would feature high on the agenda. If you asked them to share their perspectives and definitions of the term 'copyright', the result would be a lively debate with a wide range of differing opinions. There would almost certainly be as many different definitions of the word as there were people in the room. In other words, there exist several different and sometimes competing perspectives on copyright and it is important to appreciate these in order to achieve a common understanding. Paul Goldstein – one of the world's leading legal authorities on copyright – has pointed this out ('Copyright', *Journal of the Copyright Society of the USA*, vol. 38, no. 3, 1991, pages 109–22):

What is copyright? A policy maker in the United States will tell you that copyright is an instrument of consumer welfare, stimulating the production of the widest possible array of literary and artistic works at the lowest possible price. But ask the question of a practitioner on the European continent, and he will tell you that copyright is at best a watered-down version of author's right – the grand civil law

tradition that places the author, not the consumer, at the centre of protection. A low protectionist will tell you that copyright is a monopoly that undesirably drives up the price of goods in the marketplace. A high protectionist will tell you that copyright is a property right – no more, no less – and one without which we would have very few creative works in the marketplace.

Ask the question of a United States trade official and she will tell you that copyright is one of the strongest net contributors to the nation's balance of trade. Ask the question of a schoolteacher in Thailand and he will tell you that copyright is what stands in the way of getting textbooks into the hands of his students. Ask the question of an anthropologist digging through the remains of the 1976 Copyright Act a century from now and she might tell you that copyright is a symbol of a nation's cultural aspirations. Ask the same question today of a manufacturer of novelty knick-knacks and he will tell you that copyright is simply what enables him to meet his payroll at the end of the week.

Who to believe? An in-depth study of the evolution of copyright will reveal they are all right and they are all wrong. What usually happens is that people will tend to define copyright from their own viewpoint and on the basis of self-interest. The consequence is that most people have only a fragmented perception of copyright and fail to see the overall picture, which would reveal the complete function and meaning of the term.

Copyright is not about the right to copy, as the term so misleadingly suggests. Copyright reflects a nation's cultural ambition and the level of consumer welfare and it provides the fundamental conditions for trade. Copyright is thus about many different rights, economic as well as moral (Lawrence Becker, 'The moral basis of property rights', in *Property*, J. Roland Penvork, 1980):

- the right to possess or physically control something;
- the right to use or enjoy its benefits;
- the right to manage or decide how it is to be used;
- the right to receive income from it;
- the right to consume or destroy it;
- the right to modify it;
- the right to transfer it;
- the right to distribute it;
- the right to exclude others from using it.

Paul Goldstein ('copyright', *Journal of the Copyright Society of the USA*, vol. 38, no. 3, 1991) offers a more complete definition when he states that 'copyright' is about 'authorship':

By 'authorship' I mean authors communicating as directly as circumstance allows with their intended audiences. Copyright sustains the very heart and essence of authorship by enabling this communication, this connection. It is copyright that makes it possible for audiences – markets – to form for an author's work and it is copyright that makes it possible for publishers to bring these works to market.

This perception of copyright as a pre-condition for trade is becoming increasingly important. The definition should also be extended to include copyright not only as a condition for trade, but also as an object of trade.

As a trade mechanism, copyright can be used in a number of constructive ways, but it can also be applied in a negative fashion. On the one hand, copyright provides incentives and rewards to copyright-holders, stimulating the production of works. It also relates to the price mechanism and provides contractual relationships in the value circle of the publishing business. It organizes the transfer of values in a manner that is agreeable to the parties concerned.

On the other hand, copyright can be applied in a destructive manner – for instance, as a barrier to trade by monopolizing information value, restricting public and corporate access to information, denying the poor and less skilled (individual, company or nation) from acquiring knowledge, encouraging the gap between the knowledge-rich and the knowledge-poor.

Copyright can be applied in a destructive manner – encouraging the gap between the knowledge-rich and the knowledge-poor.

Copyright can also discourage individuals from using information by interpreting (and even creating) laws and practices in the copyright enforcement system that undermine the constructive intent of copyright. Typical examples are overprotective operational procedures in copyright control that are experienced as unreasonable and insulting by users, such as that commonly seen in the wording of the shrink-wrapped licence agreements that follow some software packages and that used by some collecting societies in the area of reprography (photocopying).

This duality has been well summarised by L. Ray Patterson and Stanley W. Lindberg (*The Nature of Copyright*, University of Georgia Press, 1991):

Copyright and free speech rights (a phrase we use to encompass both the free speech and free press clauses of the First Amendment) can be viewed as opposite sides of the same coin. The former is a matter of proprietary rights, the latter of society's political rights. They are bonded because both deal with the flow of information, one in the interest of profit, the other in the interest of freedom. The profit motive, however, is not a wholly reliable monitor. Like the locks on a canal, it may facilitate the flow of information, or in fact it may serve to dam that flow. This explains why the regulatory aspects of copyright must govern the proprietary aspects, for the early history of copyright – which we ignore at our peril – demonstrates how closely copyright and free speech values were (and are) connected.

Copyright as an object of trade

Copyright is also increasingly becoming an end in itself for several commercial enterprises. Copyright can be segmented into a number of different rights products that are eligible for trade in the market. Another growing area of importance is the process of administrating and clearing copyright. Due to the advances in electronic media, there is a growing number of activities in this field, which opens up a challenging market opportunity for the publishing industry.

> **Copyright is also increasingly becoming an end in itself for several commercial enterprises.**

Current systems for copyright administration

Copyright administration and clearance is a far from homogeneous market. There are different models and practices established in different parts of the world. In general, the variety of organizations involved – agencies, interest groups and business operations – is many times more complicated in Europe than in the United States. The distinctions between political, social and economic motives of some of these organizations may be difficult to find as they often operate in a grey area between acting as self-interest groups and exploiting commercial market opportunities.

The concept of 'collecting societies' was first established in the area of music in the mid nineteenth century, primarily in response to the development of broadcasting and recording technologies. Other areas, such as literary and dramatic works, followed suit. Publishers, authors and composers formed separate organizations, the prime task of which was to administer, clear copyright and ensure that the respective copyright-holders received economic compensation for the use of their works.

Today, there are a number of such collecting societies primarily concerned with collecting and distributing copyright fees. As the number of rights has expanded, so has the number of copyright organizations. Attached to the various rights is often found a corresponding copyright organization. For instance, the 'performing rights' in music are represented on an international level by the International Confederation of Societies of Authors and Composers (CISAC). Its membership consists of national organizations from all over the world. Other copyright organizations – for instance, in the fields of drama, film and television rights – are organized in a similar manner.

The evolution of copyright organizations is a fascinating study of how technology has been allowed to directly influence the organizational structure. Every time a new medium has emerged, the response has been to establish a new collecting society rather than to build on existing structures. This is no doubt weakening the effectiveness of the copyright business and will cause more and more problems as the previously distinguishable technologies merge into one multimedia industry.

The development of the photocopier is a very good example. When Xerox launched the first photocopier, and thereby revolutionized information processing, copyright-holders responded, true to tradition, by setting up a new type of collecting society called a 'reproduction rights organization' (RRO). Throughout the world, national RROs were set up to license the photocopying of protected information and combat the escalating growth of unauthorized copying and piracy. Although many of the RROs are organized in a common international forum called the International Federation of Reproduction Rights Organizations (IFRRO), this does not necessarily mean that they share common operational procedures. In fact, there are at least four very different models, which can be categorized and described as follows.

The Anglo-American model of reproduction rights organization
This model is based on a system of voluntary contracts and the RROs enter into agreement with both individual rights-holders and organizations representing rights-holders (collective agreements). Collection and distribution of remuneration (fees and royalties) are based on statistical surveys. Statistical data

will provide title-specific information, allowing for the estimation of the level of intensity of use, which, again, determines the remuneration to individual rights-holders.

The German-Spanish model
In Germany and Spain, there is statutory provision for the collection of a levy on the sales of photocopying machines. The size of the levy is determined by regulation and varies according to the type, capacity and performance capability of the equipment. It will also vary according to location and use. The levy is justified on the basis that private and personal copying is hard to track. Licensing fees for volume copying and systematic use of photocopiers are also determined by regulation. Distribution of remuneration is based on statistical surveys and is apportioned to rights-holders according to agreed source codes and the types of protected material used.

The Dutch model
In the Netherlands, the RRO operates under a statutory licensing system, principally in the government and educational area. The law authorizes the users to copy as long as remuneration is made to respective rights-holders. This affects the rights of foreign rights-holders as well. The size of remuneration is set by regulation apart from the copying of course material and readers/basic textbooks, which are negotiated.

The Nordic model
The Nordic model or, more precisely, the model of Norway, Sweden and Finland, is significantly different. These RROs will only enter into agreements with organizations representing a substantial proportion of rights-holders, such as the national association of journalists, editors, authors or publishers. Individual rights-holders cannot enter into an agreement directly – they can only do so via the respective trade organization. In Norway, the RRO is registered as a monopoly.

This model is the basis for the 'extended collective licence system', which means that whether the rights-holder is organized or not, they still fall under the responsibility of the RRO that is negotiating on their behalf. However, the remuneration collected is distributed to the RRO member organizations and the distribution data is not title-specific. This means that there is no individual tracking or identification of protected works. The individual rights-holders can only get access to the remuneration by means of a process of application for various grants announced by the rights-holders' organizations.

The publishers receive allocations of remuneration based on industry statistics. The distribution of remuneration to a particular member organization is therefore based on statistical surveys identifying the volume of types of material copied, for example, press articles, fiction, sheet music or academic literature.

This model presupposes a highly organized society where most rights-holders are represented in trade unions and associations. It assumes that rights-holders are willing to accept collective distribution of fees and give up their individual right to receive compensation for the copying of their works.

The role of collecting societies in an electronic environment

One rather traumatic issue for the RROs is the development of reproduction technology. For instance, the photocopier is now increasingly becoming digital. And a digital copier is also a printer and a computer peripheral. Suddenly the copier is part of the computer network and is a multifunctional piece of technology as it can be a copier, printer, fax, telephone, computer, television, and so on, at the touch of a button. Two questions arise. Should collecting societies also license electronic rights? If so, which collection society should administer which rights?

The technologies and markets may have converged, but the collecting societies certainly have not. What will be the role of RROs when photocopiers are no longer around? How can the copyright knowledge and resources of the RROs be put to use in the electronic age? Will they start competing with their own members and disintegrate due to internal conflict or will they provide an important service function and aid the members in creating new business areas? In that case, how can the competing objectives of the members be resolved and their interests balanced?

The technologies and markets may have converged, but the collecting societies certainly have not.

The issues at stake are both political and social, but, above all, they are economic. Automated and collective administration of intellectual property rights could potentially release substantial potent economic activity and boost growth in the global information market. However, many crucial strategic questions remain unresolved concerning how this can be achieved and what the interface between rights-holders and collecting societies should look like in the future.

6

Electronic commerce

It was in 1998 that we saw the beginning of the 'e' craze – fuelled by grossly exaggerated predictions that all kinds of commerce would migrate into so-called 'electronic commerce'. The concept of e-trade was established and businesses began to line up for the transformation, star-struck investors seeming to willingly throw their dosh around as long as the enterprise seeking investment had '.com' or '@' or 'e' in its name. There were expectations of unprecedented returns somewhere down the line when the entire world of consumers is on-line and doing all their trading on your network. Leaders from industry and government alike seemed to sing in the same chorus, making promises of the 'e heaven' soon to materialize. Some predictions went overboard, outlining a completely new world order where traditional retailers would disappear and the middleman or intermediary would not survive, as all transactions would happen on-line. Other predictions were more tempered, but still bitten by the e craze bug, describing the world of on-line commerce in terms of some kind of existential revelation.

It was in 1998 that we saw the beginning of the 'e' craze – fuelled by grossly exaggerated predictions.

While we must acknowledge the profound shifts that are taking place in the economies of the world and the importance of powerful GII networks to underpin trade, we must also be aware that realism and pragmatism are desperately needed if we are to exploit the true potential of electronic commerce. As Donald J. Johnston, Secretary General of the OECD, has said in my book *Masters of the Wired World* (Financial Times Management, 1999):

The emergence of electronic commerce – commercial transactions based on the electronic transmission of data over communications networks such as the Internet – heralds a major structural change in the economies of the OECD countries. It will

affect all aspects of the economic environment, the organization of firms, consumer behaviour, the workings of government and most spheres of household activity.

He is quite right in urging us to sit up and pay attention to the impact of information and communications technology on commerce. He is also well positioned to do so as the OECD is one of the few multinational organizations that seems to be able to carry out sound economic analysis of the trends and shifts in commerce around the world.

There are many estimates of the significance and global distribution of electronic commerce. There are large discrepancies between them, even though the sources are reputable. The reason is that we have not yet arrived at clear definitions of what 'electronic commerce' actually is and what it is supposed to embrace. Industries, governments, agencies and research organizations are all working hard to come up with new ways of categorizing and measuring commerce in the new networked environment. However, all the current published estimates seem to agree that there has been an explosion in electronic commerce and the turnover is big and the trend is growing – straight upwards (see Figure 6.1). For instance, starting from virtually zero in 1995, total electronic commerce was estimated at some $26 billion for 1997; and predicted to reach $330 billion in 2001–02 and $1 trillion in 2003–05. However, these estimates are very speculative and rank among the highest of the dozen estimates generated by various management consultancy or market research firms.

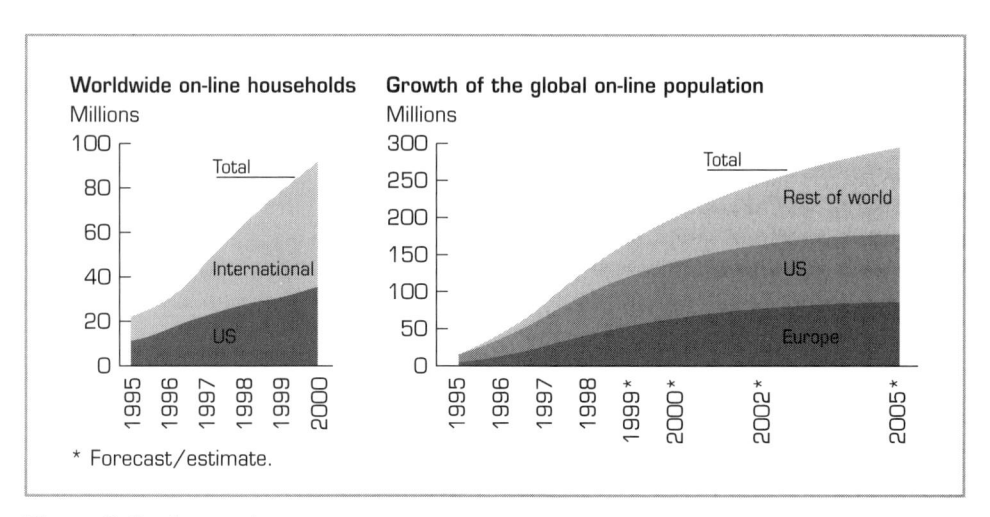

Figure 6.1: electronic commerce revenue soars
Source: Financial Times IT Review

Defining electronic commerce

Lee Stein, President of Stein & Stein and himself a successful pioneer in Internet business development and electronic commerce, brings his rather unexpected reasoning to bear on the problem and our struggle to define what we don't yet understand. Unexpected, because if we could expect anyone to be the lead singer of the e heaven choir, it would be him, given his track record in Californian-based Internet businesses. Yet, his considerable experience in making Internet virgins mature and fledglings fly has taught him, in his own words, that 'a physical world analogue needs to exist in order for an electronic business to be successful'. In my book *Masters of the Wired World* (Financial Times Management, 1999), he refers to this phenomenon as 'the analogue analogy' and explains why this is 'a fundamental requirement for the success of any player in the electronic commerce game'. His point is that 'electronic commerce' does not exist as a separate type of commerce. Rather, 'it is simply an additional channel of distribution that overlaps and coincides with all the other channels that a business has at its disposal'.

> **I shall define 'electronic commerce' as commercial transactions of data, information, products or services using on-line communication networks to place the order and exchange transactional information, but not necessarily to complete actual delivery on-line.**

In the context of this book I shall define 'electronic commerce' as commercial transactions of data, information, products or services using on-line communication networks to place the order and exchange transactional information, but not necessarily to complete actual delivery on-line.

SRI Consulting has come up with a useful graphical illustration comparing electronic – or as they call it Internet commerce – with traditional commerce (see Figure 6.2). It is useful because it reminds us of the key steps in the transactional process and illustrates examples of the choice of functions and media available to complete the process.

However, it fails to clearly show how electronic commerce can be combined with traditional commerce to generate business transactions. Most of the high-volume electronic commerce businesses are firmly based on traditional commerce – selling familiar products such as software, books and CDs, computer hardware, travel services, entertainment, food, clothes and so on (see Table 6.1).

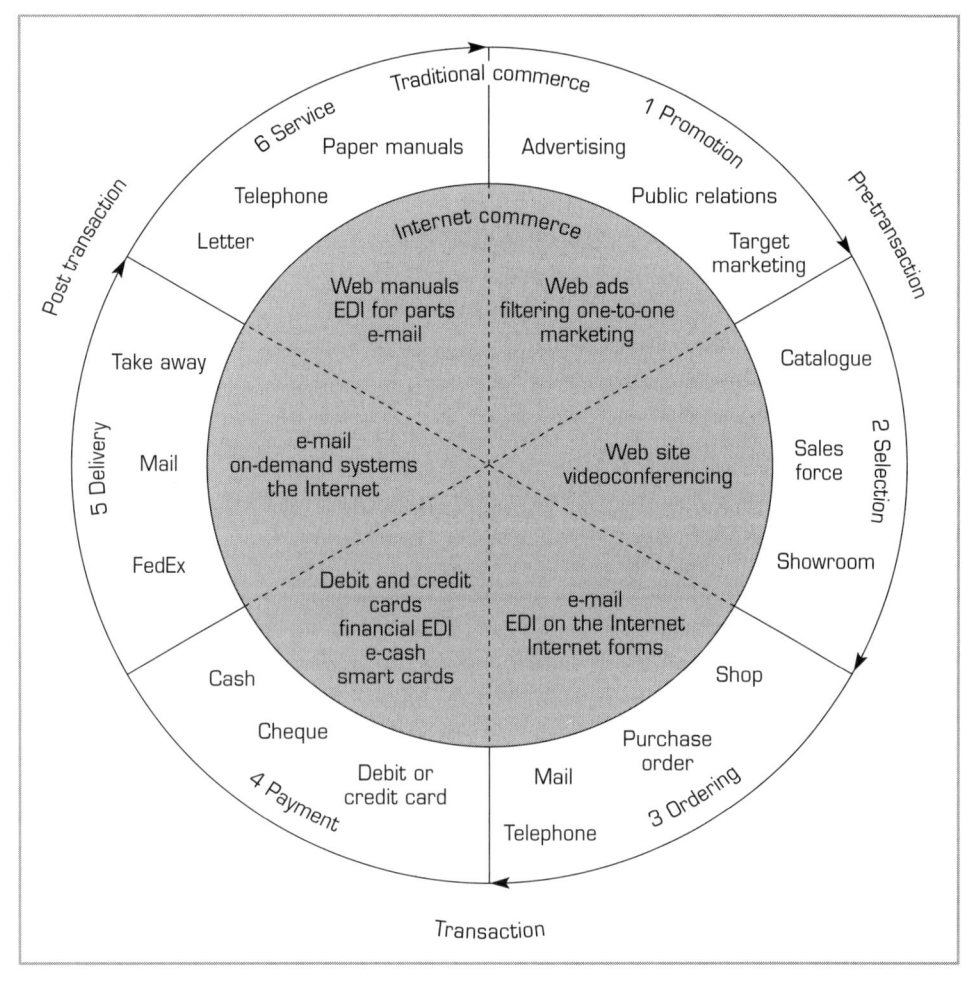

Figure 6.2: the wheel of commerce
Source: SRI Consulting

Trends in, and the value of, e-markets

Apart from the well-established electronic transactions carried out by the financial service industry, the fastest-growing area of electronic commerce is software, which, increasingly, is being traded entirely on-line, including distribution, downloading and delivery.

The market for pre-packaged software was worth $109.3 billion in 1996 and is estimated to double to $221.9 billion by 2002 (the US Department of Commerce's estimates, *US Industry and Trade Outlook*, 1998). The lead products are applications solutions — programs that perform specific industry or business functions — and the leading country is the United States, with 46 per cent of the world market ($50.4 billion) (International Data Corporation, from data quoted in *US Industry and Trade Outlook*, 1998).

According to the OECD's 1998 report *Measuring Electronic Commerce: International Trade in Software*, estimates suggest that, in 1998, electronic software distribution (EDS) amounted to 1 to 2 per cent of overall industry revenues and 10 per cent of packaged software revenues. By 2000, up to 50 per cent of packaged software is expected to be downloaded directly from the Internet and it is estimated that electronic sales will represent about 5 per cent of the total worldwide software market.

Item	Buyers (millions)	Percentage
Software	26.0	38.8
Books	13.0	19.4
Computers	10.1	15.1
Travel	7.5	11.2
Music	6.8	10.2
Food/gifts	6.5	9.7
Clothing	6.2	9.2
Investments	4.2	6.3
Consumer electronics	3.0	4.5
Auto/accessories	2.3	3.5

Table 6.1: what people buy on-line – the top 10 items purchased on-line 1997–98
Source: June 1998 ICONOCAST consensus estimate of seven research studies conducted in the past year

Information transactions – tangible versus intangible assets

Before proceeding to examine in more detail electronic commerce transactions and the key issues involved, let's take a moment to consider what actually constitutes a market and what makes it all work. What are the basic building-blocks of this marketplace and what are the conditions for market efficiency likely to be?

There must be creators, producers, products, intermediaries and consumers. There must also be marketing systems in place to facilitate the exchange of information assets. We need distribution and delivery systems providing access to information and access to consumers. There must be transactional systems to allow for charging and paying, and, last but not least, there must be rules and regulations protecting the integrity of trade from point of creation to point of consumption.

Perhaps one of the most difficult issues concerning the marketing of information and/or intellectual property rights assets in electronic form is the need for quality control, security and authenticity. Consumers need to know that what they order is what they will get. Producers need to know that what they sell will arrive intact at the point of delivery. Libraries and museums that are custodians of our cultural heritage need authentic originals in their archives. Students must be taught according to an approved curriculum of verified knowledge. Science, industry and commerce need reliable data and information that has not been tampered with.

As we move from yesterday's world of media divergence and clearly distinguishable media outputs (newspapers, books, journals, films) to a networked society of media convergence, of multimedia and digital bit streams, the ability to preserve the integrity and continued growth of intellectual creations will be a major challenge.

Traditional media industries – with authors, artists, musicians, publishers and broadcasters – are experiencing a fragmentation of their products and expressing strong concerns that digital technologies are eroding the integrity of works and dissolving traditional media responsibility. Their defence strategy is the continued protection of intellectual property rights, along with the recognition of the role of creators, publishers and broadcasters in a digital environment.

> **Traditional media industries are experiencing a fragmentation of their products and expressing strong concerns that digital technologies are eroding the integrity of works and dissolving traditional media responsibility.**

Information transactions defined

An 'information transaction' is defined as a process of value exchange between two parties, whereas 'value' is defined as information assets (including any type of media) and money. The transactional process includes, in its simplest form, two value transfers – the financial transaction to secure payment for goods and services ordered, and the transfer of the information asset. If the buyer is an end user, this will, typically, be the case. However, if intellectual property rights are attached to the asset, then there will be a third value transfer involved to allow for the transfer of rights. The buyer may only want to buy the rights and not the actual information. In that case, there will be three value transfers – money, rights and a contract. The buyer, perhaps being an agent or a rights broker, may then proceed to sell those rights to another buyer. Alternatively, if the buyer is a multimedia program developer, they may want to buy the information object, the rights and a contract to allow them to reuse and sell the material.

The challenge of security

There is much debate, and due concern, about the need to make global networks secure. The trading of information assets over global networks raises a number of security problems that need to be resolved in order to facilitate an efficient market. What kind of security we are talking about will, to some extent, depend on who is talking. 'Security' is a very widely used term that carries different meanings for different people. The participants in the Global Information Society security debate come from a variety of backgrounds and industries, so tend to have different understandings of the security issues involved.

The network provider is concerned with system performance and protection against failure and breakdowns. The bank is concerned with protection of financial transactions. The network service provider is concerned with protection of access and against unauthorized use. The content provider is concerned with protection of intellectual property rights. The law enforcement agency is concerned with access to communication channels and transactional activities to protect law and order. The consumer is concerned with protecting personal information and privacy. Resolving the security problems of the GII requires a common understanding across the board and an agreement on priorities. In this context, it is important that the players involved can appreciate all the issues at stake and not narrow down the implications to what they perceive to be important from their particular standpoint.

An 'information transaction' is defined as a process of value exchange between two parties, whereas 'value' is defined as information assets (including any type of media) and money.

Security concerns are present on several different levels and in relation to a wide range of key functions:

- law enforcement;
- national security;
- payment systems;
- intellectual property rights;
- network access and use of services;
- system performance and quality control;
- data protection;
- privacy and other consumer rights.

Security features are a fundamental part of transactional systems for information assets. Security specifications for trading information assets in the global information market need to be constructed on the basis of a number of existing standards for network communication, electronic data interchange (EDI), data storage and financial transactions, as well as new standards for more comprehensive data protection, tracking and recording of information usage. The use of cryptography, encryption technology and key management are likely to play a major role in the process of developing the level of security required for information transactions.

Cryptography and the role of encryption technology

Cryptography – the science of making (encrypting) and breaking (decrypting) secret codes – has its roots in military defence applications and intelligence surveillance. Historically, it has been the domain of government agencies concerned with national security, military defence and law enforcement. Today, governments are still the largest users of encryption technology, but its use has spread to many other application areas throughout society. The financial services sector is the second largest user. In many countries, banks are required by law to provide protection for their customers by implementing specific encryption and security standards to secure transactions and financial information. Cable and satellite television is another sector that uses specific technology to encrypt television programmes. Many closed communication and computer networks in industry also use some level of encryption to protect their data.

Software for business applications, PCs and other office communication devices is increasingly being shipped with encryption technology embedded either in specially designed security chips or in programs. This causes tension with government agencies that have a responsibility to control the export and use of encryption technology. In many countries, the manufacturing, export and use of high-grade encryption technology are strictly regulated. Some government agencies will license certain industrial sectors to use specific encryption technology. For example, the banking industry is licensed to use encryption technology based on the so-called Data Encryption Standard (DES).

One big problem for governments is that the regulations governing the use of encryption technology are not up to date in terms of defining the many new encryption techniques and emerging standards. Once again, the technology seems to be racing ahead of the legislation. This is a major concern for law enforcement agencies that do not like to lose control over the spread of encryption technology. If encryption technology was freely available in the market, it would also be freely available for criminals involved in organized crime, drug trafficking, money laundering, fraud and terrorism.

The regulation and application of encryption technology is a very contentious and difficult issue that needs urgent attention. On the one hand, national security, law and order are at stake and, on the other, the ability to create a secure trading environment for the GII. Without the use of encryption technology, it seems unlikely that information transactions on the GII will be secure. The global electronic commerce market will not take off without mechanisms being in place to secure information and intellectual property transactions, as well as the privacy, data protection and contract rights of individual consumers and suppliers. There are already several examples of companies having to withdraw encrypted products from the market, modify products to render them less secure or disable encrypted features that would have provided the security that the market requires. For example, Microsoft Network has been hampered by US export regulations on encryption technology and Netscape by French law, which does not allow the use of the company's encryption technology.

Emerging standards for encrypting information

The market for digital encryption technology is growing at a significant rate, in spite of the uncertain legal environment. In February 1995, there were 219 registered manufacturers and distributors of encryption technology in the European Union alone. This figure included 88 in the United Kingdom, 33 in Germany and 29 in France. In the United States, there were 161 companies, while Japan had only 4 (Peter N. Backe's dissertation *Industry for High-grade Personal Computer Encryption Technology in Germany and the USA*, Oxford University, March 1995). The Software Publishers Association has estimated that the potential US share of markets outside the United States for software with encryption capabilities could total US$5 billion before 2000. US software companies currently hold a 70 per cent market share in Europe.

Software encryption is based on two basic types of encryption algorithms:

- symmetrical, or, 'single-key encryption';
- asymmetrical, or, 'public key encryption'.

In symmetrical encryption, the same key is used to encrypt and decrypt the data. That is, the sender and receiver of data must have the same key. Asymmetrical encryption divides the process into two steps, using two associated keys, one private and one public. The private key is known and used only by the owner. The public key can be used by anyone who wants to send encrypted data to the corresponding private key-holder. Only the corresponding private key will be able to decrypt the data. Public key encryption lets the user encrypt information and messages as well as 'signing' them with a 'digital signature,' by generating a line of text or numbers encrypted with that person's private key. The digital signature can only be decrypted by the sender's public key and it verifies where the information or message came from.

Recently, there has been a lot of activity in this area and there are an increasing number of proposed solutions and actual products available. Most of these software packages offering encryption capability are based on proprietary encryption methods.

Although there is no worldwide agreement on one encryption standard, most products and network applications seem to be based on one of the following 'standards' for encryption algorithms.

- **DES (Data Encryption Standard)**
  A *de jure* standard.
  Adopted by the US National Institute of Standards and Technology (NIST) and approved for non-classified government data.
  A symmetrical system developed in 1977 from IBM's Lucifer algorithm, it is the most widely used standard in hardware implementations.
- **RSA**
  A *de facto* standard.
  A comprehensive set of public-key-based cryptographic algorithms developed since 1977 at the Massachusetts Institute of Technology. It is named after the inventors, Rivest-Shamir-Adleman. Several RSA algorithms are protected by US patents held by the PKP (Public Key Partners) company, formed jointly by MIT and Stanford University.
- **IDEA (International Data Encryption Algorithm)**
  A *de facto* standard.
  A symmetrical system developed by Lai and Massey in 1991, it is simple to use and relatively easy to break. It is popular in the public domain and amateur applications.

Software with encryption functions will typically integrate the use of encryption algorithms with the vendors' proprietary security features in a seamless fashion. For instance, a UK-based smart card company called Mondex uses the DES standard with its own added security software. Another company offering secure transactions, Netscape, uses RSA technology in combination with its own proprietary encryption technology called Secure Socket Layer (SSL).

Another software program that enables users to encrypt information is PGP (Pretty Good Privacy). Developed in 1991 by P. Zimmermann, it combines RSA and IDEA algorithms and has been widely distributed as freeware in the public domain over the Internet. However, Zimmermann faced legal action over the illegal export of this program and has been subject to investigation by the US Customs Service. Despite being illegal, PGP is widely used, primarily by individuals wanting to secure their e-mail correspondence, but also by reputable organizations such as Amnesty International and, unfortunately, by political extremist groups.

There is a weighty, ongoing debate concerning the need for security standards on the Internet, including the WWW. There seems to be a tug of war between those who advocate an open standards approach and those who advocate a standards approach based on proprietary technology. The well-established on-line information service providers Compuserve, Prodigy and America Online have invested in Terisa – a company recently set up by EIT and RSA Data Security to provide technology for secure Internet transactions. The standard recently chosen by the WWW consortium called the S-HTTP (Secure Hypertext Transfer Protocol) is based on the technology of EIT and RSA.

The standards debate is likely to get even more lively and confused as new proposals are put forward. RSA has been able to dominate the public-key encryption market as it is currently holding US patents on a wide range of applications. However, these patents expire during the period 1997–2001, thus opening up the market for other players.

Information encoding and identifiers

The degree of protection required will vary with the type of asset being traded. Intellectual property assets may require more complicated treatment than information assets not protected by rights. Communities of publishers, authors, broadcasters, composers and libraries, which are all concerned with protecting the integrity of works and intellectual property rights, have begun to investigate ways of encoding information assets in electronic form and implementing 'identification mechanisms' to enable them to control the use of their works in an electronic environment.

Several standards organizations currently administrating standards for traditional media or communication networks are also busy developing extensions to their existing standards and exploring new ways of marking and tracking digital information. The latter include the well-established standards developed in the 1970s for identifying printed works – the International Standard Book Number (ISBN) code for books and the International Standard Serial Number (ISSN) code for journals. There is also the International Standard Recording Code (ISRC) for identification of recorded music and the Source Identification (SID) code for identification of CD producers, both administered by the International Federation of the Phonographic Industry (IFPI). Collecting societies for various media are also busy experimenting with encoding and identification systems.

The field of digital information encoding and identification mechanisms is at a very early stage. The emerging models range from very simple protection of limited information (a header type) to very complicated models that aim to control and protect the use of information as far as possible. Technology offers many different techniques for identifying information assets in different electronic media, ranging from so-called watermarking – software that allows identifiers or messages to be embedded in electronic documents – to digital signatures using public-key encryption, to fingerprinting bit-mapped images (FBI), which could be used to identify images in electronic form.

Mechanisms for encoding and identifying information assets will be of vital importance to the development of the global electronic commerce market.

Mechanisms for encoding and identifying information assets will be of vital importance to the development of the global electronic commerce market. Buyers and sellers will need to know that intellectual property rights will be protected, original assets preserved and the integrity and reliability of trade secured. However, it is important to realize that technology is now making it possible to mark, monitor and control the use of information on a scale never known before. The implications for privacy, data protection and consumer rights need to be considered very carefully.

Transactional systems for network commerce

Much has been written about the commercialization of the Internet and the need for systems that can secure financial transactions and payment for goods and services purchased on the Web. Almost every week, somewhere in Europe, another major conference is organized on the topic of electronic commerce and information transactions. There is considerable commercial interest in developing and adopting electronic payment systems and there are numerous experiments and trials in Europe, North America, Australia, Japan and Singapore. Initiatives have come from several different camps and the most active companies are those from the software and telecommunications industries, the banking and financial sector, media conglomerates and network operators.

In the popular press, there has been much controversial coverage of 'virtual money', 'cyber-cash' or 'digital money'. Indeed, at the time of writing, it is difficult to pick up any computer magazine, business journal or even a national newspaper without headlines telling tales about virtual shopping and 'cyber-commerce'. However, these entertaining visions of future commerce could be flawed and most of them do not translate very well into the real marketplace (or should we say market space).

All this commotion, excitement and sudden interest in transactional systems is symptomatic of the fact that there is an unfulfilled need for new ways of trading information. It is ironic that the actors in the arena that have most drawn attention to this are new entrepreneurial market entrants, 'information revolutionaries' and scientists from the academic sector rather than the traditional players, which are the ones we would have expected to have seen take the lead as they have the most at stake. For instance, the banks were the last to jump on this bandwagon and most of them did so at the invitation of either a software or a telecommunications company.

Existing and emerging transactional mechanisms and models

Over the past two years, various models have been developed for handling information transactions in a networked environment. Mechanisms currently available in the marketplace can be divided into seven categories. These categories are not mutually exclusive and vendors may come up with business models that require a combination of transactional mechanisms:

- subscription;
- licensing;
- conventional credit/debit cards;
- smart cards;
- third-party clearing and brokering;
- electronic cash;
- electronic cheques.

Subscription and licensing

Subscription and licensing are familiar and well-established transactional methods for trading information on-line. The customer subscribes to a particular service and/or licensed access and use of specific content. Searching and ordering information may happen on-line, but the charging, billing and payment usually happen off-line, using conventional banking and postal services.

Credit and debit cards

The main advantages of credit and debit cards are that they represent:

- familiar transactional concepts;
- a well-proven technology;
- a long-established industry;
- well-regulated and managed services;
- a global, secure and solid infrastructure.

The first credit cards appeared on the US market in the 1920s, initially issued by petrol stations and department stores to enable their customers to use their facilities, purchase products and use their services by handing over a card rather than cash. These cards could only be used by the customer in the issuer's establishment and each card was limited to a contract between two parties – one merchant and one customer. The first multiparty cards – where groups of companies joined to issue a card – were limited to specific markets and could be used for the purpose of travel and entertainment. This was the start of American Express, Diners Club and Carte Blanche – indeed their names reflect these origins. The first general multipurpose card, BankAmericard, appeared in 1958; Visa and Mastercard followed later.

The credit/debit card business has experienced continuous growth since its inception and gone through many developments, expanding its scope and functionality, adding more and more features. There is a wide range of cards available, allowing the market to choose between dedicated one-service cards and multiservice cards. There is a growing trend of vendors teaming up with credit card companies to develop and market their own branded cards.

Today, all the major credit card companies are working to develop payment systems for electronic commerce in a Wired World. They have formed strategic alliances with companies from the telecommunications,

> **Today, all the major credit card companies are working to develop payment systems for electronic commerce in a Wired World.**

software and information industries. New collaborative projects are announced frequently. Current examples are Visa working with Microsoft and BT, Mastercard with Netscape, and American Express with America Online.

Financial transactions on the Net must be verified and cleared by whoever undertakes to process payments. The existing closed global and secure networks that these credit card companies have built up will be very useful for that purpose, putting them in a strong position as key players in the new market for electronic commerce in open global networks. The cost of building up such large-scale networks for processing transactions would be enormous for any newcomer to this market.

The market environment for financial transactional services is also very competitive and prices have been continually pushed down over the past decade. For instance, redemption of credit card slips was originally around 7 per cent discount, but today credit card discounts average around 2.5 per cent and are expected to drop even further. As Eric Hughes writes "A long-term perspective on electronic commerce" newsletter Release 1.0, EDventure Holdings, March 1995) 'Any new payment venture planning a credit card billing model that requires more than 2 per cent discounts for profitability won't be able to compete in the long term'.

There are four main disadvantages and problems with the credit model when it is applied to information transactions within global networks:

- lack of security;
- high transaction cost;
- time-consuming clearing process;
- qualifications are required to become a credit card merchant.

Lack of security The Internet is an open environment with very little security available. Sending credit card details and sensitive financial information over the Internet is not safe. Eavesdroppers, using cheap TCP/IP traffic monitors, and hackers can easily intercept and obtain credit card numbers if they are sent over the Net. This was demonstrated with the capture of the American hacker Kevin Mitnick who had a list of over 20,000 customer names and credit card numbers when he was caught.

High transaction costs The other problem facing the credit card companies is the high cost per transaction, which makes the credit card unsuitable for small transactions. Much of the information asset trade over the global networks is likely to be high volumes of very small transactions between many individual parties, but the cost per transaction will outweigh its value. Even if the credit card transaction loop is stretched between clearance and settlement in order to allow small transactions to aggregate before payments are made, it will not work – aggregated payments still have to be made between one buyer and one merchant.

This has for many years been a familiar problem in the document delivery business – publishers and authors are forever finding that proceeds from permissions sold through collecting societies and third-party information services are outstanding. The long wait for the small cheques has led some publishers to consider whether, in fact, it makes any sense to grant permissions to reproduce their works and make material available through these services. Information services would be much more economically attractive if there was a way of reducing the transaction costs and, thereby, increasing the profit potential.

Time-consuming Credit/debit cards require authorization by means of dial-up communication with clearing services that are networked to banks and credit card companies. The clearing process takes time. The settlement process is another time-consuming factor as invoices are issued.

Qualifications required to be a credit card merchant Individual traders and small enterprises that may want to trade their information assets on the networks may find it too expensive to offer the option of payment by credit cards and may not meet the criteria for qualifying as credit card merchants.

Smart cards

Credit/debit card technology has evolved with the development of microchips and computing technology. Smart cards (also called 'chip cards' or 'electronic purses') are fitted with a microprocessor that can store value and information as well as provide specified functions. Unlike a credit card, which simply has a magnetic strip with recorded information like a tiny computer disk, the smart card is like a little computer, capable of processing information as well as storing it.

There are many different applications and varieties of smart cards available in the market today. There are also some trials going on to test smart cards in electronic commerce, including services available on the Internet.

The smart card provides stored value on a card – or, put another way, it is cash on a card. The card can be 'loaded up' with cash by inserting it into smart cashpoint machines (ATMs) or by using dedicated terminals and customized telephones. A display will show the balance on the card and debits/credits made. The card can be used to make payments for all kinds of goods and services by inserting it into a smart card reader, which directly debits the card by the requested amount.

The six main advantages of the smart card model are that it:

- builds on the existing credit card industry and infrastructure;
- offers security;
- costs less;
- is efficient;
- can handle small transactions;
- provides added functionality and flexibility.

If the card is stolen, then only the current value stored on the card is lost, as opposed to an entire line of credit, which could be the case with credit card fraud. As there is no need to obtain authorization, the transaction costs are much lower than those for payment systems that require clearance from payment processors. The clearance and settlement process is instant, making this a highly efficient payment mechanism. The card can work and be economically viable for small transactions because the transaction costs are low, although the profitability of small transactions has not yet been commercially demonstrated with information in electronic form sold over networks – this is currently being explored by a number of banks and software companies. The ability to design and add different functions to the smart card is perhaps the most important feature of all. Because the card is like a miniature computer, information and special instructions can be received, stored, processed and transmitted. This has opened up a whole world of new applications for smart cards.

The smart card is a 'multipurpose card', so the same card can be used for functions as varied as those of an identity card, a door opener, a means to gain access to restricted areas, operating vending machines, using the telephone, paying for bus tickets, going shopping, paying utility and insurance bills, photocopying, borrowing books in the library, paying motorway tolls and parking, buying petrol, receiving video on demand, downloading information on the PC, home shopping, and more. The card can also be used to receive payments and information.

Smart cards have for some time been available and operational in parts of Europe. Banks in Norway, Denmark and Finland have been providing smart card services to their clients for several years. In Germany, smart cards are being used extensively in healthcare systems for patient information and billing. This successful healthcare application led the US Department of Defense

The conversion to smart card technology is already happening and the massive replacement of cards and readers and refitting of equipment is gradually going ahead.

to set up a trial using smart cards (GemPlus) for storage and transfer of medical health information. The French have taken the technology even further – their entire bank payment system, involving 22 million people, has been converted to smart card technology.

There are two main reasons for Europe being ahead of the United States in this development. First, in Europe there is a greater degree of government involvement in providing support for investment, encouraging the process of standardization and facilitating appropriate market regulation. Second, the high cost of telecommunications services in Europe compared to the United States has helped smart cards flourish among retailers as they are pleased to no longer have to carry the cost of expensive dial-up systems required to authorize credit card payments (Phil Patton, 'E-money', *Popular Science*, July 1995).

So the conversion to smart card technology is already happening and the massive replacement of cards and readers and refitting of equipment is gradually going ahead. 'This technology is sneaking into our lives through the back door,' according to Bob Gilson, Executive Director of the Smart Card Forum. The Forum is an industry group with considerable influence, representing leading banks, retailers, equipment manufacturers, software companies and government agencies involved in the development of universal standards and regulatory frameworks for smart cards.

Both Visa and Mastercard have invested substantially in smart card technology. Mastercard has a number of smart card services in Australia. Visa developed an experimental programme for the 1996 Atlanta Olympics involving the use of disposable smart cards – visitors and participants were able to use the cards for all kinds of services. Visa is also working with Microsoft to develop smart card technology for networked information services. The latter part of the 1990s has been a period of prototyping and massive experimentation with smart card applications. All the major banks and card companies, software and electronics companies, many retailers and information providers have been busy working with strategic alliances to pioneer systems.

As far as investment in the development of new transactional systems is concerned, it is clearly in the area of smart card technology that the most substantial investments are being made and also where the most significant developments are taking place.

Visa International, Mastercard International and Europay International have recently proposed 'an industry standard for smart cards' – the EMV specification (named after the three companies), which no doubt will have a significant impact on future developments. This is based on the already established ISO 7816 standard for smart cards. The EMV standard will rely on encryption technology to authenticate the user, keep data confidential and prevent data tampering.

Third-party clearing and brokering

Some companies are emerging in the marketplace that are offering credit card clearance and marketing services for electronic commerce. Essentially, they are leveraging the credit card system and acting as an intermediary between the vendor, buyer and bank. Some of these companies are dedicated to handling financial transactions for information assets being traded over open networks. First Virtual Holding is one such company that, in addition to offering a clearing and payment service, will market information assets on behalf of vendors in their own electronic shop on the Internet.

The advantage of this model is that buyers do not have to send their credit card numbers over insecure networks. The financial transactions happen off-line or only on-line in secure networks. The service company may also allow transactions to accumulate in clients' accounts before settlement, making it possible to use credit cards for smaller transactions as well. The disadvantage of this system is that it adds several steps to the information transaction process as well as an intermediary, which will have an impact on cost, profit and price.

Electronic cash

Over the last couple of years, a number of initiatives have attempted to develop solutions to the problems of facilitating transactions on-line over the open global networks. The argument is that customers (the Internet surfers) should be able to shop and perform transactions instantly on their PCs without having to wait for cheques to clear or having to use a credit card or have licensing arrangements with vendors.

The concept of 'virtual money' has been introduced under many names, including eCash, CyberCash and NetCash. The idea is that customers will be able to approach 'digital banks' on the Net that will issue electronic cash in exchange for real cash. It is a bit like buying tokens. The eCash tokens can be used for shopping with vendors that accept this form of token cash. The vendors will change the tokens back into real cash via the same 'digital bank' the customer visited.

The task of creating a new global payment system is enormous and that of introducing a new global currency is probably impossible.

One company in Holland, DigiCash, has invested considerable resources in developing a system that aims to provide complete anonymity to individuals – the identity of the buyer is hidden by means of sophisticated use of encryption technology and the transactions are not traceable. This has serious implications for law enforcement and crime control. If transactions were allowed to be anonymous, it would open the floodgates for criminal activity, including money laundering, fraud and tax evasion.

The possibility of anonymous transaction systems for trading information assets is not very attractive to information providers as they depend on close communication with their customers and the ability to track information for marketing purposes as well as legal and financial reasons.

The initial attraction of electronic cash is that it seems more secure to shift tokens over the networks rather than real money. However, electronic cash tokens represent real money value and purchasing power. Consequently, these proposed models for electronic cash can be perceived as being attempts to create new forms of currencies.

The likelihood of the world economy being receptive to new currencies that lack all the basic criteria of being able to grow value and operate financially is rather far-fetched. For instance, electronic cash does not have any national reserve or guarantor – it does not come under any national or international jurisdiction – and there is no way of earning real interest on eCash tokens. The task of creating a new global payment system is enormous and that of introducing a new global currency is probably impossible. However, these experiments are evolving in a learning process and there may be many useful functions on the way. New interesting solutions will no doubt come out of collaboration between these research-oriented initiatives and traditional players in the transactional market.

Electronic cheques

At the same stage of introductory experimentation are electronic cheques. There are a number of pilot projects investigating the use of electronic cheques in the form of encrypted e-mail messages containing the digital signature of the payer. Most of these are envisaged to work with existing financial services. NetCheque is one such project, developed at the University of South California. The user creates a cheque on screen using their digital signature, sending the electronic cheque as encrypted e-mail. The recipient forwards it electronically to the bank, which receives it as an e-mail order to transfer funds.

A problem with both electronic cash and electronic cheques is the lack of standards and guidelines. The marketplace is currently exploding with many different initiatives based on a variety of different approaches and technology. The Internet user venturing into shopping on the Net is likely to be well and truly confused and overwhelmed by the choices of payment systems being announced. Here is a list of 'electronic cash/cheque' options currently available (companies come and go every day in this business, so there is no guarantee that the names on this list will still be running when you read it):

- eCash;
- CyberCash;
- NetCash;
- Netchex;
- NetBill;
- Netcheque;
- NetMarket;
- NexusBucks;
- LETSystems;
- MagicMoney.

Electronic Data Interchange (EDI)

EDI is a well-established system for exchanging sensitive data over networks. It is included in this context as the extension of its current use could prove very interesting for conducting information transactions. EDI is defined as 'The transfer of structured data, from computer to computer, using agreed communication standards' (Joe Peppard, *IT Strategy for Business*, Longman, 1993). The transfer of data is directly usable by the recipient's computer without the need to re-key it. EDI is an interorganizational system involving two or more organizations, allowing the users to exchange standard trade documents, such as orders, invoices, price lists, product catalogues, custom declaration forms, and so on.

EDI is based on a series of standards for exchanging data over communication and telephone networks, some of which are internationally ratified – the so-called EDIFACT standards. The major standard-setting body for commercial EDI applications is United Nations/EDI for Administration, Commerce and Transport (UN/EDIFACT). EDIFACT comprises a

The extension of its current use could prove very interesting for conducting information transactions.

set of internationally agreed standards, directions and guidelines for EDI and deals particularly with the trade in goods and services between independent computer systems and networks.

EDI has been around for many years and is growing rapidly. Historically, various different industry groups got together and defined their own respective standards. For example, the car industry established the Organization for Data Exchange TeleTransmission in Europe (ODETTE)-based system and the banks established the Society for World-wide Inter-bank Financial Telecommunications (SWIFT) network.

The European Commission has long recognized the strategic importance of EDI for improving trade relations in the European Union and stimulating economic growth. The Commission has launched a dedicated programme called Trade Electronic Data Interchange (TEDIS) to carry out research, and develop solutions that can fuel the uptake of EDI applications in European industry. Several projects funded under this programme have demonstrated that EDI can be extended to the trading of information assets in electronic form and that EDI systems can be developed to handle the transfer of pictures, sound and multimedia as well as the existing alpha-numerical information. EDI is currently mostly used by companies in closed networks. However, much research and experimentation is going on to explore new EDI applications linked to the commerce on open global networks.

EDI has the inherent ability to protect data, track usage and audit information, all important features for an effective information transaction system. It is very likely that EDI will play an important role linked to transactional systems for trading information on networks. However, the high cost of European telecommunications services, ISDN and EDI software is currently a deterrent in the market uptake of EDI.

EDI has the inherent ability to protect data, track usage and audit information, all important features for an effective information transaction system.

Possible future developments

Electronic commerce has come a long way since computers were introduced in trading systems back in the early 1960s. The rapid development of technologies to underpin and facilitate on-line transactions has completely reshaped the world of commerce. Powerful computer networks have been deployed throughout the financial services industry and today it's inconceivable to imagine sectors such as banking,

Today it's inconceivable to imagine sectors such as banking, insurance and the stock market operating without e-commerce.

insurance and the stock market operating without e-commerce. Any larger scale of commerce has become totally dependent on information and communications technology and secure on-line communications.

We have seen a proliferation of new transactional tools, systems and applications emerging in the marketplace – from different types of smart cards to digital tokens. Security standards and regulations are also being put in place that will encourage electronic commerce. New software is being developed to allow more and more commercial activities to migrate on to the Net. Also, most importantly, companies are beginning to grasp the potential of electronic commerce and how it can benefit operations and customers. There is much hype and experimentation going on, as both suppliers and consumers continue to search for new ways of engaging in commercial activities. However, the novelty of the new will wear off and new patterns of commercial behaviour will take hold. E-commerce will soon become an integrated part of life for most of us and, in the future, we may very well see a 'cashless' society where the need for physical cash disappears, being replaced by information values. In the Wired World, we'll carry a piece of intelligent plastic around that is fed regularly by computers that know the digital values of the virtual real money we possess. So much easier, swifter and productive than the analogue world of traditional cash of coins, notes, cheques and paper.

7

The networked economy

It is widely recognized that a prosperous information market is essential in order to gain competitive advantage and achieve continued economic growth. During the latter part of the 1990s, the world market for information services demonstrated an annual growth rate of 11 per cent (International Trade Administration, US Department of Commerce), and as we enter the new millennium the US Department of Commerce has announced that it expects computing and communications to generate 25–40 per cent of the US's economic growth. If it happens, it will be evidence that proves Vice President Al Gore's predictions in 1995 (made in his keynote address at the G7 conference on the Global Information Society, Brussels, 27 February) to be right:

As we approach the end of the twentieth century, information is a critical force shaping the world's economic system. In the next century, the speed with which information is created, its accessibility, and its myriad uses will cause even more fundamental changes in each nation's economy.

Nine years after being elected, the Clinton and Gore Administration must take great pride and comfort in the fact that the US is well on its way to fulfilling its ambition to become the leader in the global networked economy. The early recognition of the potential of the GII and the significance of information and knowledge as the new determinants of competitiveness has no doubt given many stakeholders in the US economy a head start.

> Strategies for growth in the new economic environment must be built on effective knowledge management, the creative development of human capital and sensible, cost-effective use of information and communications technologies.

Strategies for growth in the new economic environment must be built on effective knowledge management, the creative development of human capital and sensible, cost-effective use of information and communications technologies. Success will depend on the responsiveness to change and the ability to make and implement wise decisions at great speed.

Towards the Knowledge Age

Throughout history, progress and economic growth have been achieved by means of intellectual creations and technological innovation. The ability to access information and the knowledge of what the information means have always been fundamental to the progress of humankind.

The traditional approach permits us to carve up our economic history into periods of time distinguished by certain characteristics. For instance, commonly the evolution of recent history is talked about in terms of the Agricultural Age, the Industrial Age and the Information Age (see Figure 7.1).

This simple perspective is perhaps useful in as much as it highlights major events and turning-points in our economic and political history. However, such general labels and distinctions have led many commentators to describe the development of society in terms of distinct and consecutive infrastructures and economies belonging to each age, rather than one evolving infrastructure and economy.

This is misguided as the development of society needs to be understood in terms of evolutionary and organic growth – one advance adding to another, not replacing it, as such an approach would imply. There have been shifts of emphasis in

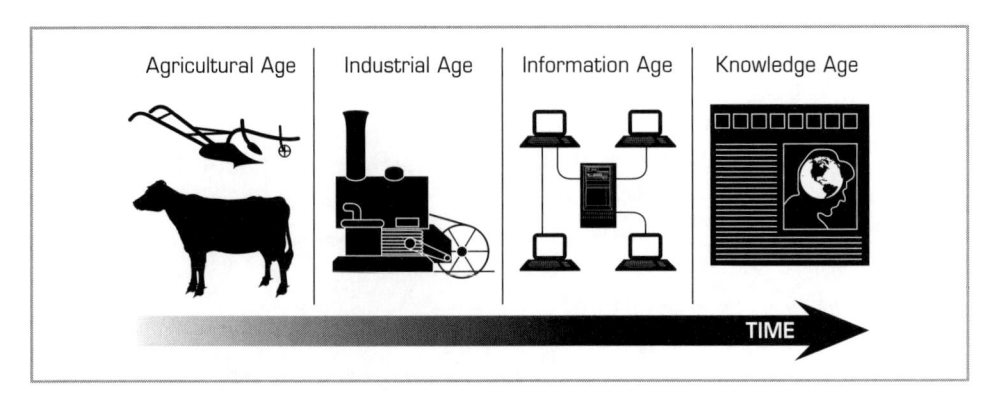

Figure 7.1: the evolution of infrastructures

the past and there will be further shifts in future as we progress towards the Knowledge Age. We no longer place the printing press and the book alone centre stage as the most important vehicle for the dissemination of intellectual works. Our attention has shifted to digital media and the Internet. It doesn't mean the book disappears. Primitive and advanced economies will coexist and old and new technologies will be combined to make up the new networked economy. We live in a world of many different infrastructures and many different economies, from the very basic to the most advanced. Rich nations are moving into an advanced networked economy and the attention has shifted from industrial production to information and knowledge. This doesn't mean that poor nations have disappeared. We cannot ignore the fact that two thirds of the world's population still live in primitive agricultural and industrial economies. For the new networked economy to be truly global, it will have to embrace the developing world and deal with the realities of the old economies as well as the challenges of the new.

The Concise Oxford Dictionary defines 'infrastructure' as 'an underlying foundation' or 'the fixed capital equipment in a country', which means things such as roads, railways, waterways, power grids, communication systems, factories, schools, universities, hospitals, and so on. During the Agricultural Age, the most important parts of the infrastructure were farms, animals and ploughs. During the Industrial Age, engines and fuels became the central parts of the infrastructure.

Today, we are in the Information Age and the infrastructure emphasizes computers and communications networks. As the information society advances towards the so-called 'Knowledge Age', the infrastructure will evolve to include a growing range of underpinning technologies, software tools and mechanisms, which will enable better use of information, as well as better storage and retrieval.

That's the infrastructure, what about the content? Why do information and knowledge play such crucial roles in the networked economy? What does it actually mean?

Human capital and knowledge management

'Change' provides fertile ground for buzzwords. 'Human capital' and 'knowledge management' probably stand to win the fashion contest for the most poetic and long-lasting buzzwords at the turn of the new millennium. This may be because there is more to it than fashion talk and advertisements from suppliers of information and communications technology looking to sell you more products and services. Buzzwords come and go, and often appear to describe what we don't yet understand. Some of them grow up linguistically and give rise to new terminology and subject disciplines. Think of 'Total Quality Management', 'business process re-engineering', 'change management' – all originally proposed as rather bizarre simplifications of business strategy by consultants eager to sell their products and services and lock in continued commitment to IT spending. The hype and the push generated by them via very successful use of buzzwords has stimulated new thinking and developments, but overrated IT systems and short-term consultancy results only in very large bills and not much useful change happening.

To define and understand terms such as 'human capital' and 'knowledge management', we need far more than buzzwords. If you really want to grasp it, you need a library of textbooks and a lifetime of experience in psychology, sociology, philosophy, history, economics, computing, media, communications, political science and management studies – and a little help from Heidi and Alvin Toffler with understanding and organizing your thoughts.

Don't think that 'human capital' and 'knowledge management' are modern inventions – they aren't. Many wise figures and political leaders of the past have pointed out the economic and cultural importance of information and knowledge. From Aristotle, Plato and Caesar to Shakespeare and Adam Smith, they all recognized that 'knowledge itself is power', although it was Francis Bacon who made this famous line his when he published *The Advancement of Learning* in 1605.

In more modern times, T. S. Eliot reflected deeply on the implications of living in an information society in 'The Rock', part 1 (1934):

'Knowledge' and 'human capital' are old concepts. What's new today is the recognition that information and knowledge have to be defined, developed, managed and exploited just like any other core assets.

Where is the Life we have lost in living?

Where is the wisdom we have lost in knowledge?

Where is the knowledge we have lost in information?

Clearly it would be wrong to assume that it is only recently, in our time, that information and knowledge have come to have such importance. That would be an insult to our ancestors. In fact, 'knowledge' and 'human capital' are old concepts. What's new today is the recognition that information and knowledge have to be defined, developed, managed and exploited just like any other core assets. To achieve this, there need to be appropriate and effective processes and systems in place. We also need to be able to measure and evaluate these assets in terms of human capital, and be able to account for such assets on the balance sheet.

In the past, the key to economic growth was industrial production. Today, as markets have matured and technology has advanced, it is no longer industrial production that is the most important economic foundation. As the networked economy develops, the essential economic resource is information and knowledge. This economic shift has caused a substantial increase in the value of media and information assets and human capital. The information and communications technology and media industries have, consequently, become vital targets for investment and concern. Research and development resources are being poured into innovation and so-called 'knowledge management'.

Competitiveness increasingly relies on the ability to grow human capital and achieve effective knowledge management. However, for most economists and advisers on economic growth, this is uncharted territory. Our governments, industries and research organizations have ample access to data and analysis of all aspects of economic growth in yesterday's world. Yet, because the world has changed with the impact of developments in technology, globalization and market convergence and consolidation, the tools and models of defining economic growth are no longer adequate. Borders are shifting, fundamental changes in the economy are taking place, which means our old maps do not fit with the new landscapes. The traditional economic indicators don't work, nor do the old categorizations of economic activities and industry sectors.

A better understanding of human capital and knowledge management is needed. We need to develop new concepts and models to enable us to get to grips with the new role of human capital stock in the economy. We need to establish new indicators and apply better tools in the analysis of the state and performance of the economy. A major challenge is that of finding ways of measuring knowledge. Not easy, as knowledge often consists of intangible assets embodied in the hearts and minds of individual people.

Economists have long understood that knowledge is intrinsically linked to the quality of labour and economic output. While economic theory recognizes the importance of knowledge, it has scarcely begun to explain its complexity. Knowledge comes in all shapes and forms, and its relationship to economic productivity is many-faceted and complicated. It is hard enough to define what knowledge is, let alone to describe or measure it.

To return to our dictionary, 'knowledge' is defined as 'the sum of what's known'; and 'to know' means what you 'have in mind', 'have learnt', 'are aware of', 'have experienced', and 'are able to recall'.

To understand how knowledge is developed, we need to understand how people communicate, form relationships and learn. We also need to differentiate between 'data', 'information', 'knowledge' and 'wisdom', which are commonly confused.

'Data' provides descriptions and facts out of context. 'Information' is data put into meaningful context. 'Knowledge' is the reasoning, experience and know-how that enable us to interpret data or information. 'Wisdom' is the ability to draw intelligent conclusions on the basis of knowledge (see Figure 7.2).

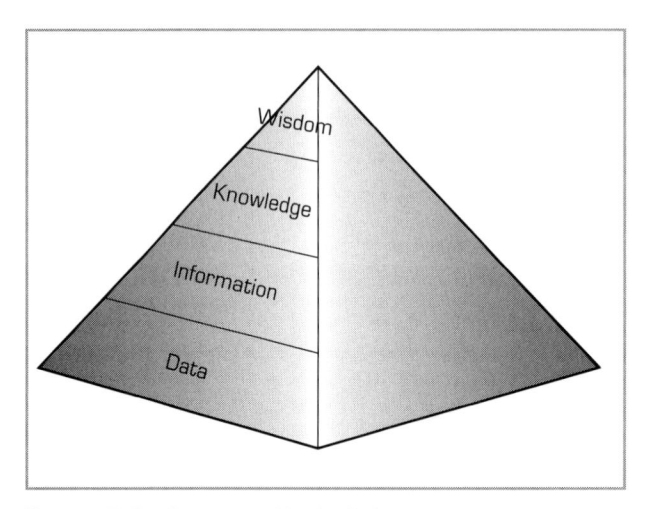

Figure 7.2: the pyramid of wisdom

There is a vital distinction that needs to be made, between 'tacit knowledge' and 'explicit knowledge'. Tacit knowledge is the kind of knowledge that is in the minds and hearts of individual people. Knowledge that is owned by the individual and can only be given or rented to other individuals or to the organization if the individual wants and is able to share their knowledge, in which case the knowledge can be made explicit. Explicit knowledge refers to the kinds of knowledge that are available and accessible as intangible or tangible assets. For instance, books and reports, databases, videos and other resources available on intranets, the Internet, television and so on. The challenge for organizations is that of defining and locating knowledge and then making tacit knowledge explicit in a culture of knowledge-sharing and development.

> 'Data' provides descriptions and facts out of context. 'Information' is data put into meaningful context. 'Knowledge' is the reasoning, experience and know-how that enable us to interpret data or information. 'Wisdom' is the ability to draw intelligent conclusions on the basis of knowledge.

'Knowledge management' has very little to do with technology: it has much more to do with understanding the value of human relationships and interactions, and how to foster and nurture a culture that encourages trust, creativity and knowledge-sharing. The best technology in the world is not going to make knowledge management initiatives succeed if the people within the organization are unable or unwilling to make their knowledge available to others. People in corporate cultures and top-down hierarchical organizations have been trained to control the ownership of knowledge as a powerful tool to maintain status. Nobody wants to lose their status and people may fear that by giving their knowledge away to others, they will become less important and this is exactly what will happen to them (see Figure 7.3).

> 'Knowledge management' has very little to do with technology: it has much more to do with understanding the value of human relationships and interactions, and how to foster and nurture a culture that encourages trust, creativity and knowledge-sharing.

'Knowledge management' straddles several subject disciplines and combines theory and practice from a range of established fields, including management studies such as economics, human resources, communications, information science, strategy, innovation and so on. The research into knowledge management also builds on work flow management, business process re-engineering, information management and so on. Experts within respective disciplines will have their particular perspective and definition of the term. IT professionals will see it as an extension of technologies designed for data storage, processing and retrieval, data warehousing, datamining, database management and so on. Human resources professionals will take a more qualitative approach and see it as a vehicle for developing a 'learning culture', creating the 'learning organization'; management consultants will define it as the omni-potential solution to everything – the central nervous system of the business. Be warned. Knowledge management should not be outsourced – every manager needs to become a knowledge manager if the business is to compete in the networked economy.

Shifting money over digital networks is easy compared to the challenge of shifting information and knowledge assets over the same networks. Money

Figure 7.3: implementing knowledge management in DigiCo
Source: The Sunday Times

is tangible and instantly convertible into a fixed physical state. Money is very content poor – in fact, the content of money is limited to globally accepted numbers and there is little ground for dispute concerning its value.

Barriers to be resolved

Information and knowledge assets are very different. They are much less tangible and more dynamic. They are content-rich and content-difficult. As established in the preceding chapters, a number of mechanisms need to be in place in order to facilitate electronic commerce and transactions of such assets over digital networks. We need mechanisms that will secure the protection of intellectual property rights, the integrity and authenticity of information, the identification of information, and the tracking and recording of information usage. There are also legal and political problems to be addressed. Equally, the problem of pricing information and knowledge assets in digital form for a global market is causing major headaches for suppliers.

In the networked economy, it is important to distinguish between electronic transactions for financial assets, for goods and services, and electronic transactions that include on-line dissemination of information assets in electronic form, in particular intellectual property rights-protected assets. Systems available in the marketplace have so far been occupied with finding solutions to problems of security with electronic financial transactions and not those integrating simultaneous transactions of money and information.

The question is, to what extent will these emerging systems be applicable and able to accommodate the on-line trade of information assets? They may be able to cope with transactions of information provided the assets are defined as 'bulk products', such as books, films, videos, CDs, cassettes, journals and magazines, but how will they cope with the mass distribution of 'items of information' from a multitude of original sources to high volumes of individual customers who each want very low volumes of information.

In order to take advantage of all the new opportunities for delivering information over networks, it will be essential to develop transactional systems that can deal efficiently with information assets delivered on demand and in fragmented or compiled form to just such a global customer base. The transactional systems that will survive in the future will have to be based on large-scale, low-cost, automated operations, with near real-time clearance and efficient settlement that can mass-process very small transactions.

Another growing requirement is the ability to use identification systems to mark and encode information, for the purpose of protecting intellectual property rights, securing authenticity and tracking information usage. This is a very difficult area, fraught with political and legal problems. There are currently many different initiatives around the world in different camps trying to develop information identifiers and standards for encoding information. It is premature to pass judgement on these developments as they are all on the drawing-board. However, this requirement has to be met for the market to function.

Copyrights have, for centuries, provided the economic foundation for the information trade. The development of digital technology and global networks has created many challenges for the copyright system. The concept of copyright has been expanded to accommodate the changes brought about by the digital revolution and the escalating growth of electronic use of published information. Critical work has been carried out and is still going on to develop the intellectual property system so that it will work as a vehicle for intellectual and economic growth in the future as well as it has in the past. Different types of information assets – such as text, music, illustrations, video, multimedia programmes, databases and so on – all depend on legal protection to survive as tradable commodities.

Effective systems are needed that allow for rapid clearance of rights, such as electronic copyright management systems. Many multimedia developers are currently frustrated with the difficulty and high cost of clearing multiple rights from multiple sources. However, the need for efficient trading systems for rights should not be confused with notions of setting up huge central control-towers directing all the distributions of proceeds from licensing electronic rights. The introduction of any compulsory scheme or licensing model would have an adverse effect on the market. The process of marketing rights and designing and implementing intellectual property rights management systems will hopefully be left to the marketplace to resolve.

A problem largely ignored by many software developers is the use of high-grade encryption technology as it is heavily regulated – indeed, in many countries, it is illegal to use and export it. The reason it is illegal is either because of national laws concerning national security and law enforcement and/or because of national laws concerning data protection, privacy and consumer rights. Many of the proposed transaction systems, trade and management systems for intellectual

> **Effective systems are needed that allow for rapid clearance of rights, such as electronic copyright management systems.**

property rights include the use of encryption technology that is not legal in many jurisdictions.

Technology is a two-edged sword – it can be used for good and bad purposes. Encryption technology can be used to secure the integrity of trade and cultural prosperity, but it can also be used as an instrument of criminal activity and unlawful behaviour. The monitoring, tracking, recording and coding of information can be used to produce better books and deliver more timely information and knowledge, but it could also be used to invade our privacy and put us under complete surveillance control, at the mercy of those who are privileged to access our personal information profile.

> **Encryption technology can be used to secure the integrity of trade and cultural prosperity, but it can also be used as an instrument of criminal activity and unlawful behaviour.**

One of the main challenges for those trying to achieve truly global transaction systems for information and knowledge assets is that of finding a viable path through the overwhelming jungle of legal implications in different jurisdictions. Regulatory frameworks and different legal regimes are in conflict and competition with each other. There is, for instance, a tug of war between competition law and intellectual property rights – between national security and privacy, between standards and consumer rights. There is also considerable confusion with regard to liability and responsibility in the convergent media market. Who is liable for information services, for the content of the information assets being disseminated over networks – the carrier, the network operator, the service provider, the publisher, the author – and who is the publisher and the author of these compiled assets?

Traditional media and communications industries are subject to a complicated regulatory framework. There are substantial differences in how these industries are regulated. For instance, the television industry is, in most countries, heavily regulated, while the press operates with a minimum of regulation, functioning instead on the principle of self-regulation. Which tradition and sets of principles are to be safeguarded in the networked information market?

> **Which tradition and sets of principles are to be safeguarded in the networked information market?**

These are crucial questions that will have a profound impact on the success of the information trade underpinning the networked economy. How they are answered will dictate many factors affecting the design of new transactional systems to facilitate this trade, as well as the trade itself.

Conditions for market efficiency and potential risk

A number of conditions need to be met for the information market to operate efficiently. There need to be:

- open markets, free competition;
- diversity, choice and availability of information products wanted by consumers;
- clearly defined roles, responsibility and accountability;
- revision, updating and improvement of regulatory frameworks;
- harmonization of competing legal regimes;
- international standards for information transaction, security and quality control;
- public policy initiatives to encourage and protect the local creation of intellectual property;
- government involvement to explore funding models for education, research, libraries and cultural heritage.

Failure to meet these conditions will undermine the development of the Global Information Society and the networked economy. The risks involved are complicated and far-reaching.

- **Less choice**
  If the market development is dominated by a few large media/information industry conglomerates, creating standards and acting as gatekeepers to information stores, consumers could risk ending up with far less choice in terms of information sources, price and technology than they have today.

- **Back to proprietary systems**
  If open systems take too long to achieve interoperable standards, they will lose the battle with proprietary system vendors already in the marketplace with solutions. Business cannot afford to wait for the ideal solution to emerge. If a proprietary system can do the job now rather than some time tomorrow, then it does not matter to business if the system is proprietary.

- **Deregulation leading to monopolistic competition**
  If deregulation of the market means that cross-media ownership rules will be abolished or substantially changed, this may lead to less competition rather than more. For instance, the relaxation of cross-media ownership rules may have been ill-conceived. The purpose of relaxing these rules was to stimulate competition and achieve diversity, but it may prove to have just the opposite effect. The trend of market concentration and vertical integration is continuing, and there is a threat of market dominance by a few very large conglomerates controlling both carriers, networks, services and content.

- **Lack of security**
  National security and law enforcement may be compromised by the increased use of encryption technology.

- **Infringement of privacy and consumer rights**
  Privacy and anonymity will be a thing of the past if many of the proposed technologies are implemented in the market. For the first time in history, it will be possible, using digital technology, to monitor and control people's use of information on a scale never seen before. The risk of constant invasion of privacy and infringement of consumer rights is very real.

- **Loss of the right of access to information and universal service**
  Human rights principles of equal access for all to information and education are at stake in the new information economy. The cost of maintaining the ambitions of international agreements on human rights, that include the principle of providing a minimum universal service, will be enormous. If governments do not hurry to define a new funding model for education, research and cultural and social welfare, then those rights will no longer exist. Information is already expensive and access to tomorrow's advanced multimedia services will be even more expensive.

Clearly there are many risks and threats to the development of a knowledge-based networked economy. These constitute both existing and potential barriers to trade. By examining the main conditions for market efficiency, it becomes apparent what those barriers are or may become. The process of harmonizing national and international law, definitions of regulatory frameworks, political intervention, standards, technological constraints, competition and market dominance are all important issues in this regard.

Projections of future developments

The task of establishing projections for the future is very much constrained by the fact that there is wide disagreement on forecasting data. The projections given here are therefore based on a mixture of data interpretations, as well as an attempt to imagine the future by gazing into a somewhat hazy crystal ball.

It is difficult to predict future developments beyond what has already been hinted at. The experts and industry leaders who have been consulted in the process of writing this book have had some very different visions and expectations. However, market observations and investment figures would indicate that the trends of globalization and market consolidation, industry convergence and strategic alliances will continue.

There is a growing shift from companies focusing with a 'single purpose' on products and market segmentation to companies focusing on service concepts and bundling products and services in an attempt to lock in loyal customer groups. Developing and managing communities of interest will be a key strategic approach and new business models are needed to leverage on-line communities and aggregation of products and services.

The trends of globalization and market consolidation, industry convergence and strategic alliances will continue.

As far as transactional technology is concerned, encryption technology and key management will deliver a range of new mechanisms that will facilitate the trading of complicated information assets, provided the legal barriers can be overcome.

Smart card technology will penetrate the market over the next decade and the executive wallet 15 years hence will be very slim indeed – maybe containing two or three smart cards and no cash. The smart card will also replace the driver's licence, ID cards and insurance certificates, and may even include your health insurance and benefits, passport and individual learning accounts.

Anonymity will be an illusion, but confidentiality may survive if governments and regulators intervene in time.

> **Anonymity will be an illusion, but confidentiality may survive if governments and regulators intervene in time.**

Global intellectual property rights management systems will be in place by 2005–10, based on an infrastructure of many interoperable systems rather than large, central facilities. Some will be collectively owned and some will be run by large media companies.

The trading of intellectual property rights will become much more market-oriented and media companies will discover many new ways to use/reuse rights, optimizing the value of their rights portfolios.

As far as technological developments are concerned, we will all be surprised by rapid change and new advancements and will see changes and new applications never imagined or predicted. The PC will still be around for years to come, but will lose massive ground to the network computer terminal and a host of new network interfaces and portable appliances. The PC or NC will be considered a utility every citizen should have access to – like water or electricity/gas or telephones.

> **The PC or NC will be considered a utility every citizen should have access to – like water or electricity/gas or telephones.**

The PC or NC will be free, together with basic software that can be downloaded from the Internet. The Internet will change beyond recognition and by 2010 we will laugh when we look back at how primitive it was in the 1990s. Internet access will also be free. However, products and services on the Internet will increasingly be charged for as the market matures and new business models emerge.

8

Wired organizations

Make haste slowly.

Gaius Suetonius Tranquillus, c. AD 69–140

The impact of the networked economy on business and society requires individual organizations to manage major processes of change at different levels. The market environment is changing rapidly. Barriers to entry are no longer what they used to be and the nature of competition is becoming much more complicated and harder to define. Industries are being deregulated, new political policies and legislation are being put in place. The effects of globalization and digitization are profound and far-reaching, leading to entirely new organizational structures and market foundations. The rules of competition are being rewritten. Every link in the value chain is being challenged as the processes of value creation change dramatically. New cost distributions, squeezed margins and significant changes to revenue earnings are putting businesses under immense pressure. Competition hits from all sides and every angle. The supply chain is getting increasingly crowded with stakeholders flocking to the customer's table to add value and fighting to grow their shares of the business. Market demands and consumer behaviour are changing as consumers get wired up and adjust to new lifestyles at home and at work.

Challenges and strategic responses of key players

Organizations have to redefine who they are and reinvent what they do in order to meet changing market demands. To survive, organizations need to acquire new knowledge and new skill-sets, which are often in scarce supply and, when found, don't easily mix with the existing culture of the organization. New people need to be recruited and existing staff must be trained and provided with the opportunities to learn. Managers need to develop new business models and drastically change organizational structures to build the new kind of capabilities needed to secure market positions and future growth.

Organizations have to redefine who they are and reinvent what they do in order to meet changing market demands.

The fast-growing number of organizations developing knowledge management strategies and systems as a key response to enable their organizations to compete in the new networked economy is a clear indicator that many recognize the need to manage human capital and intellectual properties as core assets on the balance sheet. Wired organizations with well-designed data and communications networks are in a good position to extend their business communications systems into fully-fledged platforms for effective knowledge management. 'Knowledge management' is proving to be much more than a buzzword and has given rise to a whole new discipline within business strategy and management theory. The role of the 'KMO' (knowledge management officer) is likely to stick, although no doubt there will be many different names for it depending on which side of the Atlantic and which corporate culture we are in. KMOs and their teams are likely to play a crucial role at the heart of corporate strategy, human resource management, innovation and business development (please refer to Chapter 7 for more on knowledge management).

The preceding chapters have illustrated the many opportunities of the Wired World for business development and economic growth. Digital networks have facilitated the development of electronic shopping malls where masses of information is available, together with a growing range of tangible and intangible goods and services. Navigation tools, standards and protocols allow consumers to find and purchase the information, products and services they want. For most companies, the main attraction of the digital marketplace so far has been the access to large numbers of networked customers and the potential of global electronic commerce. However, organizations have far to go in terms of learning how to leverage this connectivity and exploit the capability of the networks as vehicles for core business operations.

At the turn of the century, most organizations with their own web sites consider themselves 'wired', but they are simply using the web site for old-style marketing and information purposes – somewhere to post a glorified product catalogue, the annual report and those press releases. Organizations that have moved beyond such primitive use into actually using the networks as an integrated platform for running the business are newcomers – new market entrants with no legacy problems and plenty of entrepreneurial skills. The incumbent market operators are lagging behind, yet they are often the organizations that own the assets and resources needed to deliver substance to products and services on-line.

Organizations need to develop an overall coherent approach to the exploitation of information and communications technology, intranets, extranets and the Internet. The mistake that many managers make is to let the IT department develop on-line, Internet or e-commerce strategies rather than make sure that every business unit understands how to develop strategies to win in a networked economy. Organizations do not need an Internet strategy or an e-commerce strategy. They need business strategies that embrace the opportunities and risks of doing business on-line. The corporate strategy must be aligned to the changing landscape of the market to enable the organization to meet new market demands.

Information and media assets will increasingly account for the high volume of on-line transactions over global networks. Consequently, the so-called content industries are targets for investment and development. As leading content suppliers, both publishers and broadcasters have to learn very rapidly how to extend their respective businesses into a digital, networked environment. The publishing and media industries, together with organizations enabling access to education and culture, are the vanguard in a knowledge-based economy. These industry sectors are providers and growers of information and knowledge, of intellectual properties and human capital – the most crucial assets in the new networked economy. Let's look in turn at three types of key players within the wired content industries:

Organizations do not need an Internet strategy or an e-commerce strategy. They need business strategies that embrace the opportunities and risks of doing business on-line.

- publishers;
- broadcasters;
- advertising agencies.

See Chapter 9 for discussion of the key players in the education market, including the role of the library sector.

Publishers in a mixed media environment

Publishers have much at stake in the Wired World. I use the terms 'publisher' and 'publishing' here to refer not only to the world of print, but to all kinds of publishing products, including software, photographs, artwork, music, film, games, databases and more. The proliferation of new distribution channels has created tremendous opportunities for publishers to expand their markets. The hunger for content – a seemingly endless appetite for 'stuff' to fill up the networks – is a great challenge for those publishers who know how to embrace change and manage new channel structures (see Figure 8.1).

Figure 8.1: 'Oh baby, fill up my bandwidth!'

Media content – or, more precisely 'publishing products' – is rapidly growing in terms of its share of the value of nations' gross national product. However, if we were to set up a worldwide, country-by-country table of media output, it would provide evidence of worrying inequality. The dominance of the American media industry is staggering. Although there are many complaints about the ongoing Americanization and US invasion of national cultures, Europe and the rest of the world would do better to applaud the US for its achievements in the media and learn from its experiences. Governments and enterprises need to recognize why their own countries have not been able to match the success of the US in this respect, and they need to devise constructive strategies of their own to make their media industries more competitive.

Outside the US, media industries have not enjoyed the same prosperity and support as their US counterparts. The decline of the British film industry is a rather sad story of how a potentially very media-rich nation has been unable to grow and stay competitive and eventually has been overshadowed by the US. Many valuable British media assets were enticed abroad and quite a few bought for a penny by US investors. Film is a prime example of intellectual and cultural drain on a nation's competitive resources. The question for Britain, and indeed for other nations, is whether or not that lesson has been learnt or if the same thing will be allowed to happen all over again with the digital media and Internet.

The British filmmaker Lord Puttnam was keen to remind us that the US was the only nation to take the film industry really seriously from the start, in spite of the fact that Europe invented the cinema, developed it and even exported it to the US. Speaking at a seminar on the Global Information Society facilitated by the Oxford-Templeton Forum for Leaders of Industry and Government, at Templeton College, Oxford University on 13 May 1996, he said:

It was President Wilson who recognized, as early as 1917, that where American movies went, American goods and influence would soon follow. He put it in these terms: 'The film has come to rank as the very highest medium for the dissemination of America's plans and America's purposes.' Every US president since has upheld that view and ensured that a legislative and regulatory regime was produced to match it. It goes some considerable way towards explaining why America has so completely dominated the history of cinema, and continues to do so today.

Film and television programmes have become the biggest export asset of the United States. Of course this has huge cultural impact on the global information market and on individual countries. It raises serious questions about the competitiveness of other nations. It also begs the question, what will happen to national identity, to language and different cultures around the world?

We certainly do not want a world that has only one identity, one language and one type of culture. We must make sure that all that 'stuff' filling up the bandwidth, and that content spewing out of that 'digital hose' is not all American or, for that matter, all delivered in the English language. The fact is that, at the time of writing, nearly 70 per cent of all Internet hosts are in the English-speaking world, and the US is clearly driving the bulk of the investment activities in the market.

It should not be difficult to see why it is urgent and of paramount importance for other nations and their individual enterprises to be involved in the global information market. The European Commission is acutely aware of the need for Europe to invest and be in the driving seat. It has launched a number of initiatives designed to

Every government, every organization, every enterprise and every individual needs to come to the digital party and figure out their particular way of taking advantage of the new opportunities available in an on-line world.

improve European competitiveness, drawing on the strength of individual national cultures and intellectual creativity – but that is not enough. Every government, every organization, every enterprise and every individual needs to come to the digital party and figure out their particular way of taking advantage of the new opportunities available in an on-line world.

Publishers are getting used to having to operate in a climate of major change induced by digital technology. At first, information technology simply came in the back door. Slowly but surely, new tools were introduced and, within a few years, entire production systems had been completely revolutionized. Typesetters were made redundant and printing works closed down. The old cut-and-paste editing tables and the slow analogue editing techniques used in film and television disappeared as computer-based editing systems took over.

Now information technology is revolutionizing publishers' markets. Technology know-how can no longer remain the domain of just the IT and production departments. All those involved in management and in all the creative, marketing and distribution functions need to learn how to use it.

Publishers are experiencing a kaleidoscope of emerging new business opportunities, driven by new market demands for publishing products. Traditional roles are changing, industries and markets are converging and entirely new patterns of competition are emerging.

Technological progress has made it possible to disseminate and manage information in new ways. Electronic mixed-media publishing, digital libraries, distance learning, teleworking and on-line shopping are developing rapidly, changing the way people learn, work, shop and play. When leading politicians and leaders of industry speak of the 'Global Information Society' or the Information Superhighway, they have in mind a much more advanced version of what is currently available via the Internet, on-line databases and CD-ROM(s). They foresee a time, in the relatively near future, when all cultural products are available in digital form, stored in vast, searchable databases and delivered via transparent telecommunication networks to high-resolution PCs, NCs and television sets. Many librarians and educationalists share this expectation of access for everyone, to everything, anytime, anywhere. Publishers and broadcasters around the world are busy establishing how best they can respond to this development.

Although more and more information is being made available in electronic form, the market for printed products continues to grow. So does the market for television, video, film and games. It is not a question of one medium eradicating the other. There are significant shifts in growth patterns for different publishing and broadcasting products, caused by changes in market behaviour, which publishers and broadcasters must pay careful attention to as this will have strategic implications for and a significant impact on their distribution and sales.

A major challenge for publishers is that of acquiring the understanding of how to combine different media formats and take advantage of new distribution channels. The publishing process is no longer simple and linear in form. The value and business cycles have become more complicated to manage, with many more elements being added. It is necessary to redefine the market and the process of publishing in order to take advantage of the changing market. Publishers need to come up with business strategies that will fit the new market terrain in order to remain competitive.

A major challenge for publishers is that of acquiring the understanding of how to combine different media formats and take advantage of new distribution channels.

Many publishers are unwittingly sitting on potential goldmines of poorly exploited copyrights, human talents and resources, but many fail to see how these valuable assets can be optimized in the new networked economy. They simply do not have the vision or management capability to change and expand their business in tune with the changing market. Instead, they opt for the ostrich position, trying to stick with the old ways. In the short term, such a resistant strategy may seem to be holding for some successful publishers. This can be observed in particular in the very successful book publishing industry. However, in the long run, these publishers will no doubt lose out as the accumulating loss of business opportunities mounts up.

Some publishers seem to behave as if, somehow, they are exempt from the world economy and the fast-changing market environment. In spite of numerous wake-up calls, many are still sound asleep, lost in a dream of yesterday's reality, pretending business can go on as usual while the new competition is allowed to gain market share and seize future growth. However, publishers in denial will not survive unless they are able to deal with the fact that the publishing business is very much subject to the same forces of change as the rest of the economy. Traditional publishers in particular seem to be desperately slow to respond to the challenges of globalization, convergence, digital technology and societal change. If only more publishers would rise to the challenge and seize the opportunities with the same vigour and enthusiasm as other winning enterprises.

Perhaps then there would be more meaningful, quality content available in the market for customers to enjoy in digital form.

We cannot dismember ourselves from the general economy and create a world of our own where the industry of yesterday can remain intact. We cannot avoid the impact of major changes taking place in society. Publishers in particular should embrace change and welcome the avalanche of new publishing opportunities that technological development has brought about. Publishers are uniquely positioned to make sense, and profits, out of digital opportunities. There is a growing market demand for publishers to change and deliver their products and services in a variety of ways. Customers want more and better choice. Customers are no longer the same as those which publishers courted in the pre-digital era. Customer behaviour is changing rapidly and, if publishers want to grow and continue to build loyal customer relationships, they too will have to change and adapt to life in the Wired World.

Customers are no longer satisfied with expensive bulk products. Publishers are very good at producing bulk – books and journals, newspapers and magazines, videotapes and CDs. However, customers want cheaper bulk and more service. They also want more functionality and interactivity. This means on-line products and services, which require new and very different business models from those used in the past. Customers want to access materials and resources in the most satisfying and efficient manner possible. With the proliferation of new distribution channels and media platforms available, publishers are under real pressure to offer choice and flexibility. It is not a question of either/or, but of this and that. Publishers need to extend existing product lines into a digital environment where they can provide a much richer and more complicated content diet for their content-hungry customers.

Managers are trying to understand the meaning of convergence and finding ways to address the impact of it on their core businesses. As we have seen, traditional distinctions between markets, media forms and industries no longer work. There's a need for a more holistic management approach to business, markets and customers. Convergence does not mean that everything goes into one big melting pot for universal digital bits as the popular rhetoric seems to convey. For publishers, convergence means a need to build new customer relationships and find a new approach to a very different market landscape.

Convergence means a need to build new customer relationships and find a new approach to a very different market landscape.

In a knowledge-based economy, there is a value shift in terms of capital resources. Intellectual properties, creativity, knowledge, experience and other forms of human capital become central and, indeed, more important than more tangible capital assets of the likes of industrial goods and money. This is good news for authors and publishers, for booksellers and libraries – in fact, for all the stakeholders in the publishing industry. Why? Because suddenly we have a new economy that puts intellectual property and human capital centre stage. If anyone understands how to generate growth in this emerging knowledge economy it ought to be publishers. For centuries, publishers have had the privilege of perfecting the art of managing human capital and, with authors, creating and delivering intellectual properties. This legacy ought to provide publishers with a solid competitive advantage. However, if publishers fail to adapt their skills and resources to the new market demand, they will quickly lose that advantage. Even with powerful brands such as Oxford or Harvard, the BBC or Disney, future prosperity is not guaranteed. All brands will die if their owners fail to reinvent their businesses in line with what the customers want and the market will take.

> **For centuries, publishers have had the privilege of perfecting the art of managing human capital and, with authors, creating and delivering intellectual properties.**

Organizations from across the board, in both public and private sectors, are trying to understand what has essentially been the publishers' core business since the invention of the printing press and the camera. It seems that everybody wants to be involved in the so-called 'content industries'.

However, content is not king, and neither is technology, nor distribution. It is the customer who is king! To succeed and prosper as publishers and broadcasters in a mixed media environment, it is essential to grow new customer relationships and understand changing market demands. Only by paying close attention to what customers want or need and are prepared to pay for, will publishers and broadcasters succeed.

Will the grand old publishing houses still be 'grand' in 25 years from now? Will they still produce top-selling titles and have the exclusive rights to mankind's greatest modern literary works? Will they instead fail to absorb change and, slowly but surely, see their dominance in the information and media markets diminish? Will they dismiss the great new publishing opportunities as passing fads and gimmicks? If so, more competitive players will be free to reap the rewards of what was once very safe turf where only a limited number of publishers were allowed to play. Already there are many new players on this turf. The clever ones stand ready to execute an aggressive acquisition strategy in any situation where those grand old figures of publishing decline invitations to go digital or show any signs of delaying involvement. In fact, the takeover or elimination of old players by new competition is now a well-known phenomenon in the publishing industry. The acquisition rate has gone through the roof, particularly during the period 1992–99, and many publishers have gone through several ownership changes.

Traditionally, publishers have been organized in different sectors, depending on what they publish and the media they publish in; for example, commercial book publishing, academic publishing, scientific, technical and medical journals and books, magazines, newspapers, photographs or illustrations, classical or popular music, films, videos or games, and so on. However, the development of digital publishing technologies and the deregulation of markets have removed many of the old boundaries between different publishing activities. The technology and means of production, dissemination and delivery are now often the same for the different types of media products. A digital transmission may contain a television or a radio broadcast, a newspaper, a piece of music, a film, book, journal article, photograph, WWW or Internet pages or, for that matter, a telephone conversation. The same transmission network can be used for different types of delivery. The technical skills required for publishing these 'strings of digital bits' are also very similar across the different forms of media.

Understanding process and managing bits

It is no longer so much the nature of the individual types of publishing products or services that matter as the nature of the market segment for which they are intended. Publishers that may have been very product-driven in the past are now recognizing the need to be more market-driven and customer-oriented. Increased competition and fast-changing market dynamics have forced many to review their business strategies and market understanding. Publishing is not limited to publishing individual titles and building up collections or lists of individual titles. The concept of publishing has expanded from traditional 'bulk publishing' mentioned earlier to what may be referred to as 'process publishing' and 'bit publishing' (see Figure 8.2).

Publishers will continue to publish 'bulk' products such as books, magazines, television programmes, videos, music and software on compact discs, but they are also increasingly developing various services as part of their product portfolio. The idea of making what are called 'hybrid products' is receiving a lot of attention. A

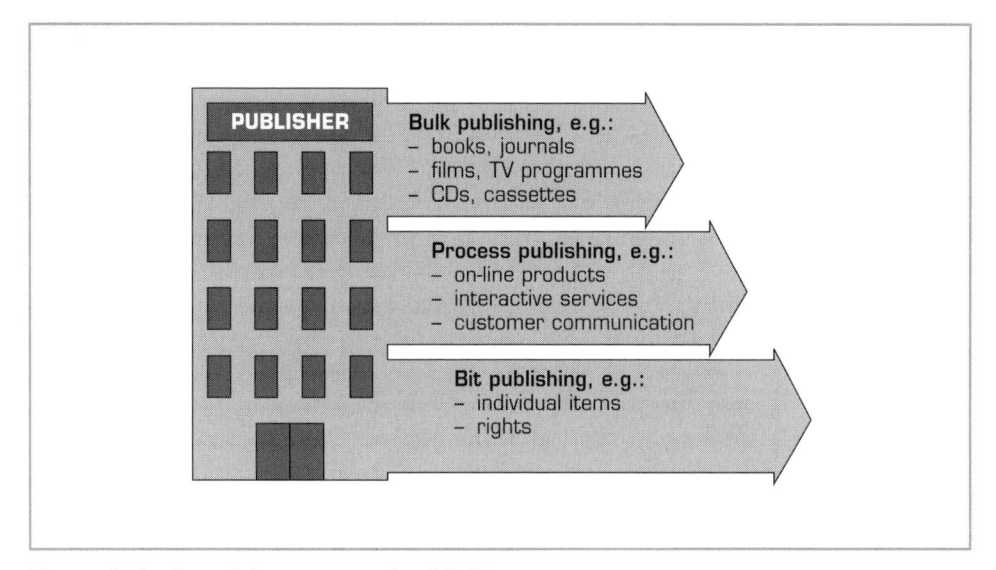

Figure 8.2: the triple concept of publishing

'hybrid product' is a series of interlinking publishing products packaged together to add more value and functionality. For instance, it could consist of a textbook in science, a multimedia science encyclopaedia on CD-ROM, a science video game, television programmes, on-line tutorials and an interactive laboratory on the Internet. In interactive on-line publishing, the process of interaction with customers can itself be a publishing product.

In addition to 'bulk' and 'process', publishers are increasingly dealing in 'bits' too. Publishers are keen to exploit their intellectual properties. They are often in an excellent position to take advantage of the growing market demand for material that can be used as part of multimedia products or included in various types of compilations of information or entertainment. Publishers can supply endless 'bits of stuff'; they can sell and license rights for single parts of publications, for example to be used in other media or by individual customers for some particular purpose.

Publishers are also finding opportunities to extend their branding by developing product lines of related and integrated products and services. By 1999, most national newspapers around the world had launched their newspaper sites on-line. Many of them have been quick to discover that on-line newspaper publishing opens entirely new ways of delivering publishing content. It goes far beyond simply making electronic versions of the printed format.

There seem to be three different trends emerging among newspaper publishers. One is that of simply offering electronic access to the printed newspaper edition. Publishers either put their newspapers up on the Net themselves or they choose to do so via an on-line service provider or they do both.

The second trend is the concept of 'personalized newspapers'. This idea was pioneered at the Media Lab at the Massachusetts Institute of Technology in the United States. Readers will tell the publisher details of who they are, their areas of interest and what sort of information they would like to have in their newspapers. The publisher will use this information to build up 'personal reader profiles' and deliver individual editions to each individual reader – that is, newspapers tailored to individual preferences and tastes. It is a sort of '*Daily Me*' type of newspaper, rather than a '*Daily World*'. Although these experiments are exciting, I cannot help wondering what the world would be like if people were to only hear, read and see what they indicated an interest in or specifically asked for. Would it be the end of personal growth?

> **I cannot help wondering what the world would be like if people were to only hear, read and see what they indicated an interest in or specifically asked for. Would it be the end of personal growth?**

The third trend is to develop 'hybrid products', combining the print edition with on-line news services, archives of back issues/programmes on CD-ROMs or videos. They represent an advance in searchable databases targeted at professional, academic and educational markets.

Many publishers are building product portfolios based on flexible lists of titles targeted at specific customer groups. They are developing powerful product lines where individual titles can be quickly added, amended or removed, according to market demand. The ability to optimize and develop brands is essential in order to succeed and attract consumer loyalty in an ever more competitive marketplace.

Not all publishers find this transition to the new networked economy easy. Over the years, many traditional publishers have adopted an introvert perspective on the world (see Figure 8.3). They do not venture often enough outside their traditional publishing culture and activity. As a result, they fail to take notice of just how much things have changed.

The introvert perspective assumes linearity and passivity in terms of relationships in the value chain. Authors are there as suppliers of the raw material. Such publishers seem to have an image of authors as a creative water tap in the publisher's

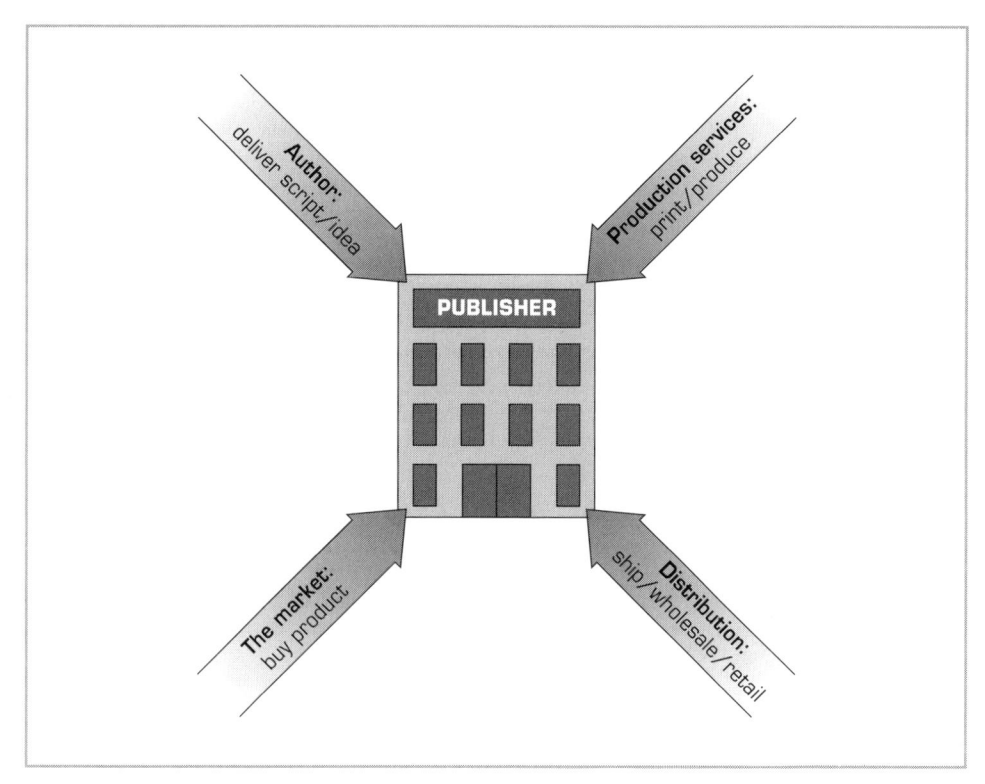

Figure 8.3: the introvert perspective of the 'old-style' publisher

kitchen, publishers being able to turn on the tap of creativity whenever they need it. Production services are simply mechanical facilities to get a job done. The distribution system moves the products out in the way it has always done. The object of the relationship with customers is that they purchase the products. It is a one-way story all the way.

Such an introvert perspective is no longer sustainable. The development of the information market has changed and broadened the traditional roles of the players in the marketplace and their relationships. The process of invention, production, distribution and consumption is no longer simple and linear (see Figure 8.4).

> **The introvert perspective assumes linearity and passivity in terms of relationships in the value chain.**

It is often a challenge for larger publishers to see the business opportunity presented by grouping together individual titles that traditionally belong in different corners of the enterprise. They need to reorganize internally in order to improve

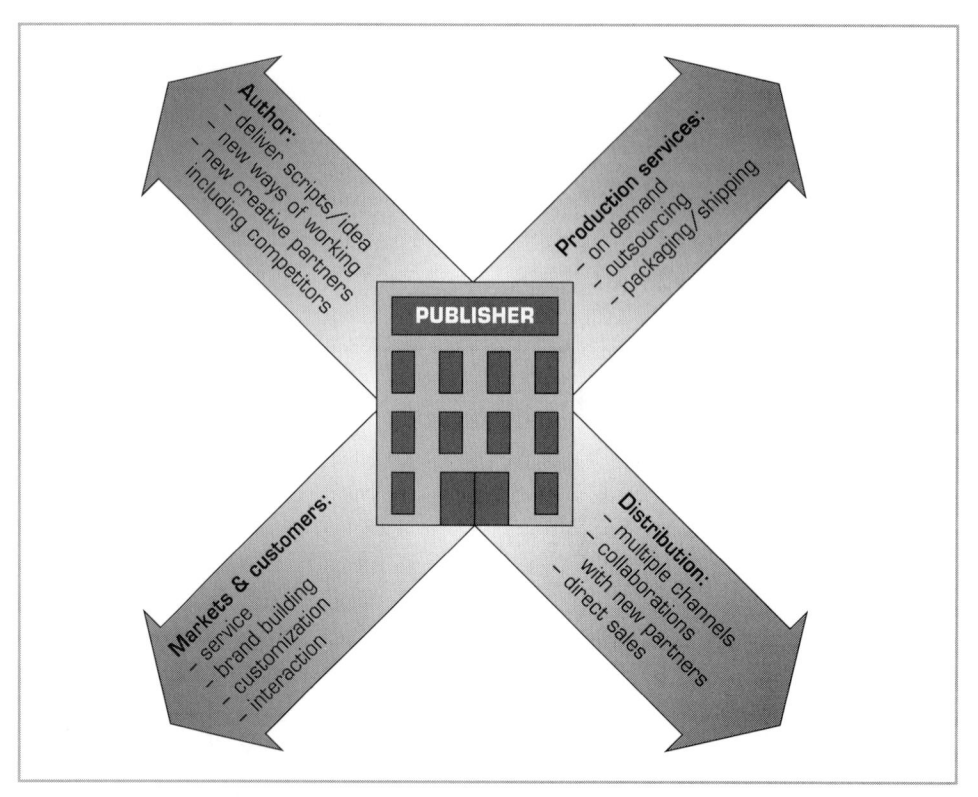

Figure 8.4: the extrovert perspective of the 'new-style' publisher

the exploitation of their intellectual property rights. Strategic portfolio management of rights is essential in order to succeed in building dynamic lists across different subject areas and editorial groups.

Mixed-media product lines and the expansion of different forms of publishing cannot be achieved without new skills and resources. Consequently, publishers enter into all sorts of collaborations with external partners, from so-called third-party multimedia developers to network operators, service providers, software companies and so on. Managing external partnerships well is critical and the key to long-term success.

Publishers and broadcasters also need to develop good internal partnerships between different business units within their own organization, in order to pool the necessary expertise and resources to innovate, seize opportunities, achieve critical mass and economies of scale.

Digital television

The world of television is being turned upside down as a result of advances in digital technology, computing and broadband communications. The deregulation of the communications and media industries and the globalization of markets are compounding this revolutionary impact. The last decade of the twentieth century has seen a proliferation of new TV channels and bandwidth availability. As we exit the twentieth century and move into the next, a great many of us have sophisticated satellite systems capable of delivering more than 1200 television channels into our living rooms. Gone are the days of terrestrial television and linear programming dictated by a handful of powerful broadcasters. We have moved into a multichannel media reality driven by an ever-increasing degree of choice and fierce competition.

The world of television is being turned upside down as a result of advances in digital technology.

For programme makers and broadcasters, digital television has the double impact of, on the one hand, profoundly changing the ways in which programmes and services are made and, on the other, bringing fundamental change to the way in which media distribution, sale and consumption take place.

New tools, digital production, distribution and delivery systems require not only a massive investment in technology, but also considerable investment in human resources and training to develop the new skill-sets and competences needed for the development of digital television. Stakeholders in the television industry have no choice but to make such investments today if they want to survive and prosper tomorrow. The challenge for traditional television companies is how to extend what they do into this new multichannel environment. They will not be able to switch overnight from analogue to digital or from terrestrial to satellite. For years to come, they will have to continue to service an existing customer base with a mixed penetration of 'old' and 'new' technology. The challenge for broadcasters is to be available on all media platforms and manage a multichannel distribution structure – from conventional terrestrial analogue aerial and cable to digital terrestrial, cable and satellite, including Web TV and the Internet.

The convergence of technologies, industries and markets will eventually dissolve many traditional boundaries. We can already see a blurring between computing, telecommunications, television and publishing. The merger mania and massive consolidation happening within and between these industry sectors are speeding up this process. Microsoft's recent deals and acquisitions in the telephony, satellite and cable TV companies is just one powerful example of the rapid move towards a very different media and communications industry.

Broadcasters will have to work increasingly hard to maintain and develop identity and brands to secure a leading role as media content providers. The competition is fierce and constantly moving. Success will very much depend on the abilities to embrace and manage change and make the right strategic investments in innovation and product/service development. Strategic partnerships with key players (including competitors) is also vital to gain core competence and market reach, as well as shared risk and access to funding. Increased competition and falling market shares, combined with an ongoing and escalating cost of technology investment, mean that broadcasters will have to do more for less and constantly innovate and find new, creative ways of making and delivering content and services.

Digital television also means that national governments lose the last grip they had on controlling the media output within the boundaries of their countries. Satellite television and Internet communications cuts across national borders. Global players already dominate the media industry. Digital television has immense implications for the development and execution of media policy, and media policy is crucial as an instrument of democracy, value creation and quality control. It has always been, and always will be, an important national concern, due to the power of the media and its role in shaping cultural identity, language and opinion. In a digital environment, media policy makers and regulators can no longer be effective unless they also work together and co-operate on an international level. There are many obstacles in the process of achieving a more global and harmonized media policy to underpin the development of a prosperous, diverse and high-quality media industry. Nations across the world vary in their approach and there are significant differences between the approaches of China, the US and countries in Europe, Australasia and Africa.

The clash of cultures and approaches to media policy is clearly demonstrated by the ways in which public service broadcasting operates in different countries. In the US, commercial television dominates and public service broadcasting is practically bankrupt, constantly struggling to find the funding and the talent it needs to operate. With the advent of digital television, public service broadcasters risk being reduced to 'digital have-not beggars', completely side-stepped by well-funded media conglomerates. Without substantial support from state subsidies and public funds or much better means of generating commercial revenues and attracting media spend, the future for public service broadcasting looks bleak in many countries.

With the advent of digital television, public service broadcasters risk being reduced to 'digital have-not beggars', completely side-stepped by well-funded media conglomerates.

At the other end of the scale, in the UK we see an entirely different story. The BBC has taken a leading role in the race to build and extend services for the digital media market. Still primarily funded by the 'ancient' model of the licence fee, the BBC has so far managed to evolve what it does best, delivering high-quality programming into a multichannel television environment. However, the pressure is on to secure the substantial funding required to maintain and develop the BBC's position in the new and rapidly changing market environment. The BBC is at the mercy of the UK government's media and communications policy as well as being at risk from changes in international agreements and regulations. Will this great flagship of the best in broadcasting continue to stand out as a global example of excellence in the digital world of tomorrow? Much will depend on the vision, leadership and strategic approach of the BBC's top management team and its ability to secure the continued support of its governors and the government.

> With the blurring of boundaries, the globalization of markets, and with the location of the home base no longer relevant, it is hard to avoid wondering if the notion of a digital licence fee-payer in cyberspace is viable.

So far, the licence fee has provided a cornerstone for the BBC. There is no guarantee, however, that the licence fee model will survive for ever or even for quite a few years to come. Nor is the income from the licence fee likely to be sufficient to fund the transformation of the BBC into a major player in the new digital television reality.

The BBC already operates in the global market and is increasingly successful with its overseas activities. Digital television and broadband communication networks largely ignore national boundaries, so how will the BBC distinguish between its programming and services for the British public and its output in other countries? Does it continue to make any sense to maintain the strict division about what the BBC does for the British public and what it does overseas? Does the British public mind paying a licence fee to enable the BBC to compete abroad as long as it provides a solid service at home? The BBC has always been meticulously careful to separate the funding and operation of its main concern – which is to provide high-quality broadcasting services to the British public – from its growing commercial activities organized under the name BBC Worldwide. Has the time come to review the necessity of that traditional 'wall of China' between the public and commercial roles of the BBC? Perhaps it is no longer sustainable in a digital world. As long as the BBC enjoys the benefit of collecting over £2 billion in licence fee revenues, regulators and the BBC's competitors will always ask: 'What exactly is the BBC licence fee-payer in the UK being asked to pay for?' So far, the question has been easy to answer and the licence fee model has stood the test of time and proved a very productive business model. However, with the blurring of boundaries, the globalization of markets, and with the location of the home base no longer relevant, it is hard to avoid wondering if the notion of a digital licence fee-payer in cyberspace is viable.

Transforming advertising

The information and media industries rely heavily on advertising revenues. Any significant shifts in advertising spending figures will have an immediate impact on cash flows and levels of media output. How advertisers choose to spend their advertising budgets will be a main driver in the shaping of the global media market. It will be critical for publishers, broadcasters, network operators and information service providers to find ways of capturing and holding on to their shares of the advertising market.

How advertisers choose to spend their advertising budgets will be a main driver in the shaping of the global media market.

There will be significant changes in media advertising as this market develops. It may not worry the media industry much yet, as advertising spending patterns have yet to absorb the impact of the Internet and other digital media platforms and the new forms of advertising. Many advertisers still define advertising that uses new media channels as a research activity. However, this is rapidly changing as the new media channels mature and new business models are worked out.

Advertising rates on the Internet are, in many cases, based on a combination of a monthly fixed charge and a charge for the number of actual 'hits' – that is, the number of times (or number of users by whom) the advertisement is accessed. Rates vary tremendously. Some offer space for between $10,000 to $30,000 per month or $15,000 to $18,000 per million hits. If you want to place an ad banner on one of the leading Internet portals, it could cost you millions! Many Internet advertisers have learnt that simply placing banners on web sites does not automatically create customers, nor is it any guarantee that Internet users will click on the banners and arrive at their web sites. Internet users are often in need of help to navigate and locate products and services. If advertisers could find more creative ways of adding value to the experience of being on the Web, they would be much more likely to succeed. Advertising on the Internet is all about mastering the interactive communication with Web customers and understanding what people want to do on-line.

The new Wired World of connected consumers brings many exciting opportunities for advertising. Advertising agencies and their clients are busy experimenting with new methods and new channels for advertising. Traditionally, media advertising has been split into five main revenue streams – magazines, newspapers, radio, television and film. Now there are many more to consider, including cable networks, on-line information networks, on-line banking, interactive television, digital radio, multimedia games and the phenomenal growth of the Internet and WWW with all its networks and different applications.

The competition for advertising revenue will be fierce as the media market continues to expand. Advertisers will bask in a world full of advertising space and thrive in a buyer's market. The choices advertisers make determine the funding of the media. Allocation of advertising spending money will drive the process of convergence and market concentration even further, as many players in the global information market will have to join forces to be able to demonstrate a market reach attractive enough to advertisers.

The networked market is also changing the style and presentation of advertising. Never before in our history have advertisers had so much information about their markets and access to so many tools to accumulate knowledge about their individual customers. Market intelligence has never been as intelligent as it is today. Advertisers can make use of sophisticated customer profiles, enabling them to target customers with very specific advertising that has been tailored to individual interests, tastes and buying power. This is called 'personalized advertising'.

Network advertising also means exciting possibilities for interaction between advertisers and customers. This in turn means new opportunities for developing customer relationships. Closer communication with customers can only be a good thing for advertisers. Feedback and input from customers will improve the ability to deliver competitive products. Advertisers will learn more about customers and customers will learn more about what the advertisers have to offer and, thus, be able to make more informed purchasing decisions.

> **The choices advertisers make determine the funding of the media.**

Direct marketing over networks can be convenient for customers, especially if it is integrated with features such as automated ordering facilities, secure payment and delivery on demand. Direct marketing can also be more profitable for companies as the cost of sales is reduced and intermediaries can be removed from the equation. However, direct marketing also puts new pressure on companies as they will have to make decisions about how to organize their marketing operations. A growing number of organizations are developing their own direct marketing systems, including direct mail order. Many choose to outsource their direct marketing operations and make use of the broad range of advertising and marketing services available.

Another interesting development is the upsurge in 'collaborative advertising', which is when companies from different sectors collaborate on joint advertising schemes and/or enter into partnerships in order to combine their products and services in new ways. In the past, it was unthinkable to associate certain products with others. Today, though, it seems only natural to bundle disparate products together to promote particular images, values and lifestyles. For instance, who would have thought that it could make sense to bundle subscriptions to the *British Medical Journal* with classic cars, good wine selections and holidays abroad? Once that threshold is crossed, it pushes back the frontiers of advertising and opens endless new opportunities for original advertising of products and services.

Network advertising can be integrated with the actual product or service in entirely new ways. A television soap opera, for instance, can be built around a series of products that feature in the programme. Advertisers can use all kinds of programming to create interactive services – even sports and news. Viewers can select and order products they see in the programmes, be it an item of clothing worn by a soap character, trainers worn by an athlete, or a shirt worn by a politician. Perhaps the Queen's hats will even appeal to viewers.

'Interactive' advertising is changing the focus of advertising from individual product-pushing to concept-building. Advertisers increasingly seek to understand the individual circumstances of customers and their needs and wants. They are selling products and services with a view to supporting certain lifestyles and/or work styles.

> **'Interactive' advertising is changing the focus of advertising from individual product-pushing to concept-building.**

The evolution of new types of advertising also means that advertising agencies will have to develop new skills and ways of working with clients. Clients will need to be much more involved in the design and process of advertising. The relationship between the client and the advertising agency will change as a result and they will have to come much closer to each other's business.

The concept of each customer receiving only the advertising to which they are susceptible is attractive to both customers and advertisers. However, this development can also have implications for the individual's right to privacy as it presupposes the detailed recording and usage of personal information. It also raises concern over media ethics, advertising standards and consumers' rights of protection. The risk of potential abuse of new forms of powerful advertising will no doubt be on the political agenda very soon, if it is not there already. There is, for example, considerable unease in the regulatory camps dealing with the laws of advertising, privacy, consumer rights and the media. It will be a real challenge to redefine the regulatory framework in such a way that it will stimulate the economic growth of the global information market while safeguarding the principles of media regulation and advertising standards that have delivered the quality and richness of the media content we have available today.

Value creation and changing business models

Established concepts used for developing business models no longer fit in a digital environment as these concepts fail to properly accommodate the new market dynamics and changing business parameters. For instance, widely used concepts such as the 'value chain' and 'product lifecycle' presuppose a notion of linearity, and dictate a sequential order in the business process, that often doesn't

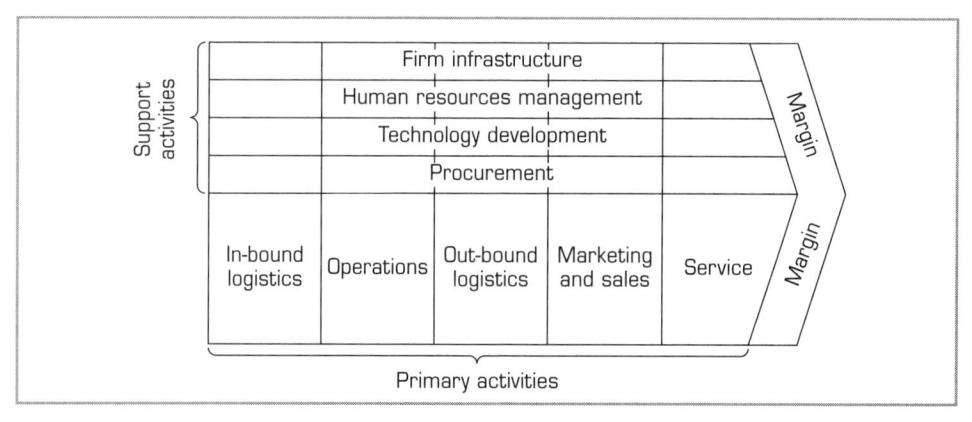

Figure 8.5a: the traditional generic value chain concept
Source: Michael E. Porter, *Competitive Advantage*, 1985

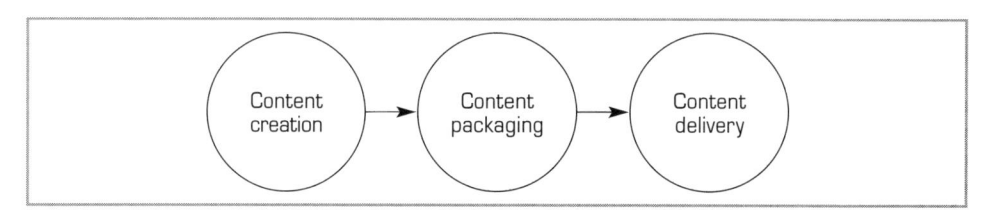

Figure 8.5b: the value chain concept applied to the publishing industry
Source: Michael E. Porter, *Competitive Advantage*, 1985

Widely used concepts such as the 'value chain' and 'product lifecycle' presuppose a notion of linearity, and dictate a sequential order in the business process, that often doesn't happen in cyberspace.

happen in cyberspace (see Figure 8.5). To take the example of publishing, the value chain for this is often described in terms of three main parts:

- creative input;
- editing/production;
- distribution/output.

However, such traditional and linear models are no longer adequate. There are many more links in the value-creation chain and also many more participants looking to secure their place in it. With the arrival of digital media and interactive publishing, the framework for creating value looks more like a circle. Many wired organizations have now begun to look for new value-creation concepts and models. For many organizations, it would be more useful to drop the concept of the linear value chain and develop concepts of value circles or value matrices that could also define and capture the value creation in interactivity and customer/community relationships (see Figure 8.6).

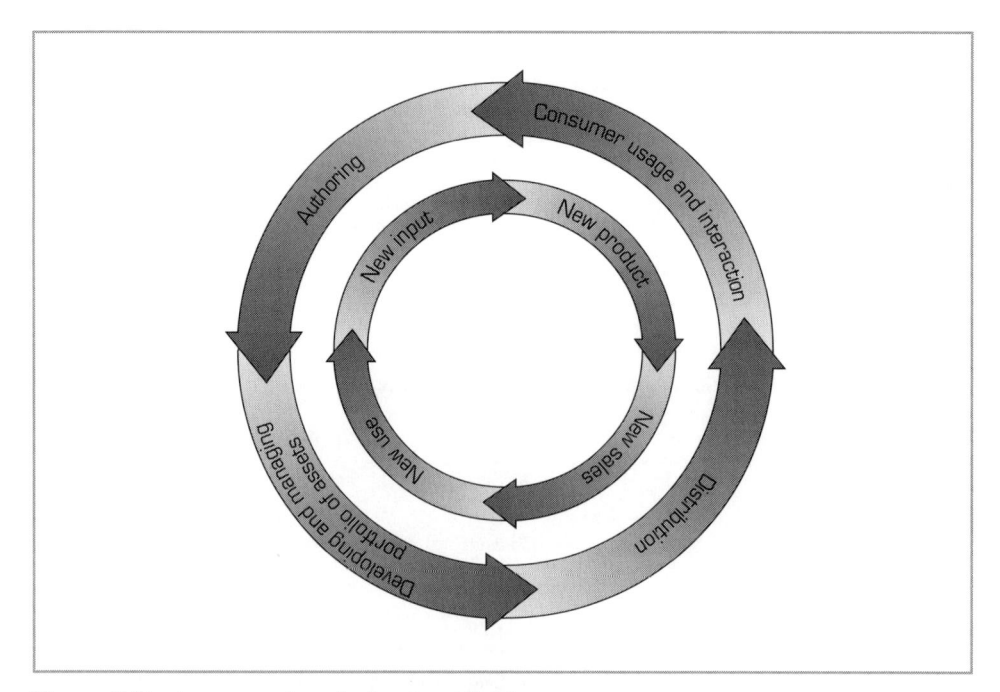

Figure 8.6: the new value circle of publishing

As for the 'product lifecycle', this is a concept borrowed from biology. It implies that something is 'born', goes through the process of 'growing up', 'matures' and inevitably 'dies' (see Figure 8.7). There are, of course, well-proven business strategies on offer to deal with each of these four evolutionary stages in the life of the product.

The idea that the life of a product should follow the four main phases of biological life forms is quite absurd, if you think about it. Why do we accept such a notion? Is it useful? There are plenty of examples of products that never die or seem to just leap into the market without any 'growing pains'. There are also examples of 'dead' products coming back to life and finding a place in the market.

The product lifecycle concept can be dangerous and cause strategic vision impairment. It often narrows down the scope of perceived market opportunity. The product lifecycle can stop us from understanding how products and services 'live' in the market. One of the important challenges in the new networked economy is to optimize the value of assets by understanding how they interrelate and can be combined. Quite often, this will extend and enrich the 'life' of individual products and services – that is, products and services in digital form will not die, but change and evolve into something new.

> **Products and services in digital form will not die, but change and evolve into something new.**

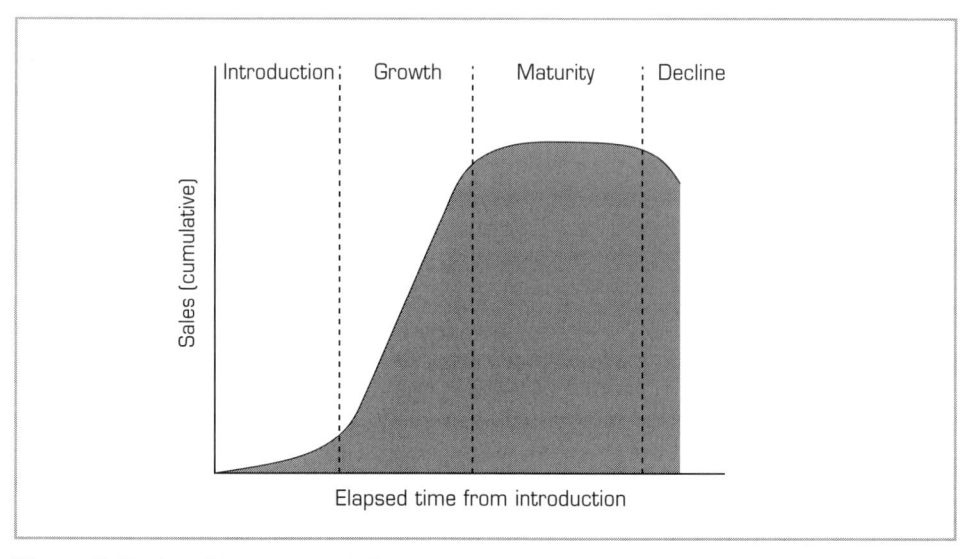

Figure 8.7: the old concept of the product lifecycle
Source: Michael J. Baker, *Marketing: Theory and practice*, 1995

Publishers and broadcasters will have to rethink current business models that are based on the assumption that the market consumes all information and media packaged in bulk products and fixed linear programming schedules. The scenario for trading assets over networks in the global media market allows for media consumption on demand – the consumer paying for actual information/media use. On-demand publishing/broadcasting requires new business models that will capitalize on the changes taking place in the market.

Some of the most significant changes in the buying behaviour of information/media consumers are that, in a networked environment, they are:

- much more selective than before, targeting the specific information they require;
- being aided by browsers, menus, indexes and search software;
- being served and controlled by intelligent agents, user profiling and information gatekeepers;
- expecting a high degree of functionality – for instance, being able to interact with the information, compile and customize information from a variety of sources;
- wanting to obtain the information/media services instantly;
- increasingly, only prepared to pay for actual use and wanting access to preview information/media content, to 'try it on before they buy'.

Other significant business model considerations are:

- the merging of telecommunications and computing, publishing and broadcasting;
- the continuing process of market consolidation and dominance of global players;
- the growing importance of consumers' time and exposure to choice as competing factors as, given the proliferation of new channels, products and services, consumers have limited time to spend and limited capacity to absorb choice – for example, more time spent on the Internet means less time spent watching television and reading books and vice versa (see Figure 8.8);
- the expectation that voice traffic telephony will be free and, in any case, only amount to 1 per cent of total telecommunications/Internet traffic – the remaining 99 per cent being data by 2002;
- the trend towards giving hardware, software and killer applications away for free in order to build and keep a customer base – for example, the Netscape browser, mobile phones, digital television set top boxes and satellite dishes, PCs and NCs;

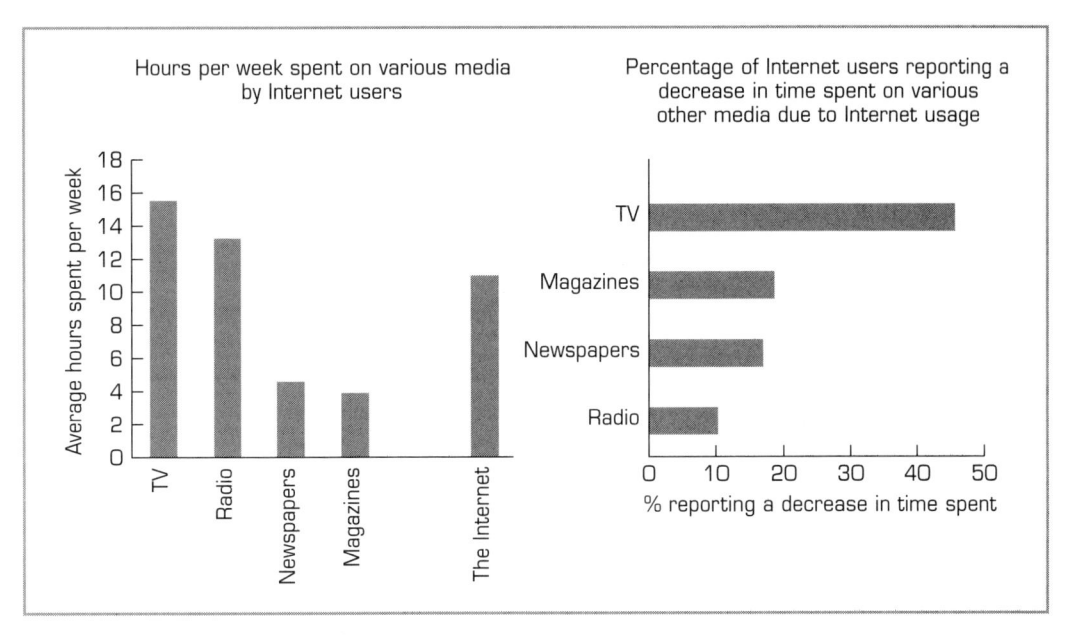

Figure 8.8: competing for time

- the suggestion that computing and network communications are becoming basic utilities that every citizen should have access to for free, funded by advertising rather than customers;
- the fact that, so far, most of the money made on the Internet is that made by short-term financial investors on highly inflated Internet stock transactions based on fictitious and unsustainable market evaluations;
- many major Internet transactions are done by swapping Internet stocks – the so-called illusionary money business, where you pay be x billion dollars' worth of Internet stock for an x per cent stake in an Internet company – real money does not actually change hands.

The impact digital technologies and networks have had, and will have in the future, on the ways in which value is created, added and exploited in the market is beyond doubt. We need to revise and extend existing concepts and business models and develop new ones if necessary. However, we must be careful not to throw the baby out with the bathwater. There are essential resources, basic functions, fundamental principles and areas of responsibility that still apply and need to remain intact. Authorship, publishing, film and TV programme making, advertising, retailing and electronic transmission and delivery (broadcasting/telecommunications) will continue to be primary functions and areas of value creation. There are also basic and well-proven theories of markets and economics that will work just as effectively in a networked economy.

Growing and managing communities of interest

The concept of 'communities of interest' (COIs) has attracted a lot of attention and become a focal point for discussion of new business models for the Internet. It is, of course, a very old concept that has probably been around since the dawn of humanity and served as a basic framework for developing all kinds of business models. Think of the old trading markets where people would gather and share common interests and exchange goods and services. Think of how society has always tended to have a host of clubs and groups, institutions, professions and so on. Taking part in, and belonging to, communities of interest is a fundamental function of human existence. That's perhaps why they work so well on the Internet and in an environment where the business models must be, first and foremost, sensitive to the art of building and managing relationships.

Communities of interest first started to build up around main web sites on the Internet where growing numbers of users were aggregated around a set of common interests and resources. The Well is a classic example of how they can evolve over time in a bottom-up, organic fashion, driven by individual users and their communication needs. Many Internet sites that hold the best clues to business model development are such non-commercial sites. They are often 'old' and well-established on-line communities that demonstrate what people want to do on-line and what adds value. The craftsmanship and understanding of human nature that are essential in order to build and manage such groups are very much lacking in on-line businesses, although some very good commercial sites and on-line services are emerging based on communities of interest. These are notably within specific and topical areas, such as education, business information, healthcare, music, travel and sports.

High-traffic web sites that have managed to aggregate high volumes of users, content and resources are often referred to as 'portals' and these serve as important gatekeepers of on-line business and distribution. Typical examples of so-called mega-portals are global sites such as Yahoo! and AOL. There are very few mega-portals, but an enormous array of portals are targeted at specific markets and topic areas. There are also more and more sophisticated portals emerging that are targeting the needs and wants of individual customer groups in very well-defined markets (see Figure 8.9).

Communities of interest are also created within corporate networks (intranets or extranets) where groups of personnel and business partners belong to different communities depending on their roles and functions within the organizations. Corporate extranets could function like an individual portal for specific business communities.

Clusters of communities of interest are often found linked to a common portal or several portals, such as mega-portals or other main portal sites focusing more vertically on specific market segments and areas of interest. The business of interlinking and integrating sites requires careful model planning to secure important revenue streams and attractive deals.

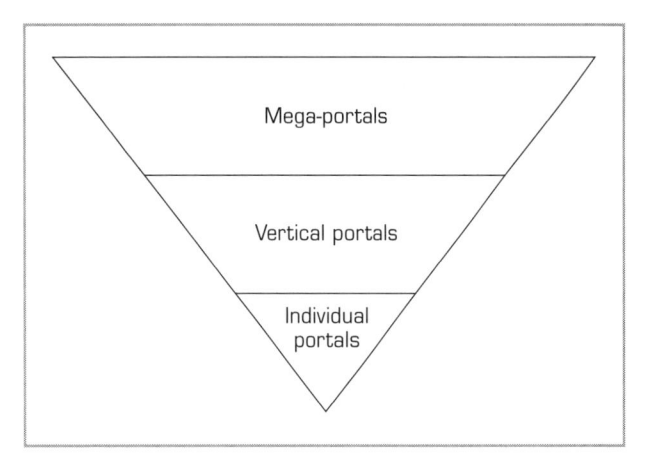

Figure 8.9: the mega-portals are gatekeepers for more targeted portals

According to Sentilhes and Davison, veterans of digital business development, the defining characteristics of a successful vertical portal (see Figure 8.10) include:

- development of content, community, and e-commerce features to serve a specific interest community;
- aggregation of a large, but often fragmented global audience;
- aggregation of an e-commerce offering from diverse vendors of interest to the community;

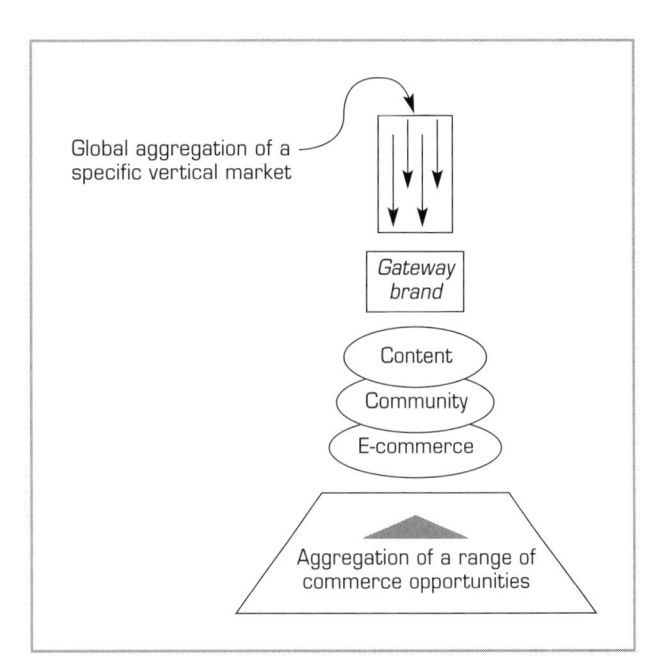

Figure 8.10: building business on-line in vertical markets
Source: Sentilhes and Davison

Wired organizations 135

- development of a strong brand focused on the specific audience;
- refinement of the 'experience dimension' in all levels of interactivity and e-commerce;
- personalized one-to-one marketing relationships.

It is important for business organizations to understand that the value-creation process depends on the on-line customer experience and the quality of the relationship created by the vendors. The customer experience includes a whole range of activities and functions, and the actual commercial transaction is a small part of the overall experience. On-line customers are used to, and expect to have, free access to rich content resources. They also demand privacy and the freedom to communicate and participate via e-mail, chat rooms, discussion groups and so on, without the intrusion of commercial enterprise. Business organizations that want to succeed on-line need to be prepared to invest in developing and providing a whole range of complimentary and people-sensitive services in order to win interest or loyalty from customers. To achieve this, organizations will have to reinvent the way they do business and adopt a much more holistic and embracing approach to business development. The likelihood is that no single organization will be able to do that alone, so the importance of forming sustainable partnerships becomes critical.

The strategic alliance syndrome

The current Wired World market scenario is dominated by players from traditionally separate industries, each providing their independent infrastructures, be they in telephony, broadcasting, cable television, on-line business information, publishing or other areas. These key players have for some time been planning for a future where these infrastructures will merge or interconnect. The expectation is that the separate means of communication will be integrated in digital services to be provided throughout society. The stakeholders are consequently investing in developing new applications that can take advantage of the new GII services.

As a result, companies are realizing that, if they are to respond to this market development, they will need resources and skills outside their traditional domains. Consequently, all the key commercial players busy shaping the GII have reached outside their own entities to form relationships with others in combined efforts to create products and services for the global networked market.

The convergence of technologies is causing fundamental changes to the structure of traditional industries. New business models require new market positions. Collaboration across industrial and cultural borders is needed to succeed in the new environment. The strategic response of many companies is one of growth by means of acquisitions and/or strategic alliances as part of a process of vertical or horizontal integration.

This growing trend of strategic alliances in the market has been going on since the early 1980s. However, in the past, strategic alliances have usually been limited to those between two companies – that is, joint ventures. Today, we see groups of companies establishing formal links with each other. There is an increasing trend for industrial sectors to merge activities and build collaborations across a wide spectrum of skills and resources. Software, computer and consumer electronics companies, telecommunication and cable operators, network service providers, broadcasters, publishers, chip manufacturers, banks, distributors and retailers are all forming alliance groups in order to develop new products and services. As Benjamin Gomes-Casseres writes ('Group versus group: How alliance networks compete', *Harvard Business Review*, vol. 72, July–August 1994):

A new form of competition is spreading across global markets: group versus group. Call them networks, clusters, constellations, or virtual corporations, these groups consist of companies joined together in a larger overarching relationship.

9

Public services

Many governments see the Global Information Society as an opportunity for social, cultural and economic reform. Information networks offer many new opportunities to rationalize public sector activities and operate public services more efficiently. The establishment of an information infrastructure can also add value to the quality of the Welfare State by offering new means of delivering education, providing healthcare services and stimulating cultural activities. Governments and their administrations play an important role in setting policies and determining regulatory frameworks. As we have seen with recent political campaigns, many of them actively pursue an agenda of building a Global Information Society, launching initiatives aimed at stimulating private investment and facilitating growth in the information market.

There is a general economic climate and political attitude throughout the competitive world that favours the freedom of market forces and a transfer of public ownership and responsibilities to the private sector. This is manifesting itself in a number of ways, most notably in the increasing number of public companies being privatized and the deregulation of industrial sectors. The predominant political and economic conviction is that the building of open competitive markets and the commercial enterprise are key to efficiency and economic growth.

However, there are several sectors of the Global Information Society that will never be able to operate by commercial rules alone, such as health, education, culture and scientific research. These will continue to need public funding and support. They will remain a primary concern and responsibility of democratic governments and public organizations.

Reinventing government

Information and communications technology and the emergence of the GII have, and will continue to have, an enormous impact on what governments do in terms of policy development, regulation and the funding and operation of public services. The convergence of technologies and markets needs to be matched by a process of appropriate integration of government sectors, roles and responsibilities. Just as the private sector is under immense pressure to reinvent its businesses and change organizational structures, so are governments and the public sector. The old-style hierarchical organizational model with its inherent top-down management approach is just as inappropriate and outdated for governments in the new networked economy as it is for private enterprises. That's why we see many governments and public-sector organizations undergoing major surgery and changing both internally and externally.

In 1993, the US Clinton and Gore Administration set out to 'use IT to reinvent government' and, over a four-year period, reduced the federal workforce by 351,000 employees, eliminated 250 programmes and agencies and saved $137 billion. In 1997, Al Gore launched another initiative called 'Access America', designed to make government 'more productive, open, responsive and user-friendly', Al Gore ('Putting people first in the Information Age' in my book *Masters of the Wired World*, Financial Times Management, 1999). Gore also put forward the concept of 'virtual government' and described how information and communications technology and networks can be used to create virtual organizations that can improve the information processing and knowledge-sharing needed to deliver government functions. Virtual government networks can provide one-stop shops for citizens and customers, greatly improving the efficiency of service and process.

> **Just as the private sector is under immense pressure to reinvent its businesses and change organizational structures, so are governments and the public sector.**

At the International Telecommunication Union Congress on 12 October 1998, Al Gore announced a 'Digital Declaration of Interdependence,' in which he spells out 'five great challenges that . . . can create a brighter world for us all.

- We must improve access to technology so everyone on the planet is within walking distance of voice and data telecommunications services within the next decade . . .
- We must overcome our language barriers and develop technology with real-time digital translation so anyone on the planet can talk to anyone else . . .

- We must create a Global Knowledge Network of people who are working to meet our most important challenges in education, healthcare, agricultural resources, sustainable development, and public safety . . .
- We must use communications technology to ensure the freeflow of ideas and support democracy and free speech . . .
- We must use communications technology to expand economic opportunity to all families and communities around the globe.

Parallel to the US developments, in the UK, Tony Blair's government embarked on a very similar agenda and declared its ambition for the 'UK to become the leading digital economy in Europe' by 'taking the lead in the use of digital technologies' (Peter Mandelson, 'The digital government' in my book *Masters of the Wired World,* Financial Times Management, 1999). The government's Green Paper published in 1998 outlines how these digital technologies will impact communications between a government and the citizens. Targets have been set across the board to implement information and communications technology. For instance, the government itself wants 90 per cent of all central government's routine purchases of goods to be made electronically by 2001 and 25 per cent of government services to be made available electronically by 2002.

The UK government has also introduced what it calls the concept of 'joined-up government' to improve and integrate communications and operational processes across separate government departments and agencies. Several organizational initiatives have been, and are being, put in place to ensure efficient cross-sector communications and a coherent approach to government activities. One such example is the Creative Industries Task Force, which has been established to stimulate and facilitate the development of intellectual capital and access to cultural resources in a networked environment. Members of this influential task force come from several government departments as well as the private sector.

Education, culture, media, communications, industry and so on can no longer be governed as distinctly separate sectors. These traditional governmental structures have major legacy problems that need to be overcome. Departments and agencies need to be redefined and reshaped to meet the new demands of the changing landscape in which they operate. A much higher degree of collaboration and integration is required to achieve a productive governance model and avoid confusion and overlap.

The education sector has been targeted by most governments as the most urgent and critical in terms of its need for a digital makeover.

Throughout the EU and the OECD member states there is much work and attention given to the exploitation of information and communications technology to develop 'open government', modernize administrations and improve governance and management of public services. The EU's fifth Framework programme (1998-2002) allocates large investments to the research and development of the networked economy and includes a programme called 'Creating a User-friendly Information Society', specifically targeted at reinventing and improving public services such as health, culture, environment, transport and so on. The EU is also making funds available to support innovation and growth in European industries. EU member states are all concerned with the US dominance in the information and communications technology and content industries, and are looking for ways of securing cultural diversity and local growth of their own economies and talents.

> Economic growth now depends on the intellectual capacity of a skilled workforce and the efficient management of human capital.

Digital technologies and the rules of the new networked economy have shrunk our planet, blurred traditional borders between nation states and shifted the world's power structure, and, as a result, governments more than ever need to collaborate on the international level to solve common challenges. International organizations such as the OECD, EU, UN or World Bank play a crucial role in facilitating cross-border collaboration and enabling nations to learn from each other and combine forces to achieve results.

The education sector has been targeted by most governments as the most urgent and critical in terms of its need for a digital makeover. Huge amounts of money have been poured into wiring up schools, libraries and universities and into training teachers and learners in information and communication technology in the hope that this will improve educational standards and equip our nations to compete in the next millennium.

Lifelong learning and the rapid transformation of the education sector

Education has moved to the top of the political and commercial agenda. This is a direct consequence of the shift towards a new networked economy, where the key resources are information and knowledge. Economic growth now depends on the intellectual capacity of a skilled workforce and the efficient management of human capital.

Information technology has brought sweeping changes across society, affecting most professions and functions. The need for learning new skills and acquiring new knowledge is predominant. It is no longer sufficient to limit the individual's time spent in education to the years of childhood and youth. Neither is the traditional formal education provided by schools and universities adequate. The need for retraining and continuous access to education has boosted the development of the concept of 'lifelong learning'. Many nations are working hard at developing and implementing comprehensive reforms designed to deliver an educated workforce fit to succeed in the new networked economy. The entire education sector is the subject of scrutiny and reorganization. We see the emergence of new educational structures, new policies and new regulations.

The development of the Global Information Society has a profound impact on the educational market and places new demands on the creation and delivery of educational materials and services. The arrival of digital communications networks in schools, libraries, universities, homes and offices offers a range of opportunities for learning and is fast changing the way in which education takes place.

Education is widely recognized as being a fundamental key to wealth creation and competitiveness in the current global information economy. Consequently, there are enormous pressures on the educational sector to come up with efficient ways of delivering appropriate and effective education across complicated and ever-growing fields of knowledge. Not only is there pressure to change what and how people learn, but there is also considerable economic pressure to establish new funding models that can sustain the delivery of education and lifelong learning to a fast-growing number of individuals. This is bringing about change in the relationship between the public and private sectors and demands a rethink of how operators in the education market may work together to solve common challenges.

Investment in the development of information and communications technology and networks for learning

During 1996 and 1999, many countries embarked on ambitious and comprehensive investment programmes designed to exploit the use of information and communication technology for effective delivery of education. As mentioned earlier, a great deal of money has been spent, and still is being spent, on PC equipment and wiring up schools, colleges, universities and libraries. At the turn of the century, many nations have reached their targets in terms of building up the infrastructure and network connectivity. However, there are deep concerns about getting the expected returns on these investments in technology and they stem from the following three main problems.

The spiralling cost of technology relative to the total education spend

The costs of maintaining and updating fast-changing technology and software are ongoing costs that require a fundamental redirection of education funds. The big question is what should the new distribution of the education spend look like? How much should be allocated to the acquisition of content as opposed to technology and in relation to other traditional expenditure, such as teachers' salaries, training, school buildings, books and materials.

Education authorities and policy makers are battling with the need to balance scarce funds appropriately. Some have been misled by consultants and suppliers of information and communications technology into believing that investment in technology would bring significant cost savings when, in fact, the opposite is true. Investment in the technology and learning networks means we need to spend more on education, not less. We have no choice if we want our nations to be competitive. The investment will bring no cost savings in the education budget – on the contrary, it is an ongoing commitment to a whole set of new cost items that have to be added to the budget.

What should the new distribution of the education spend look like?

However, if efficient exploitation of information and communications technology can be achieved and provided more educational content is made available, studies show there are good opportunities for cost benefits resulting from a more effective delivery of education. Yet so far, most of the investment has been made in technology and communications networks, not in content and in skill development. Given the funding crisis in education and the immense pressure on education authorities to manage the education spend as efficiently as possible, as well as cut costs wherever possible, there are clear uncertainties as to whether or not there will be funds available for the expensive creation and supply of educational software and multimedia, let alone to update software and hardware required for a state-of-the-art infrastructure.

The lack of educational content

There is a content crisis looming over the networked education sector due to an acute lack of quality learning materials in multimedia form suitable for use in a networked environment. Most available software on the market has been developed by software companies with little understanding of how you set about creating effective learning materials. The market is also dominated by the US software industry, and what works in an American context is not necessarily transferable to other educational markets around the world.

> There is a content crisis looming over the networked education sector.

There is a growing resource of 'homemade' educational software created by teachers and members of staff within schools, colleges and universities – often with the help of IT or software companies. This is a very worthwhile activity, but it can never replace the high-quality learning materials traditionally created by educational authors, publishers and broadcasters, nor service the need for educational software that meets national standards.

The lack of quality materials available on the Internet or multimedia CDs, for example, is holding back the uptake and use in the market. Many teachers and learners will give examples of how they purchased CDs that were used once and never again, or how the Internet distracts learners from the learning tasks at hand.

An associated problem is the fact that the supply chain is very fragmented in the education market. The creators and suppliers of educational software and multimedia products come from many places and from different industries and there is no single industry as such. Consequently, there is no single voice communicating with governments or the educational sector on how best to work together to develop the educational software market.

> For learners to learn, teachers need to be educated, and providers of learning materials themselves need to learn how to create and deliver resources in new ways.

The skills shortage

New skills and know-how are required to make use of information and communications technology and networked resources. For learners to learn, teachers need to be educated, and providers of learning materials themselves need to learn how to create and deliver resources in new ways. There is an all-round problem with skills shortages – with regard to technology, content and usage. Unlike the corporate sector, schools and colleges do not have professional IT departments with round-the-clock support and help desks. Neither do they have the training budgets to frequently send librarians, teachers and parents on courses to update their IT skills. Authors, publishers and broadcasters need to move up the learning curve too and acquire new skill-sets to enable the supply of educational software and multimedia products. Users need to adapt to new ways of learning and develop skills to master complicated resources and communication processes. This market will not take off until suppliers and users have the necessary skill-sets and resources to make use of educational software.

Global overview of ICT initiatives in education

The US

President Clinton and Vice President Gore have consistently demonstrated their ongoing commitment to information and communications technology investments and the development of their original GII agenda designed to strengthen US competitiveness and improve public services. After nearly a decade of pioneering the use of multimedia and network applications, the US is enjoying a head start in many areas, providing valuable learning experiences and inspiration for other nations and similar programmes throughout the world.

Education is a major area of investment and Al Gore's ambitious plans are reflected in his announcement in 1998 of four national goals:

- every classroom should be connected to the Internet and other advanced telecommunications services by 2000;
- all children should have access to modern, multimedia computers;
- all teachers should have the training and support that they need to use technology effectively in the classroom;
- high-quality educational software and content should be available to support learning in all subjects.

The US government is investing over $700 million to help states and local communities meet these four national goals (*Masters of the Wired World*, Financial Times Management, 1999).

Another interesting government intervention from the US is the introduction of new regulation to secure affordable network access by means of special discount rates for education – the 'e-rate'. This is an extension of the definition of universal service, including discounted telecommunications services and Internet access for schools, libraries, and rural healthcare centres. These e-rate discounts were authorized by the Telecommunications Act of 1996, and are being implemented by the Federal Communications Commission.

The Clinton and Gore Administration announced its 'Next Generation Internet' (NGI) initiative on 10 October 1996. The NGI is an ongoing research project that is designed to establish the foundations for the networks and networked applications of the twenty-first century in the same way that previous research networks, such as the ARPANET and the NSFNET, led to today's Internet. The US government's investment is mounting to $110 million per year, in addition to significant resources from leading high-tech companies and research universities.

The UK

In 1996, the Department for Education and Employment (DfEE) in the UK launched two major programmes aimed at exploiting information and communications technology in education as part of the government's overall strategy for lifelong learning and developing the UK into a learning society – the National Grid for Learning (NGfL) and the University for Industry (UfI). Another initiative was launched in 1999 called the Individual Learning Accounts (ILAs), which is a brand new concept of funding and encouraging lifelong learning.

The National Grid for Learning is 'a framework for a learning community designed to raise standards and improve Britain's competitiveness, and which embraces schools, colleges, universities, libraries, home and the workplace' ('Connecting Schools, Networking People' BECTA publication, April 1998). The following targets for education have been set (see the official DfEE web site for a full description of each of these targets):

- by 2002, all schools, colleges and libraries and as many community centres as possible should be connected to the Grid;
- by 1999, all newly qualified teachers to become technology-literate and, by 2002, serving teachers to be confident and competent to teach using the equipment within the curriculum;
- by 2002, most school-leavers to be technology-literate, based on prescribed standards;
- by 2002, the UK to become a centre for excellence in the development of network-based software content for education and lifelong learning, and a world leader in the export of learning services;
- from 2002, general administrative communications to schools by UK education departments, OFSTED and non-departmental public bodies, and the collection of data from schools, should largely cease to be paper-based.

For 1998–99 alone, the UK government allocated £100 million for schools to spend on information and communications technology. An additional fund of

£300 million from National Lottery money was announced in 1998 to be spent on information and communications technology training of teachers and librarians, and on the digitization of educational content. A further £450 million has been promised by the government to support the NGfL in 2000–02. The initial focus of the NGfL is the school sector, but there are plans to expand the Grid to embrace home-based learning, higher education and learning in the workplace.

The University for Industry (UfI) is a good example of how a government can ensure such a development gets started and serve as an incubator for a new operation that, in turn, can be run and exploited by the private sector. The government provided the initial funding of £20 million and a conceptual framework for a new organization that could respond to the changing educational needs of industries and enable existing education providers to develop new educational products and services.

After two years of planning and development under the management of the DfEE's transition team, the UfI was incorporated as a private enterprise in 1999 and is charged with the expectation of becoming a key player in the UK education market. The Secretary of State for Education, David Blunkett, stated in March 1998:

Within five years we intend the University for Industry to play a leading role in the learning revolution – and we intend it to be a respected part of national life.

The idea behind the Individual Learning Accounts is that any individual citizen can open a savings account with a bank and accumulate money to be spent only on learning. The account-holder is given access to careers guidance and information about educational opportunities by means of a network of advisers attached to the participating bank. The account-holder will be able to purchase learning materials, courses and other educational services from accredited education providers, such as via the UfI or the NGfL or direct from universities and educational publishers.

The government is spending £150 million on a pilot scheme involving 1 million employees who will each receive £150 in their ILA provided they contribute £25 of their own money too. The scheme is being managed by local training councils and chambers of commerce and depends on a partnership model between industry and the government.

Depending on the outcome of the pilot exercise, the government plans to launch the ILA scheme nationwide by spring 2000. There are also plans to implement smart card technology to enable account-holders to monitor credits and learning progress made.

Major international efforts

Wiring up the education sector and connecting learners to the Internet instantly opens up possibilities for direct communications and links with individuals and organizations far beyond national boundaries. What, for many governments, started out as a national agenda to build a national information infrastructure, soon grew to embrace the Global Information Infrastructure. For the first time in history, learners and schools across the world can connect to the same networks and gain access to unprecedented amounts of educational resources and shared learning experiences.

The World Bank Group has, ever since its inauguration in March 1946, seen education as a key instrument for economic and human development and an important weapon in the battle to overcome poverty around the world – a prime objective of the organization. Part of its mission statement reads: 'To help people help themselves and their environment by providing resources, sharing knowledge, building capacity, and forging partnerships in the public and private sectors.' The World Bank is now the largest provider of development assistance in the world, servicing more than 100 developing countries with over $20 billion in new loans every year. Education is a fast-growing sector and, in 1998, it became the second largest sector for lending, receiving 11 per cent of the total allocation of funds.

As James D. Wolfensohn, President of the World Bank Group, stated in the bank's annual report of 1998:

We share the same world and we share the same challenge. The fight against poverty is the fight for peace, security and growth for us all . . . What we as a development community can do is help countries – by providing finance, yes; but, even more important, by providing knowledge and lessons learnt about the challenges and how to address them. . . .

The World Bank Group has a crucial and influential role to play in enabling a truly multinational membership of the Global Information Society and thereby contributing to the development of democracy and stability worldwide. Its unique ownership, comprising as it does more than 180 member states as shareholders, the five largest being France, Germany, Japan, the UK and US, and its ability to tap the world's capital markets and leverage the contribution of rich member states, are essential reasons for the organization's success in raising money for development at low rates of interest.

In 1997, the World Bank Group launched a major programme called 'The World Links for Development' (WorLD) to link up schools in developing countries with schools in industrialized countries so teachers and students can work together on research and learning via the Internet. By 2000, the target is to link up 1200 schools in 40 developing countries with partner schools in Australia, Canada, Europe, Japan and the US, reaching over 300,000 teachers and students every year. The WorLD programme is a flagship example of what can be achieved by means of partnerships between governments and business communities, and between east and west, north and south.

James D. Wolfensohn, commenting on the vision for the WorLD programme in the 1998 annual report of the World Bank Group, says, inspiringly:

I want . . . a partnership for creating and sharing knowledge and making it a major driver for development. The challenge is to harness technology to link people together and to leverage its impact for development. We are linked by a common humanity, and are united in an historic undertaking to improve the human condition.

The WorLD programme's network of schools is connecting to other networks of schools and educational communities around the world, multiplying its reach and richness of resources. Examples of some of these are the European Schoolnet (EUN), Education Network Australia (EdNA), KONET World in Japan, Canada Schoolnet, Schools Online in the US, Schoolnet SA in South Africa and the International Education and Resource Network (iERN).

There are also many subject- or project-oriented Internet sites building educational communities based on specific topics or programmes. One such example is the Global Learning and Observations to Benefit the Environment (GLOBE) programme, which is a worldwide network of students, teachers and scientists working together to study and understand the environment. Over 5000 schools in more than 70 countries are working with research scientists to learn more about our planet and help in the collection of local scientific data, which is disseminated to scientists via the Internet, who in turn provide feedback and input to science education.

The call for public- and private-sector partnerships

It is not only the political and economic environment that has changed, educational institutions – schools, colleges and universities – are all busy adapting to the impact of information technology. Publishers and broadcasters also have to change the way they create and deliver learning materials. Telecommunications and other communication network providers are developing educational services.

Technology and software providers are busy developing a range of applications and system solutions to support educational activities.

Governments and other funders of education, educational institutions, publishers and broadcasters, channel owners/operators and technology/software companies – what all these market operators have in common is that no one can succeed alone in delivering education in a networked mixed media environment. The need for collaboration between different types of organizations becomes essential.

What is emerging is a series of partnerships and clusters of alliances between different types of organizations combining their resources to facilitate the delivery of education over networks. Schools, universities and libraries, publishers and broadcasters, are partnering with telecommunications and software providers. The number of initiatives in the so-called lifelong learning market is growing at an exponential rate and the demand for educational multimedia content is mounting. Learners are given access to educational multimedia content in a variety of new ways. The expectation is that individuals are going to be connected to digital networks, capable of delivering broadband content. People all over the world will be able to receive educational content via the telephone, TV screen, PC and a range of new electronic delivery devices.

> **No one can succeed alone in delivering education in a networked mixed media environment.**

The production and supply of learning materials has, in the past, been based on single delivery platforms, such as print or television or PC software. The Internet and multimedia resources are changing the way in which learning materials are created and delivered. Educational publishers are increasingly looking for ways to deliver materials across a number of different media and delivery platforms. There is a trend towards multiple platforms, where the same educational content can be packaged and delivered in a variety of ways to meet the needs of different markets.

So far, the major investments in both public and private sectors have been made in infrastructure and technology. Governments across the world have made available considerable funds for the purpose of wiring up nations, including the provision of IT equipment and Internet connections in libraries, schools, colleges and universities. However, far too little attention has been given to what learners and teachers would actually want to do with this technology and the kind of content the digital pipes will be filled with.

As the information infrastructure and on-line connectivity become a reality, the attention shifts from technology to content. The enormous investment in networks and technology is worthless without meaningful content and effective education. Many are beginning to voice their concern about the current mismatch of funds being spent on technology, content and human educational resources.

The escalating growth of information and knowledge has put enormous pressures on the funding of education and research. Libraries, archives and museums are also struggling with a severe inequality between what is expected of them, their given mandates and available funds.

Ironically, the same information technology that has put so much pressure on the educational system is also proposing solutions and ways of meeting the crisis and improving the capacity of the system. Global networks and access to vast know-ledge stores are creating exciting opportunities for delivering educational products and services in new ways. The explosion in distance learning projects and businesses provides many illustrations and good indicators for a more effective provision of education in a networked economy.

The private sector's new-found love of education is driven by the perception of a great market opportunity.

Education is receiving a lot of commercial interest, too, and this is something new. The private sector's new-found love of education is driven by the perception of a great market opportunity. Its involvement brings much-needed investment in the education sector. However, not everybody is comfortable with this. As the former European Commissioner of Education, Edith Cresson, said pointedly in a speech at the Network Economy Conference in Paris (28 February, 1995): 'business people are no angels!'

Lord Puttnam is a businessman and filmmaker who early on recognized what he calls the convergence between education, entertainment and business. He launched the idea of creating an 'Education Hollywood' in Great Britain, capitalizing on the country's main export asset – the English language – and its considerable experience and skill in publishing educational materials. He has attracted support and involvement from a number of organizations in both public and private sectors. Together with the British Council, the BBC, the Open University and others, he is promoting the idea of building a 'World Learning Network'.

Both public and private sectors recognize the value of education and its critical role as a catalyst for a healthy networked economy. Indeed, the quality and success of education will be fundamental to how the Global Information Society develops. As Edith Cresson also said at the conference: 'Well-educated, well-trained, highly motivated and creative people . . . These are the best assets for Europe to live and prosper in the digital world of the next millennium.'

There is much confusion and frustration, though, about what the interface between private and public sectors should be, in particular regarding the future operation of educational systems, libraries and other cultural institutions. What happens to the nature and role of companies when their employees all become lifelong learners? What happens to the nature and role of schools and universities when most learning takes place outside the educational establishment and far beyond the narrow time constraints of K12 and traditional higher education?

In many countries, there is heated debate over roles and responsibilities and the division of labour between the public and private sectors. How far does public responsibility extend? How much should the private sector take charge of? Who will pay for the custody of, and access to, the world's growing knowledge stores? Who will pay for the continued creation of new knowledge?

> **Who will pay for the custody of, and access to, the world's growing knowledge stores? Who will pay for the continued creation of new knowledge?**

One thing is clear, the taxpayer alone will not be able to foot the bill for public services in a knowledge-based economy. The market will only pay for what it favours or is commercially viable. There is a desperate need for new funding models for education, research and culture. Policy makers are busy searching for solutions and looking at what can be achieved by collaborative effort between the public and private sectors. However, the details of what will be shared responsibility models remain hazy and will no doubt be the subject of much debate.

The educational sector will probably alleviate some of the economic pressures by securing more involvement and support from the private sector. Private enterprise is excited about the scores of identifiable consumers in this sector and the promise of new potential buyers of educational products and services. However, there will always be a need for significant public funding and government involvement in education. Also, the library system, as we have defined it, will have great difficulty operating without considerable public and non-profit funding, although many library services can be successfully privatized, as they have been in several countries, most notably in the United States and in Britain. However, today's market forces do not consider the needs of future generations. What our great-grandchildren may need simply does not feature in our current commercial equations.

The role of the libraries as the appointed custodians of our cultural heritage is widely accepted, but not often enough applauded. Libraries across the world should be recognized for what they do and the kinds of challenges they face in their struggles to cope with exponential information growth. This sector needs much more involvement from governments, the private sector and individuals who can help solve the crisis of the world's growing information mountains.

Paper alone can no longer carry the volumes of published knowledge. The world now depends on information technology to provide the means to handle the growing literature, cultural heritage and scientific and scholarly information, and to achieve effective methods for storage, distribution and retrieval. Essentially, this means substantial investment in digital technology and a complete overhaul of libraries' operations.

Libraries have come a long way since the first was founded in 1250 BC by King Ramses II of Egypt with a stock of 20,000 papyrus scrolls. The more famous library of Alexandria was founded during the early part of the third century BC with a collection of 200,000 scrolls of papyrus and linen. Today, the largest library in the world is the national Library of Congress in the US. By the end of 1994, it had a collection of over 28 million books in 470 languages and a digital store of 35 information databases with access to over 26 million records. The Library's databases have around 20 million users located in 100 countries around the world. In Europe, the largest national library is the British Library with over 18 million books.

Libraries' policies vary from country to country. For instance, electronic storage and distribution of works subject to copyright are permitted in the United States, subject to certain restrictions and conditional requirements, but in most European countries it would be illegal for libraries to do this. Many libraries have not yet been given the digital mandates they need in order to maintain their traditional roles and continue to provide an adequate level of service to their users.

Today's market forces do not consider the needs of future generations. What our great-grandchildren may need simply does not feature in our current commercial equations.

The problem of incompatible national policies and systems for libraries causes problems and friction on an international level. The digital networks of the

Global Information Society operate across national borders. It does not matter which country you are in, you can always log on to the information databases of, for instance, the Library of Congress or the British Library and download the information you need. So, which national jurisdiction applies? A library cannot control through which jurisdictions the information is transmitted or which network connections are used for each of the millions of electronic requests it receives. Libraries' policies and systems need to be harmonized across the world and standard solutions need to be resolved on a multinational level.

> **Power will not be in the hands of the nation state, but in the digital hands of those who master the networked economy of the Wired World.**

This is a contentious political issue as it stirs up national feelings about the right to determine a nation's cultural policy irrespective of what other nations do. National control over internal affairs is a well-established principle and not many politicians would dare to rock that boat. However, times are changing and the new networked economy disregards national borders. Membership of the Global Information Society is what matters and control over national affairs and the nature of citizenship is changing. Power will not be in the hands of the nation state, but in the digital hands of those who master the networked economy of the Wired World.

10

People

The individual citizen and the Wired World

There are several visions and very different expectations of what the Wired World is all about. On the one hand, people eagerly promote the positive benefits of the GII and a connected society: more efficiency, commerce, access to education, knowledge and culture, 'open joined up' government. Leaders from government and industry across the world have given individual citizens enormous promises of prosperity, democracy and a better world that will somehow be magically achieved by an Internet connection, which supposedly provides unlimited access to knowledge and all the joys of global togetherness. On the other hand, we have other leading thinkers ringing alarm bells and voicing deep concerns about the negative impacts of technological progress and the direction the new networked economy is taking. The fact that we live in a divided and unequal world with much suffering is not likely to be changed or fixed by the Internet. Those of us who are privileged to work and play in the affluent part of the world can easily lose sight of the real state of the world as a whole. It is a world of warring regions and groups of people, widespread poverty, rising levels of illiteracy, crime, violence and corruption in which two thirds of the population is starving and the rest is dieting. The Wired World sceptics have a frightening vision of an even more divided world where the gap between the haves and have nots will be deepened even further as a result of the impacts of technology and the GII. However, whatever your attitude is – whether your vision is positive or negative – all of us are, beyond doubt, witnessing a time of momentous change in the history of humanity. For individual citizens across the globe, the Wired World brings complicated challenges and new opportunities. There are valuable benefits to be enjoyed, but also less desirable consequences to deal with.

The private sector continues to be the main driver behind the new networked economy and it is commercial enterprise that is pushing to bring you the magical connections to the Wired World. Why? Because they want to sell you 'stuff'. One of the most influential businessmen of our time, Bill Gates, sums it all up in his book *The Road Ahead* (Penguin, 1995):

If you are watching the movie *Top Gun* and think Tom Cruise's aviator sunglasses look really cool, you'll be able to pause the movie and learn about the glasses or even buy them on the spot – if the film has been tagged with commercial information . . . if the movie star carries a handsome leather briefcase or handbag, the highway will let you browse the manufacturer's entire line of leather goods and either order one or be directed to a retailer.

Twenty-four-hour screen shopping in the global supermarket, narcissistic obsessions with materially rich lifestyles, the polished superlooks of mass-produced superstars and virtual imagery may go down well in the United States, but the idea that to be able to shop instantly on a scale never known before or to look like a movie star are the ultimate fruits of technological advance, is a shallow one. A quote from Leacock Stephen Butler (*The Public Speaker's Treasure, Collins Dictionary of Quotations*, Collins, 1995) comes to mind: 'Advertising may be described as the science of arresting human intelligence long enough to get some money from it.'

There is much more to the Global Information Society than a 'global supershop'. Connectivity to an ever-growing range of different activities and functions has the potential to change and enrich our lives is so many ways. It's up to each and every individual person, organization and government to decide how best to make use of the powerful tools of a connected Wired World.

It is true that there will always be cultural differences; what is perfectly acceptable and desirable in one culture will be rejected and frowned upon in another. Take the example of advertising in Europe, which is very different to advertising in the United States. In fact, what works and what is acceptable varies greatly from country to country. Like people in the past, people in tomorrow's world will continue to have different objectives and agendas, different tastes and preferences to those in today's world. Globalization does not mean the eradication of languages and cultures, nor does it mean the end of local differences and ideological and political conflicts.

We must not limit the wonders of the Global Information Society to a gigantic shopping venture. The existential notion of 'I shop therefore I am' represents a kind of consumerist madness, which can have a corrupting and devastating effect on the values of education, art, music, culture and so on.

'I connect therefore I am' is another definition of life that is apparent in today's Wired World, where tools of technology seem more important than what can be achieved with original thought. We need to balance our investment in the Global Information Society so that the individual citizen can enjoy the richness of human life today as well as in the future. We will be wise to recall the judgement of King Thamus described in the third chapter of this book. He warned his chief inventor about being blinded by enthusiasm for a new invention and so unable to see the implications of what it could do to people and society. He pointed out the dangers of what might happen when people 'receive a quantity of information without proper instruction' and when 'they are filled with the conceit of wisdom, rather than real wisdom: people will appear to be knowledgeable, but be mostly ignorant and consequently a burden to society'.

We must look beyond connectivity to a life of creativity. It is the intellectual capacity and creativity of the individual that will enable us to put the Global Information Infrastructure to good use. People are needed to build that Global Information Society – they are the core asset in the new networked economy; technology is not. Simply being connected to the grid of a Wired World is of little value; knowing what to do with it is the challenge.

Alvin and Heidi Toffler are two of the world's most outstanding observers of societal change. Their work has had, and continues to have, a significant influence on world leaders in business and politics as well as individuals from all walks of life. Together they've written what can be referred to as the ultimate trilogy on the subject of change – *Future Shock* (on the source and impact of change, Macmillan, 1991), *The Third Wave* (on the process and direction of change, Collins, 1981) and *Powershift* (on the control and management of change, Bantam, 1990). The Tofflers have described in great detail

In the new networked economy, no single manager or individual will be in charge.

the massive processes of change taking place in our times at all levels of society. They stress that each and every one of us has responsibility for change and for shaping the new civilization for ourselves as well as for future generations: 'The responsibility for change lies with us. We must begin with ourselves, teaching ourselves not to close our minds prematurely to the novel, the surprising, the seemingly radical' (*Creating a New Civilization*, Turner Publishing Inc, 1994). The Tofflers also explain how some generations are born to create and others to maintain a civilization, and make it so clear to us why our generation has 'a destiny to create'.

Whatever happened to the original existential notion of the French philosopher René Descartes that read 'I think therefore I am'? Many of us live a life that leaves so little room for reflection and thought. Being part of the Wired World also means that we are bombarded with information and media services around the clock. We are feeling the impact of dynamic changes on all levels in society, as we are forced to respond and react rather than think and understand. We surf the headlines, rather than study the details, we pretend we read our fast-filling in-trays and all the e-mail, yet we never have the time to do so properly. We would probably like to read more details and communicate more widely, but do not have the time. It is that horrible contemporary disease again of having to do everything in a hurry and being overloaded with information, and it is spreading like a plague. It seems that the managerial as well as the personal challenge is to rise above the coping strategy and stop pretending that we understand it all and that we have the control other people expect us to have.

In the new networked economy, no single manager or individual will be in charge. Business processes can no longer be broken down into separate parts, isolated tasks and operations as they have been in the past. What's needed is a much more holistic approach – an understanding of a highly complicated, integrated and connected business reality. The notions of management, control and leadership will have to change fundamentally for organizations and individuals to prosper. Companies that resist such change and, instead, cling on to their old organizational structures and management styles will not be able to compete in the long run. This loss of control and ability to know all you need to know about your particular reality, your organisation or subject area is frightening. It terrifies corporations as well as individuals. What is needed is reorganization and education. People will need to learn new ways of managing operations and doing their work. 'Lifelong learning' is not just a soundbite or something of relevance only to your children or your employees. 'Lifelong learning' implies a new lifestyle and approach to life that holds the key to survival for everybody. 'Flat organizations' and the move from bureaucracy to 'ad hocracy', are not just fads either, they imply an entirely new way of working and require a deep understanding of change at managerial level and a new or re-educated breed of managers.

> **'Lifelong learning' implies a new lifestyle and approach to life that holds the key to survival for everybody.**

There is something wonderfully liberating and democratic about the Wired World – the way in which the networks of the GII are empowering individuals and stripping institutional authorities of the ability to abuse their traditional power. The Internet has blossomed as a people's medium and, in many instances, has demonstrated its ability to deliver 'power to the people'. However, as a medium for commerce and governance, the Internet is still in its infancy. The Internet has its roots as a communications medium for people around the globe and ought, therefore, to be able to provide a good bedrock for our newly Wired World. What the shape of this bedrock will be and how the many new opportunities will be exploited is, for most of us, unclear. Time will tell, and you and I can make the difference.

The opportunities and impact of teleworking

At the turn of the century, 'teleworking' is fast becoming a major new type of work organization, actively promoted by governments and industry. Although up until 1999 only a relatively small percentage of those who make up the total workforce have become 'teleworkers', 0.5–9.7 per cent depending on which country you're looking at – the number of teleworkers is expected to grow substantially over the next decade with the impact of GII penetration, explosion of commerce and, most importantly, critical barriers and conditions for effective teleworking being resolved.

The European Commission's 'Status Report on European Telework' in 1998 showed enormous discrepancies between countries and regions, as well as industry sectors and types of organizations involved in teleworking (see Table 10.1).

Not surprisingly, there is significant correlation between, on the one hand, the degree of GII connectivity and access to advanced technology and services, and, on the other, the growth and success of teleworking. Countries or areas of high multimedia technology penetration and connectivity – such as Scandinavia, the Netherlands, UK and France – have also been able to experiment and make substantial progress with telework, and therefore have a much higher number of teleworkers than other countries which are lagging behind in GII development and exploitation. However, technology and connectivity is only a small part of what is needed to facilitate teleworking. It is an entirely new form of work organization.

There are many definitions of 'teleworking' which makes it difficult to gather quantitative data. At one end of the scale, 'teleworking' is used as a loose, all-embracing term to cover any kind of work that is enabled by information and

Country	Corporate telecommuters ('000)[a]	All teleworkers ('000)[b]	ETD estimates[c]			
			Teleworkers		Percentages of workforce	
			Formal ('000)	Total ('000)	Formal	Total
Austria	8	29	5	50	0.2	1.5
Belgium	46	30	5	200	0.1	5.3
Denmark	43	18	100	250	3.9	9.7
Finland	36	26	15	150	0.6	6.3
France	148	417	30	240	0.1	1.1
Germany	139	294	400	600	1.1	1.9
Greece	n/a	31	2	20	0.1	0.5
Italy	51	188	40	250	0.2	1.2
Ireland	n/a	51	10	50	1.2	6.1
Luxembourg	n/a	2	n/a	n/a	n/a	n/a
Netherlands	157	52	200	600	3.0	9.1
Portugal	n/a	48	3	60	0.1	1.3
Spain	9	192	5	80	0.0	0.6
Sweden	80	33	30	180	0.9	5.4
UK	307	1,199	280	1,800	1.1	7.0
Total	1024	2,610	1,125	4,530	0.9	4.07

Table 10.1: the estimated number of teleworkers in Europe, late 1997
a IDC, based on remote access
b Jala International
c The figures for the countries, synthesized from a range of sources to provide a common basis, do not necessarily match data from particular sources provided in individual country summaries.
Source: European Commission, 'Status Report on European Telework', DGXIII, 1998

communications technology and takes place at a geographical distance from where work results are needed. At the other end of the scale, it refers only to workers using computers, telephony and communication networks to work from home rather than at established business premises. For the purpose of this book, the broader definition will be used, which includes the following work scenarios.

- **Home-based**
  Employees or individuals working primarily from home instead of at other business premises belonging to employers, customers, suppliers or business partners

- **Mobile**
  Employees or individuals using information and communications technology to enable them to do mobile work and spend time with customers to deliver a range of services and capabilities that previously would have involved office-based staff or visits to a company's offices.

- **Local support centres**

    People who do not want, or are unable, to work from home, but would like to avoid the cost, time and effort of travelling to work, can telework at local support centres that provide office facilities, information and communications technology and services. Such local support centres are sometimes referred to as 'telecentres' or 'telecottages' and may also be able to provide teleworkers with access to education and skills development, as well as social networking with other teleworkers.

The exploitation of the GII and information and communications technology profoundly changes the way work is carried out throughout the value and supply chains. Work functions that previously were done manually by people are now automated and done by computers. The need for workers to be physically present at the same work premises or close to customers has often disappeared as jobs can be carried out at a distance effectively, in whatever part of the world makes the most sense. The deep digitization of work processes causes widespread dislocation of traditional work operations and results in the need to relocate many work functions, processes and tasks. Entirely new work flow systems are being designed and implemented, and individuals have to rapidly adapt to them if they are to be employable.

Teleworking is also increasing the competition for labour and affects many kinds of sourcing and outsourcing of workers and services performed by them. Physical location and available space no longer matter the way they did. Work can be done from thousands of miles away, sourced and outsourced across national borders. Teleworkers can work in virtual and geographically dispersed teams around the world.

The European Commission has identified the following key benefits of teleworking in the information society.

- **Information society technologies (IST)**

    The critical use of electronic network technologies in enabling, or promoting, these core characteristics, thereby profoundly affecting all types of work, whether or not traditionally considered as teleworking. Teleworking thus has spill-over effects on all work.

- **Place and time constraints lifted**

    Constraints on the physical location of the parties involved in work (employees, employers, colleagues, partners, customers, suppliers and so on) are partially or totally relaxed and can be determined instead by what is best or most convenient for all concerned.

The timing of work can be adjusted to take account of the needs of all the parties involved in the work. For example, it is possible to fit in family needs or work co-operatively across national boundaries or time zones, thereby fully exploiting the 24-hour day.

- **Employment market extended**
  Both employers' labour markets and individuals' job markets are widened in terms of geographical extent as well as in professional range and quality.

- **Organizational transformation**
  Work takes place in disaggregated, often dispersed, smaller organizational units displaying delayered, flatter hierarchical structures and exhibiting a large amount of delegation and horizontal communication (both within and outside the organization).

  Organizational boundaries and permanence tend to break down, with more work being performed in virtual organizations and teams set up for the duration of the task.

- **Management and work relationships**
  Management becomes focused more on strategic development, creating appropriate work cultures, facilitating teams and measuring work by output or results than on control, detailed decision making or measurement of time expended.

  Work relationships become much more complicated, multifarious and equal, with specific parties often playing more than one role (such as customer, manager, supplier, partner, colleague, work executor).

  Greater trust becomes key to most, if not all, work relations, and all parties involved in the work develop flexible attitudes.

- **Work processes and tasks**
  Decisions about, and responsibilities for, work are delegated to the executors of the work.

  Work becomes fully networked, covering physical interaction as well as interaction and communication over the telecommunications network.

  Work becomes more project-like, with specific goals, budgets, processes, organization and time horizons.

  Work becomes more dynamic and flexible in response to rapidly changing market situations.

- **The individual**
  The individual takes more responsibility for their own development of skills, competence and career paths.

The individual develops the skills of working independently but also co-operatively in both physical and networked contexts. These encompass professional expertise as well as all-round competences such as use of ISTs, common sense, organizational talents, work management, planning, human relationship and teamworking skills.

The individual's ability to integrate work with personal and family life is enhanced.

Teleworking is promoted by many of our political leaders as a key to competitiveness, as it will boost employment opportunities and make businesses more efficient. We're told teleworking could potentially also have positive environmental effects as traffic congestion would ease as people no longer had to travel to work every day. Teleworking is also described as an opportunity to improve the quality of life of individuals and families. Also, teleworking opens up opportunities for participation in the global economy to previously excluded social groups or disadvantaged poorer nations.

Alvin Toffler has described how teleworking and advances in information and communications technology services may bring back to the home many core functions that were taken away from it as a consequence of the Industrial Revolution. Education, healthcare, work, culture were all centred on the home in the pre-industrial era. However, with the Industrial Revolution came factories and office buildings – people had to leave their homes to go to work. Education became increasingly institutionalized and children were sent away to school. Hospitals took care of the ill, and cultural establishments aggregated cultural assets and took care of entertainment and leisure. Now we see people taking a greater responsibility for their own lives and power is shifting back to the individual and the home, away from large institutions. There is a 'demassification' process going on, to use the Tofflers' terminology. During the industrial era – which the Tofflers refer to as the 'Second Wave' – people lived and worked in a 'mass society' that reflected and required 'mass production'. Civilization became increasingly 'massified' and homogeneous – mass manufacturing, mass media, mass education, mass religion and so on. In the new networked economy, we feel the impact of the Tofflers' 'Third Wave' era. The comeback of individualistic lifestyles and the return of the individual at the centre. It could also mean the return of the extended family. With the collapse of the nuclear family of the industrial era, we see the emergence of new and complicated

Individuals as well as companies and governments need to understand and respond appropriately to a rapid fragmentation of a familiar reality, learning to deal with an entirely different and unfamiliar heterogeneous, far more complicated and integrated world.

family structures embracing all kinds of family types from single-parent families to live-alones to once, twice, multiple times married and divorced couples to homosexual and lesbian partnerships.

Organizations will need to completely change their approach to the management of human resources as well as the way in which markets are understood and operations are carried out. Individuals as well as companies and governments need to understand and respond appropriately to a rapid fragmentation of a familiar reality, learning to deal with an entirely different and unfamiliar heterogeneous, far more complicated and integrated world.

There are currently plenty of barriers to the uptake and implementation of teleworking that need to be overcome if we are to be able to reap its much heralded benefits, namely:

- attitudes to teleworking, organizational culture and structure;
- employment and contract law, internationally harmonized regulatory frameworks;
- development of organizational policies, procedures and practices;
- social isolation of teleworkers;
- skills problems and knowledge shortage, the need for training;
- information and communications technology capability and access;
- cost of rapidly changing technology and software.

Teleworking has significant societal, economic and strategic business implications that need to be much better understood in order to secure competitiveness and prosperity in the new networked economy. Grasping the full potential and meaning of teleworking is an essential key to success.

Net addiction and other cyberspace side-effects

What happens in a Wired World society where screens and computers dominate the way we work, learn, play and live? What happens when technology has soaked into the very fabric of our surroundings and penetrated all aspects of our lives? Will we have a good life and will it be a better world? Will we instead all graduate from being couch potatoes to become mouse potatoes or some other kind of interface potato beyond the familiar remote control and mouse?

There are serious side-effects and justified concerns about the negative impacts of technology and media. People are spending more and more time in front of screens, be they televisions, Game Boys, or computer monitors. We have a limited number of hours in the day, yet we spend more and more of them in front of those screens as media and communication consumers or teleworkers. We are living in a screen society dominated by a digital, virtual world that keeps stealing our analogue time and remote world out there, constantly distracting us from what's near and dear and that which brings meaning to our personal lives.

Many social commentators and writers have begun to warn us about the effects on social discourse from technology and screen overdosing, and other damage it can do. Clifford Stoll is an 'astronomer, computer jock and weekend plumber' who lives in California and, by his own admission, has been an Internet user for the past 15 years. He has little time for what he calls the 'technocratic belief that computers and networks will make a better society' (*Silicon Snake Oil: Second thoughts on the Information Highway*, Doubleday, 1995). He dismisses the notion that somehow 'access to information, better communications, and electronic programs can cure social problems'. He reminds us that 'the most important interactions in life happen between people and not computers'.

The fact is that on-line communications and interactions do not measure up to good old-fashioned face-to-face human contact and relationships. In cyberspace, you don't have to respond to people in the same way.

Cyberspace enthusiasts and e-community promoters will argue that virtual communities are full of real people and real social interactions. However, the fact is that on-line communications and interactions do not measure up to good old-fashioned face-to-face human contact and relationships. In cyberspace, you don't have to respond to people in the same way. You don't have to live up to expectations or meet legitimate demands or stick with any kind of communication if you don't like it. You can hide, pretend, evade and escape for ever and nobody will know, and you won't grow much either. Cyberspace is not a substitute for your personal space – your nearspace – which is far more precious and educational. Cyberspace is just a poor complement, a tool to help you augment your nearspace. As Clifford Stoll says in *Silicon Snake Oil*:

Computer networks isolate us from one another, rather than bring us together. We only need to deal with one side of an individual over the Net. And if we don't like what we see, we just pull the plug . . . By logging on to the networks we lose the ability to enter into spontaneous interactions with real people. Evening time is now spent watching a television or a computer terminal – safe havens in which to hide. Sitting around a porch and talking is becoming extinct, as is reading aloud to children.

There are psychological and sociological surveys emerging describing serious defects among children and adults exposed to too much screen and cyberspace activity. This comes as no surprise to those who are familiar with the literature on the social impacts of television, video and computer games. There is even a range of new psychological disorders being classified by established authorities. In a recent case of parental negligence and child abuse in the UK, the courts attributed the cause of the crime to one such disorder – 'Internet Addiction Syndrome'. A single mother of three young children was found to spend up to 18 hours a day on-line while her children were left alone locked up in the bedroom with no toys and hardly any food. Marriages are reported to break up because husbands spend all their time on the Net. Children demonstrating expert cyberspace skills and who have no problems finding their way around the Internet have been found, in some cases, to be totally incapable of having human conversation and forming real relationships.

An increasing number of people seem to be unable to distinguish between cyberspace and the media world, and their personal lives and circumstances. This breakdown of the border between illusion and reality causes psychiatric problems and identity crises. The attachment and glorification of media personalities and soap characters, and the dependence on fabricated pop stars and sports idols, are just some indicators of this phenomenon. It is not the fault of technology and the Internet, but of society as a whole. However, the technology and the media have the power to amplify problems to a point where it takes clever management to counter-attack and correct such negative outcomes. Children need to be taught how to use the media and the Internet and how to integrate it into real life. We must strike a balance between life spent in front of screens and being wired to cyberspace, and life spent with real people, in the unwired surroundings of nature and nearspace.

Children need to be taught how to use the media and the Internet and how to integrate it into real life.

The digital divide

As much as we may want to, we will not be able to sustain a belief that we live in a Global Information Society with access for every citizen in the world. As we move closer to a new century, there are still more telephones in Manhattan or London than in the whole of Africa. Nearly 70 per cent of the world's Internet hosts are in the English-speaking world. As Stoll puts it 'The dream of a harmonious world with equal opportunities for all seems further away than ever before, with the communication revolution transforming many countries into knowledge-based societies, the less-developed countries will be left out of the process, light years behind the rest of the world.'

The US has the lead and still dominates the construction and economic stakes of the GII. However, even in the US, there is evidence of the gap widening between the haves and have nots. A survey carried out by the US government in 1997 (*Falling Through the Net II: New data on the digital divide*, US National Telecommunication Administration, US Central Bureau of Consensus and US Department of Commerce) concluded that, although the uptake of technology and on-line communications have increased dramatically, the so-called 'digital divide' – the gap between those who have access to telephones, computers and on-line communications and those who do not – is widening compared to 1994 when a similar survey was carried out (see Table 10.2).

The so-called 'digital divide' – the gap between those who have access to telephones, computers and on-line communications and those who do not – is widening compared to 1994.

The findings clearly demonstrate the correlation between high income, education and race, and access to technology and communications. The penetration of technology and connectivity was growing rapidly in the high-income groups – predominantly well-educated, white households

Year	Computer	Modem	Phone	e-mail
1994	24.1	11	93.8	3.4
1997	36.6	26.3	93.8	16.9

Table 10.2: percentages of US households with a computer, modem, telephone and e-mail – 1994 and 1997

– with little or no change in the lower-income brackets and racial groups, particularly disadvantaged blacks and Hispanics (see Table 10.3).

Race/origin	Under $15,000	$15,000–$34,999	$35,000–$74,999	$75,000+
White, not Hispanic	15.4	28.0	55.1	76.3
Black, not Hispanic	6.3	18.2	40.2	64.1
Other, not Hispanic	19.1	38.5	62.6	81.0
Hispanic	7.8	16.6	36.8	72.8

Table 10.3: percentages of US households with a computer, by income and race/origin, 1997

There are, it is estimated, 880 million adults in developing countries and 200 million in the industrial world who can neither read nor write effectively. The challenge for all nations must be to tackle this growing problem and work towards a more inclusive society. Technology and the GII could enable us in that process instead of amplifying and worsening the gap between rich and poor.

Arne Fjoertoft, the Secretary General of the Worldview International Foundation, has dedicated a lifetime of work towards closing such gaps and building bridges between the East and the West, the North and the South. He has a background in television and media and is acutely aware of the power and positive potential of the GII to help build a better world. However, he warns us that, at this moment in time, we are not heading in the right direction and need to change both policies and investment strategies, as well as attitudes, to reverse the process (in 'Challenging the digital divide', in my book *Masters of the Wired World*, Financial Times Management, 1999):

The gap has traditionally been between one of basic need issues, but the communication revolution is dramatically increasing the gap as it represents the very foundation of development – access to information and knowledge, the raw material for sustainable growth.

The Global Information Society versus information city states

We need to consider the long-term consequences of developing the Global Information Society. The assessment of the new economic opportunities must be balanced by an understanding of the social and political implications of the decisions we make. We live in a world of division – between the privileged few and the underprivileged many, between North and South, between the affluent and the starving. If we are not careful, the Global Information Society will be reserved for those who can afford the membership fee. To ensure that access to the benefits of the Wired World is open to all, we depend on intervention and commitment from our political leaders to develop and implement a public policy for the Global Information Society. Otherwise, we could be heading towards a world of even greater division, where the gap between the knowledge-rich and the knowledge-poor will continue to widen. Riccardo Petrella, head of science forecasting at the European Commission, has drawn up what is a quite frightening future scenario, all based on hard data. Ten years from now, he argues, we will live in a world governed by a network of global information city states. The borders between these information hubs will have more significance than national borders. The individuals who will have access to these information networks will, at best, constitute an eighth of the world's population – hardly a development that will foster democracy. His message stands in sharp contrast to the message we hear from many of the Wired World missionaries who would like us to believe that everyone will have access and that the stairway to heaven is to acquire an ever-growing range of information products.

The question we need to ask is what kind of society do we want? Are our aspirations all democratic and truly global or simply commercial and, at best, multinational? We have the opportunity to use the Global Information Society and the potent power of the networked economy to help us deal with the biggest problems facing our world – the imbalance of wealth, unemployment, poverty, scarcity of resources, pollution, crime and wars. There are many wonderful examples of how the GII can be used to deliver better education and resources to more people. And there are encouraging examples of previously underprivileged people being empowered by means of information and communications technology and access to knowledge. Developing countries can leapfrog to a knowledge-based economy, provided the wealthy nations will give them half the opportunity to do so. The overriding question all nations – rich or poor – need to answer is this: are we aspiring towards creating a better world or are we satisfied with continued economic growth for ourselves in the short term?

> **The question we need to ask is what kind of society do we want? Are our aspirations all democratic and truly global or simply commercial and, at best, multinational?**

> **Developing countries can leapfrog to a knowledge-based economy, provided the wealthy nations will give them half the opportunity to do so.**

The choice is ours. Whatever course and decisions we choose to take, future generations will live with the consequences. Let's hope wisdom will prevail and that our legacy will be a good one, for never before has humankind had such a great opportunity to further democracy and build a truly global village.

Appendix 1

Chapter 1 of the Bangemann Report

Europe and the global information society
Recommendations to the European Council

In its Brussels meeting of December 1993, the European Council requested that a report be prepared for its meeting on 24–25 June 1994 in Corfu by a group of prominent persons on the specific measures to be taken into consideration by the Community and the Member States for the infrastructures in the sphere of information.

On the basis of this report, the Council will adopt an operational programme defining precise procedures for action and the necessary means.

Brussels, 26 May 1994

The information society – new ways of living and working together

A revolutionary challenge to decision makers

Throughout the world, information and communications technologies are generating a new industrial revolution already as significant and far-reaching as those of the past.

It is a revolution based on information, itself the expression of human knowledge. Technological progress now enables us to process, store, retrieve and communicate information in whatever form it may take – oral, written or visual – unconstrained by distance, time and volume.

This revolution adds huge new capacities to human intelligence and constitutes a resource which changes the way we work together and the way we live together.

This revolution adds huge new capacities to human intelligence and . . . changes the way we work together and the way we live together.

Europe is already participating in this revolution, but with an approach which is still too fragmentary and which could reduce expected benefits. An information society is a means to achieve so many of the European Union's objectives. We have to get it right, and get it right now.

Partnership for jobs

Europe's ability to participate in, to adapt and to exploit the new technologies and the opportunities they create will require partnership between individuals, employers, unions and governments dedicated to managing change. If we manage the changes before us with determination and understanding of the social implications, we shall all gain in the long run.

Our work has been sustained by the conviction expressed in the Commission's White Paper, 'Growth, Competitiveness and Employment', that ' . . . *the enormous potential for new services relating to production, consumption, culture and leisure activities will create large numbers of new jobs* . . . ' Yet nothing will happen automatically. We have to act to ensure that these jobs are created here, and soon. And that means public and private sectors acting together.

If we seize the opportunity

All revolutions generate uncertainty, discontinuity – and opportunity. Today's is no exception. How we respond, how we turn current opportunities into real benefits, will depend on how quickly we can enter the European information society.

In the face of quite remarkable technological developments and economic opportunities, all the leading global industrial players are reassessing their strategies and their options.

A common creation or a still fragmented Europe?

The first countries to enter the information society will reap the greatest rewards. They will set the agenda for all who must follow. By contrast, countries which temporize, or favour half-hearted solutions, could, in less than a decade, face disastrous declines in investment and a squeeze on jobs.

Given its history, we can be sure that Europe will take the opportunity. It will create the information society. The only question is whether this will be a strategic creation for the whole Union, or a more fragmented and much less effective amalgam of individual initiatives by Member States, with repercussions on every policy area, from the single market to cohesion.

The only question is whether this will be a strategic creation for the whole Union, or a more fragmented and much less effective amalgam of individual initiatives by Member States.

What we can expect for . . .

- *Europe's citizens and consumers:*
  a more caring European society with a significantly higher quality of life and a wider choice of services and entertainment;
- *the content creators:*
  new ways to exercise their creativity as the information society calls into being new products and services;
- *Europe's regions:*
  new opportunities to express their cultural traditions and identities and, for those standing on the geographical periphery of the Union, a minimizing of distance and remoteness;
- *governments and administrations:*
  more efficient, transparent and responsive public services, closer to the citizen and at lower cost;
- *European business and small- and medium-sized enterprises:*
  more effective management and organization, access to training and other services, data links with customers and suppliers, generating greater competitiveness;
- *Europe's telecommunications operators:*
  the capacity to supply an ever wider range of new high value-added services;
- *the equipment and software suppliers; the computer and consumer electronics industries:*
  new and strongly-growing markets for their products at home and abroad.

The social challenge

The widespread availability of new information tools and services will present fresh opportunities to build a more equal and balanced society and to foster individual accomplishment. The information society has the potential to improve the quality of life of Europe's citizens, the efficiency of our social and economic organization, and to reinforce cohesion.

The information society has the potential to improve the quality of life of Europe's citizens, the efficiency of our social and economic organization, and to reinforce cohesion.

The information revolution prompts profound changes in the way we view our societies and also in their organization and structure. This presents us with a major challenge: either we grasp the opportunities before us and master the risks, or we bow to them, together with all the uncertainties this may entail.

The main risk lies in the creation of a two-tier society of haves and have nots, in which only a part of the population has access to the new technology, is comfortable using it and can fully enjoy its benefits. There is a danger that individuals will reject the new information culture and its instruments.

Such a risk is inherent in the process of structural change. We must confront it by convincing people that the new technologies hold out the prospect of a major step forward towards a European society less subject to such constraints as rigidity, inertia and compartmentalization. By pooling resources that have traditionally been separate, and indeed distant, the information infrastructure unleashes unlimited potential for acquiring knowledge, innovation and creativity.

Mastering risks, maximizing benefits

Thus, we have to find ways to master the risks and maximize the benefits. This places responsibilities on public authorities to establish safeguards and to ensure the cohesion of the new society. Fair access to the infrastructure will have to be guaranteed to all, as will provision of universal service, the definition of which must evolve in line with the technology.

A great deal of effort must be put into securing widespread public acceptance and actual use of the new technology. Preparing Europeans for the advent of the information society is a priority task. Education, training and promotion will necessarily play a central role. The White Paper's goal of giving European citizens the right to lifelong education and training here finds its full justification. In order best to raise awareness, regional and local initiatives – whether public or private – should be encouraged.

Preparing Europeans for the advent of the information society is a priority task. Education, training and promotion will necessarily play a central role.

The arrival of the information society comes in tandem with changes in labour legislation and the rise of new professions and skills. Continuous dialogue between the social partners will be extremely important if we are to anticipate and to manage the imminent transformation of the workplace. This concerted effort should reflect new relationships at the workplace induced by the changing environment.

More detailed consideration of these issues exceeds the scope of this report. The group wishes to stress that Europe is bound to change, and that it is in our interest to seize this opportunity. The information infrastructure can prove an extraordinary instrument for serving the people of Europe and improving our society by fully reflecting the original and often unique values which underpin and give meaning to our lives.

At the end of the day, the added value brought by the new tools, and the overall success of the information society, will depend on the input made by our people, both individually and in working together. We are convinced that Europeans will meet this challenge.

Time to press on

Why the urgency? Because competitive suppliers of networks and services from outside Europe are increasingly active in our markets. They are convinced, as we must be, that if Europe arrives late our suppliers of technologies and services will lack the commercial muscle to win a share of the enormous global opportunities which lie ahead. Our companies will migrate to more attractive locations to do business. Our export markets will evaporate. We have to prove them wrong.

Tide waits for no man, and this is a revolutionary tide, sweeping through economic and social life. We must press on. At least we do not have the usual European worry about catching up. In some areas we are well placed, in others we do need to do more – but this is also true for the rest of the world's trading nations.

The importance of the sector was evident by its prominence during the Uruguay round of GATT negotiations. This importance is destined to increase.

We should not be sceptical of our possibilities for success. We have major technological, entrepreneurial and creative capabilities. However, the diffusion of information is still too restricted and too expensive. This can be tackled quickly through regulatory reforms.

Public awareness of the technologies has hitherto been too limited. This must change. Political attention is too intermittent. The private sector expects a new signal.

Political attention is too intermittent. The private sector expects a new signal.

An action plan

This report outlines our vision of the information society and the benefits it will deliver to our citizens and to economic operators. It points to areas in which action is needed now so we can start out on the market-led passage to the new age, as well as to the agents which can drive us there.

As requested in the Council's mandate, we advocate an action plan based on specific initiatives involving partnerships linking public and private sectors. Their objective is to stimulate markets so that they can rapidly attain critical mass.

In this sector, private investment will be the driving force. Monopolistic, anti-competitive environments are the real roadblocks to such involvement. The situation here is completely different from that of other infrastructural investments where public funds are still crucial, such as transport.

This sector is in rapid evolution. The market will drive, it will decide winners and losers. Given the power and pervasiveness of the technology, this market is global.

The market will drive . . . the prime task of government is to safeguard competitive forces . . .

The prime task of government is to safeguard competitive forces and ensure a strong and lasting political welcome for the information society, so that demand-pull can finance growth, here as elsewhere.

By sharing our vision, and appreciating its urgency, Europe's decision makers can make the prospects for our renewed economic and social development infinitely brighter.

New markets in Europe's information society

Information has a multiplier effect which will energize every economic sector. With market-driven tariffs, there will be a vast array of novel information services and applications:

- from high-cost services, whose premium prices are justified by the value of benefits delivered, to budget-price products designed for mass consumption;

- from services to the business community, which can be tailored to the needs of a specific customer, to standardized packages which will sell in high volumes at low prices;
- from services and applications which employ existing infrastructure, peripherals and equipment (telephone and cable TV networks, broadcasting systems, personal computers, CD players and ordinary TV sets) to those which will be carried via new technologies, such as integrated broadband, as these are installed.

Markets for business

Large and small companies and professional users are already leading the way in exploiting the new technologies to raise the efficiency of their management and production systems. And more radical changes to business organization and methods are on the way.

Business awareness of these trends and opportunities is still lower in Europe compared to the US. Companies are not yet fully exploiting the potential for internal reorganization and for adapting relationships with suppliers, contractors and customers. We have a lot of pent-up demand to fill.

Business awareness of these trends and opportunities is still lower in Europe compared to the US.

In the business markets, teleconferencing is one good example of a business application worth promoting, while much effort is also being dedicated worldwide to the perfection of telecommerce and electronic data interchange (EDI).

Both offer such cost and time advantages over traditional methods that, once applied, electronic procedures rapidly become the preferred way of doing business. According to some estimates, handling an electronic requisition is one tenth the cost of handling its paper equivalent, while an electronic mail (e-mail) message is faster, more reliable and can save 95 per cent of the cost of a fax.

Electronic payments systems are already ushering in the cashless society in some parts of Europe. We have a sizeable lead over the rest of the world in smart card technology and applications. This is an area of global market potential.

Markets for small- and medium-sized enterprises

Though Europe's 12 million SMEs are rightly regarded as the backbone of the European economy, they do need to manage both information and managerial resources better.

They need to be linked to easy access, cost-effective networks providing information on production and market openings. The competitiveness of the whole industrial fabric would be sharpened if their relationships with large companies were based on the new technologies.

Networked relationships with universities, research institutes and laboratories would boost their prospects even more by helping to remedy chronic R&D deficiencies. Networking will also diminish the isolation of SMEs in Europe's less advantaged regions, helping them to upgrade their products and find wider markets.

Markets for consumers

These are expected to be richly populated with services, from home banking and teleshopping to a near-limitless choice of entertainment on demand.

In Europe, like the United States, mass consumer markets may emerge as one of the principal driving forces for the information society. American experience already shows that the development markets encounter a number of obstacles and uncertainties.

Given the initial high cost of new pay-per-view entertainment services, and of the related equipment, as well as the high cost of bringing fibre-optics to the home, a large mass consumer market will develop more easily if entertainment services are part of a broader package. This could also include information data, cultural programming, sporting events, as well as telemarketing and teleshopping. Pay-per-view for on-line services, as well as advertising, will both be necessary as a source of revenue. To some extent, existing satellite and telephone infrastructure can help to serve the consumer market in the initial phase.

At the moment, this market is still only embryonic in Europe and is likely to take longer to grow than in the United States. There, more than 60 per cent of households are tapped by cable TV systems which could also carry text and data services. In Europe, only 25 per cent are similarly equipped, and this figure masks great differences between countries, e.g. Belgium (92 per cent) and Greece (1 per cent).

Another statistic: in the United States there are 34 PCs per 100 citizens. The European figure overall is 10 per 100, though the UK, for instance, at 22 per 100, is closer to the US level of computer penetration.

Lack of available information services and poor computer awareness could therefore prove handicaps in Europe. Telecommunication networks are, however, comparable in size and cover, but lag behind in terms of utilization. These networks, therefore, can act as the basic port of access for the initial services, but stimulation of user applications is still going to be necessary.

Such structural weaknesses need not halt progress. Europe's technological success with CD-ROM and CD-I could be the basis for a raft of non-networked applications and services during the early formative years of the information society. These services on disk have considerable export potential if Europe's audio-visual industry succeeds in countering current US dominance in titles.

In terms of the market, France's Minitel network already offers an encouraging example that European consumers are prepared to buy information and transaction services on screen, if the access price is right. It reaches nearly 30 million private and business subscribers through 6 million small terminals and carries about 15,000 different services. Minitel has created many new jobs, directly and indirectly, through boosting business efficiency and competitiveness.

In the UK, the success of the Community-sponsored 'Homestead' programme, using CD-I, is indicative, as is the highly successful launch of (an American) dedicated cable teleshopping channel.

Meanwhile in the US, where the consumer market is more advanced, video-on-demand and home shopping could emerge as the most popular services.

Audio-visual markets

Our biggest structural problem is the financial and organizational weakness of the European programme industry. Despite the enormous richness of the European heritage, and the potential of our creators, most of the programmes and most of the stocks of acquired rights are not in European hands. A fast-growing European home market can provide European industry with an opportunity to develop a home base and to exploit increased possibilities for exports.

Linguistic fragmentation of the market has long been seen as a disadvantage for Europe's entertainment and audio-visual industry, especially with English having an overwhelming dominance in the global market – a reflection of the US lead in production and, importantly, in distribution. This lead, which starts with cinema and continues with television, is likely to be extended to the new audio-visual areas. However, once products can be easily accessible to consumers, there will be more opportunities for expression of the multiplicity of cultures and languages in which Europe abounds.

. . . once products can be easily accessible to consumers, there will be more opportunities for expression of the multiplicity of cultures and languages in which Europe abounds.

Europe's audio-visual industry is also burdened with regulations. Some of these will soon be rendered obsolete by the development of new technologies, hampering the development of a dynamic European market. As a first step to stimulating debate on the new challenges, the Commission has produced a Green Paper on the audio-visual industry.

Appendix 2

Speech of US Vice President Al Gore
International Telecommunication Union
Monday 21 March 1994

I have come here, 8000 kilometres from my home, to ask you to help create a Global Information Infrastructure. To explain why, I want to begin by reading you something that I first read in high school, 30 years ago.

'By means of electricity, the world of matter has become a great nerve, vibrating thousands of miles in a breathless point of time . . . The round globe is a vast . . . brain, instinct with intelligence!'

This was not the observation of a physicist – or a neurologist. Instead, these visionary words were written in 1851 by Nathaniel Hawthorne, one of my country's greatest writers, who was inspired by the development of the telegraph. Much as Jules Verne foresaw submarines and moon landings, Hawthorne foresaw what we are now poised to bring into being.

The ITU was created only 14 years later, in major part for the purpose of fostering an internationally compatible system of telegraphy.

For almost 150 years, people have aspired to fulfil Hawthorne's vision – to wrap nerves of communications around the globe, linking all human knowledge.

In this decade, at this conference, we now have at hand the technological breakthroughs and economic means to bring all the communities of the world together. We now can at last create a planetary information network that transmits messages and images with the speed of light from the largest city to the smallest village on every continent.

I am very proud to have the opportunity to address the first development conference of the ITU because the President of the United States and I believe that an essential prerequisite to sustainable development, for all members of the human family, is the creation of this network of networks. To accomplish this purpose, legislators, regulators, and businesspeople must do this: build and operate a Global Information Infrastructure. This GII will circle the globe with Information Superhighways on which all people can travel.

These highways – or, more accurately, networks of distributed intelligence – will allow us to share information, to connect, and to communicate as a global community. From these connections we will derive robust and sustainable economic progress, strong democracies, better solutions to global and local environmental challenges, improved healthcare, and – ultimately – a greater sense of shared stewardship of our small planet.

The Global Information Infrastructure will help educate our children and allow us to exchange ideas within a community and among nations. It will be a means by which families and friends will transcend the barriers of time and distance. It will make possible a global information marketplace, where consumers can buy or sell products. I ask you, the delegates to this conference, to set an ambitious agenda that will help all governments, in their own sovereign nations and in international co-operation, to build this Global Information Infrastructure. For my country's part, I pledge our vigorous, continued participation in achieving this goal – in the development sector of the ITU, in other sectors and in plenipotentiary gatherings of the ITU, and in bilateral discussions held by our Departments of State and Commerce and our Federal Communications Commission.

The development of the GII must be a co-operative effort among governments and peoples. It cannot be dictated or built by a single country. It must be a democratic effort.

And the distributed intelligence of the GII will spread participatory democracy.

To illustrate why, I'd like to use an example from computer science. In the past, all computers were huge mainframes with a single processing unit, solving problems in sequence, one by one, each bit of information sent back and forth between the CPU (Computer Processing Unit) and the vast field of memory surrounding it. Now, we have massively parallel computers with hundreds – or thousands – of tiny self-contained processors distributed throughout the memory field, all interconnected, and together far more powerful and more versatile than even the most sophisticated single processor, because they each solve a tiny piece of the problem simultaneously and when all the pieces are assembled, the problem is solved.

Similarly, the GII will be an assemblage of local, national, and regional networks, that are not only like parallel computers but in their most advanced state will in fact be a distributed, parallel computer.

In a sense, the GII will be a metaphor for democracy itself.

Representative democracy does not work with an all-powerful central government, arrogating all decisions to itself. That is why Communism collapsed.

Instead, representative democracy relies on the assumption that the best way for a nation to make its political decisions is for each citizen – the human equivalent of the self-contained processor – to have the power to control his or her own life.

To do that, people must have available the information they need. And be allowed to express their conclusions in free speech and in votes that are combined with those of millions of others. That's what guides the system as a whole.

The GII will not only be a metaphor for a functioning democracy, it will in fact promote the functioning of democracy by greatly enhancing the participation of citizens in decision making. And it will greatly promote the ability of nations to co-operate with each other. I see a new Athenian Age of democracy forged in the fora the GII will create.

The GII will be the key to economic growth for national and international economies. For us in the United States, the information infrastructure already is to the US economy of the 1990s what transport infrastructure was to the economy of the mid twentieth century.

The integration of computing and information networks into the economy makes US manufacturing companies more productive, more competitive, and more adaptive to changing conditions and it will do the same for the economies of other nations.

These same technologies are also enabling the service sectors of the US economy to grow, to increase their scale and productivity and expand their range of product offerings and ability to respond to customer demands.

Approximately 60 per cent of all US workers are 'knowledge workers' – people whose jobs depend on the information they generate and receive over our information infrastructure. As we create new jobs, 8 out of 10 are in information-intensive sectors of our economy. And these new jobs are well-paying jobs for financial analysts, computer programmers, and other educated workers.

The global economy also will be driven by the growth of the Information Age. Hundreds of billions of dollars can be added to world growth if we commit to the GII. I fervently hope this conference will take full advantage of this potential for economic growth, and not deny any country or community its right to participate in this growth.

As the GII spreads, more and more people realize that information is a treasure that must be shared to be valuable. When two people communicate, they each can be enriched – and unlike traditional resources, the more you share, the more you have. As Thomas Jefferson said, 'He who receives an idea from me, receives instruction himself without lessening mine; as he who lights his taper at mine, receives light without darkening me.'

Now we all realize that, even as we meet here, the Global Information Infrastructure is being built, although many countries have yet to see any benefits.

Digital telecommunications technology, fibre-optics, and new high-capacity satellite systems are transforming telecommunications. And all over the world, under the seas and along the roads, pipelines, and railroads, companies are laying fibre-optic cable that carries thousands of telephone calls per second over a single strand of glass.

These developments are greatly reducing the cost of building the GII. In the past, it could take years to build a network. Linking a single country's major cities might require laying thousands of kilometres of expensive wires. Today, a single satellite and a few dozen ground stations can be installed in a few months – at much lower cost.

The economics of networks have changed so radically that the operation of a competitive, private market can build much of the GII. This is dependent, however, upon sensible regulation.

Within the national boundaries of the US we aspire to build our information highways according to a set of principles that I outlined in January in California. The National Information Infrastructure, as we call it, will be built and maintained by the private sector. It will consist of hundreds of different networks, run by different companies and using different technologies, all connected together in a giant 'network of networks', providing telephone and interactive digital video to almost every American.

Our plan is based on five principles: first, encourage private investment; second, promote competition; third, create a flexible regulatory framework that can keep pace with rapid technological and market changes; fourth, provide open access to the network for all information providers; and fifth, ensure universal service.

Are these principles unique to the United States? Hardly. Many are accepted international principles endorsed by many of you. I believe these principles can inform and aid the development of the Global Information Infrastructure and urge this Conference to incorporate them, as appropriate, into the Buenos Aires Declaration, which will be drafted this week.

Let me elaborate briefly on these principles.

First, we propose that private investment and competition be the foundation for development of the GII. In the US, we are in the process of opening our communications markets to all domestic private participants.

In recent years, many countries, particularly here in Latin America, have opted to privatize their State-owned telephone companies in order to obtain the benefits and incentives that drive competitive private enterprises, including innovation, increased investment, efficiency and responsiveness to market needs.

Adopting policies that allow increased private-sector participation in the telecommunications sector has provided an enormous spur to telecommunications development in dozens of countries, including Argentina, Venezuela, Chile, and Mexico. I urge you to follow their lead.

But privatization is not enough. Competition is needed as well. In the past, it did make sense to have telecommunications monopolies.

In many cases, the technology and the economies of scale meant it was inefficient to build more than one network. In other cases – Finland, Canada, and the US, for example – national networks were built in the early part of this century by hundreds of small, independent phone companies and co-operatives.

Today, there are many more technology options than in the past and it is not only possible, but desirable, to have different companies running competing – but interconnected – networks, because competition is the best way to make the telecommunications sector more efficient, more innovative – and more profitable as consumers make more calls and prices decline.

That is why allowing other companies to compete with AT&T, once the world's largest telephone monopoly, was so useful for the United States. Over the last ten years, it has cut the cost of a long-distance telephone call in the US more than 50 per cent.

To promote competition and investment in global telecommunications, we need to adopt cost-based collection and accounting rates. Doing so will accelerate development of the GII.

International standards to ensure interconnection and interoperability are needed as well. National networks must connect effectively with each other to make real the simple vision of linking schools, hospitals, businesses, and homes to a Global Information Infrastructure.

Hand in hand with the need for private investment and competition is the necessity of appropriate and flexible regulations developed by an authoritative regulatory body.

In order for the private sector to invest and for initiatives opening a market to competition to be successful, it is necessary to create a regulatory environment that fosters and protects competition and private-sector investments, while at the same time protecting consumers' interests.

Without the protection of an independent regulator, a potential private investor would be hesitant to provide service in competition with the incumbent provider for fear that the incumbent's market power would not be adequately controlled.

Decisions and the basis for making them must also be made public so that consumers and potential competitors are assured that their interests are being protected.

This is why in the US, we have delegated significant regulatory powers to an independent agency, the Federal Communications Commission. This expert body is well-equipped to make difficult technical decisions and to monitor, in conjunction with the National Telecommunications and Information Administration and the Department of Justice, changing market conditions. We commend this approach to you.

We need a flexible, effective system for resolution of international issues, too – one that can keep up with the ever-accelerating pace of technological change.

I understand that the ITU has just gone through a major reorganization designed to increase its effectiveness. This will enable the ITU, under the able leadership of

Mr Tarjanne, to streamline its operations and redirect resources to where they are needed most. This will ensure that the ITU can adapt to future and unimaginable technologies.

Our fourth principle is open access. By this I mean that telephone and video network owners should charge non-discriminatory prices for access to their networks. This principle will guarantee every user of the GII can use thousands of different sources of information – video programming, electronic newspapers, computer bulletin boards – from every country, in every language.

With new technologies like direct broadcast satellites, a few networks will no longer be able to control your access to information – as long as government policies permit new entrants into the information marketplace.

Countries and companies will not be able to compete in the global economy if they cannot get access to up-to-date information, if they cannot communicate instantly with customers around the globe. Ready access to information is also essential for training the skilled workforce needed for high-tech industries.

The countries that flourish in the twenty-first century will be those that have telecommunications policies and copyright laws that provide their citizens access to a wide choice of information services. Protecting intellectual property is absolutely essential.

The final and most important principle is to ensure universal service so that the Global Information Infrastructure is available to all members of our societies. Our goal is a kind of global conversation, in which everyone who wants can have his or her say.

We must ensure that whatever steps we take to expand our worldwide telecommunications infrastructure, we keep that goal in mind.

Although the details of universal service will vary from country to country and from service to service, several aspects of universal service apply everywhere. Access clearly includes making service available at affordable prices to persons at all income levels. It also includes making high-quality service available regardless of geographic location or other restrictions such as disability.

Constellations of hundreds of satellites in low earth orbit may soon provide telephone or data services to any point on the globe. Such systems could make universal service both practical and affordable.

An equally important part of universal access is teaching consumers how to use communications effectively. That means developing easy-to-use applications for a variety of contexts, and teaching people how to use them. The most sophisticated and cost-efficient networks will be completely useless if users are unable to understand how to access and take full advantage of their offerings.

Another dimension of universal service is the recognition that marketplace economics should not be the sole determinant of the reach of the information infrastructure.

The President and I have called for positive government action in the United States to extend the NII to every classroom, library, hospital, and clinic in the US by the end of the century.

I want to urge that this conference include in its agenda for action the commitment to determine how every school and library in every country can be connected to the Internet, the world's largest computer network, in order to create a Global Digital Library. Each library could maintain a server containing books and journals in electronic form, along with indexes to help users find other materials. As more and more information is stored electronically, this global library would become more and more useful.

It would allow millions of students, scholars and businesspeople to find the information they need whether it be in Albania or Ecuador.

Private investment ... competition ... flexibility ... open access ... universal service.

In addition to urging the delegates of this conference to adopt these principles as part of the Buenos Aires Declaration, guiding the next four years of telecommunications development, I assure you that the US will be discussing in many fora, inside and outside the ITU, whether these principles might be usefully adopted by all countries.

The commitment of all nations to enforcing regulatory regimes to build the GII is vital to world development and many global social goals.

But the power of the Global Information Infrastructure will be diminished if it cannot reach large segments of the world population.

We have heard together Dr Tarjanne's eloquent speech setting forth the challenges we face. As he points out, the 24 countries of the OECD have only 16 per cent of the world's population. But they account for 70 per cent of global telephone mainlines and 90 per cent of mobile phone subscribers.

There are those who say the lack of economic development causes poor telecommunications. I believe they have it exactly backwards. A primitive telecommunications system causes poor economic development.

So we cannot be complacent about the disparity between the high- and low-income nations, whether in how many phones are available to people or in whether they have such new technologies as high-speed computer networks or videoconferencing.

The United States' delegation is devoted to working with each of you at this Conference to address the many problems that hinder development.

And there are many. Financing is a problem in almost every country, even though telecommunications has proven itself to be an excellent investment.

Even where telecommunications has been identified as a top development priority, countries lack trained personnel and up-to-date information.

And in too many parts of the world, political unrest makes it difficult or impossible to maintain existing infrastructure, let alone lay new wire or deploy new capacity.

How can we work together to overcome these hurdles? Let me mention a few things industrialized countries can do to help.

First, we can use the Global Information Infrastructure for technical collaboration between industrialized nations and developing countries. All agencies of the US government are potential sources of information and knowledge that can be shared with partners across the globe.

The Global Information Infrastructure can help development agencies link experts from every nation and enable them to solve common problems. For instance, the Pan American Health Organization has conducted hemisphere-wide teleconferences to present new methods to diagnose and prevent the spread of AIDS.

Second, multilateral institutions like the World Bank can help nations finance the building of telecommunications infrastructure.

Third, the US can help provide the technical know-how needed to deploy and use these new technologies. USAID and US businesses have helped the US Telecommunications Training Institute train more than 3500 telecommunications professionals from the developing world, including many in this room.

In the future, USTTI plans also to help business people, bankers, farmers, and others from the developing world find ways that computer networking, wireless technology, satellites, video links, and other telecommunications technology could improve their effectiveness and efficiency.

I challenge other nations, the development banks, and the UN system to create similar training opportunities.

The head of our Peace Corps, Carol Bellamy, intends to use Peace Corps volunteers both to help deploy telecommunications and computer systems and to find innovative uses for them. Here in Argentina, a Peace Corps volunteer is doing just that.

To join the GII to the effort to protect and preserve the global environment, our Administration will soon propose using satellite and personal communication technology to create a global network of environmental information. We will propose using the schools and students of the world to gather and study environmental information on a daily basis and communicate that data to the world through television.

But regulatory reform must accompany this technical assistance and financial aid for it to work. This requires top-level leadership and commitment – commitment to foster investment in telecommunications and commitment to adopt policies that ensure the rapid deployment and widespread use of the information infrastructure.

I opened by quoting Nathaniel Hawthorne, inspired by Samuel Morse's invention of the telegraph.

Morse was also a famous portrait artist in the US – his portrait of President James Monroe hangs today in the White House. While Morse was working on a portrait of General Lafayette in Washington, his wife, who lived about 500 kilometres away, grew ill and died. But it took seven days for the news to reach him.

In his grief and remorse, he began to wonder if it were possible to erase barriers of time and space, so that no one would be unable to reach a loved one in time of need. Pursuing this thought, he came to discover how to use electricity to convey messages, and so he invented the telegraph and, indirectly, the ITU.

The Global Information Infrastructure offers instant communication to the great human family.

It can provide us with the information we need to dramatically improve the quality of their lives. By linking clinics and hospitals together, it will ensure that doctors treating patients have access to the best possible information on diseases and treatments. By providing early warning on natural disasters like volcanic eruptions, tsunamis, or typhoons, it can save the lives of thousands of people.

By linking villages and towns, it can help people organize and work together to solve local and regional problems ranging from improving water supplies to preventing deforestation.

To promote . . . to protect . . . to preserve freedom and democracy, we must make telecommunications development an integral part of every nation's development. Each link we create strengthens the bonds of liberty and democracy around the world. By opening markets to stimulate the development of the Global Information Infrastructure, we open lines of communication.

By opening lines of communication, we open minds. This summer, from my country, cameras will bring the World Cup Championship to well over one billion people.

To those of you from the 23 visiting countries whose teams are in the finals, I wish you luck – although I'll be rooting for the home team.

The Global Information Infrastructure carries implications even more important than soccer.

It has brought us images of earthquakes in California, of Boris Yeltsin on a tank in Red Square, of the effects of mortar shells in Sarajevo and Somalia, of the fall of the Berlin Wall. It has brought us images of war and peace, and tragedy and joy, in which we all can share.

There's a Dutch relief worker, Wam Kat, who has been broadcasting an electronic diary from Zagreb for more than a year and a half on the Internet, sharing his observations of life in Croatia.

After reading Kat's Croatian diary, people around the world began to send money for relief efforts. The result: 25 houses have been rebuilt in a town destroyed by war.

Governments didn't do this. People did. But such events are the hope of the future.

When I began proposing the NII in the US, I said that my hope is that the United States, born in revolution, can lead the way to this new, peaceful revolution. However, I believe we will reach our goal faster and with greater certainty if we walk down that path together. As Antonio Machado, Spanish poet, once said, 'Pathwalker, there is no path, we create the path as we walk.'

Let us build a global community in which the people of neighbouring countries view each other not as potential enemies, but as potential partners, as members of the same family in the vast, increasingly interconnected human family.

Let us seize this moment. Let us work to link the people of the world. Let us create this new path as we walk it together.

Appendix 3

Speech of US Vice President Al Gore
15th International ITU Conference
Monday 12 October 1998

This is the third time in four years I have had the honour of speaking to this distinguished audience. The first time, I travelled 8000 kilometres from the White House to Buenos Aires. The second time, I spoke to you by way of satellite in Kyoto, and invited you to come here this year. I want to thank all of you for the distances you travelled to be here today, and, on behalf of President Clinton and the American people, I want to welcome all of you to the United States of America.

As we gather today to talk about technology and the future, I want to share with you a list I found not long ago in an airline magazine of 31 signs that technology has taken over your life. According to the list, you know technology has taken over your life:

- if you know your e-mail address, but not your telephone number;
- if you rotate your computer screen saver more than your tyres;
- if you have never sat through a movie without having at least one electronic device on your body beep or buzz;
- And, my personal favorite, number 23: if Al Gore strikes you as an 'intriguing fellow'.

I didn't get it.

We meet today in Minnesota: the land of 10,000 lakes, at the very centre of North America. One of our great writers, Sinclair Lewis, once wrote that 'to understand America, it is merely necessary to understand Minnesota. But to understand Minnesota, you must be an historian, an ethnologist, a poet, and a graduate prophet all in one'.

Of course, people might say the same thing about the Global Information Infrastructure – a network of networks that transmits messages and images at the speed of light and on every continent ultimately linking all human knowledge.

Its creation is so revolutionary – the changes it has wrought are so vast – that even those of us who have worked on it for years cannot predict its full impact.

For all the stunning capabilities of the Global Information Infrastructure, we must remember that at its heart it is a way to deepen and extend our oldest, and most cherished global values: rising standards of living and literacy, an ever-widening circle of democracy, freedom, and individual empowerment.

And, above all, we must remember that – especially in this global economy and Information Age – we are all connected, from Minnesota to Mongolia, from Madrid to Mali.

That is what I want to talk about today. Thanks to the people in this room – and people listening around the world – this is truly an open moment in world history, a moment when we can come together across our communications networks to rediscover and renew our shared values – and build the twenty-first century our children deserve.

That is a vision that was not even imaginable back in 1947, when the International Telecommunication Union last met in the United States. That year, two scientists working at Bell Labs – John Bardeen and Walter Brattain – made an amazing discovery. Using a little slab of germanium, a thin plastic wedge, a shiny strip of gold foil, and a makeshift spring fashioned from an old paper-clip, they were able to boost an electrical signal by more than 450 times. They called their invention a 'transistor'.

Incidentally, one of those two scientists – Walter Brattain – first learned about quantum mechanics less than five miles from where we meet today, as a doctoral student at the University of Minnesota.

There are now more than half a billion transistors manufactured – every second. Every hour, more than a trillion of them are packed into everything from computers to car engines, satellite systems to gas pumps. Within two years, a single microchip will routinely contain one billion transistors – and the patterns etched on them will be as complicated as a roadmap of the entire planet. Fifty years ago, it cost $5 for every transistor. Today, it costs 1/100th of a cent. In just a few years, it will cost a billionth of a cent.

I once used the old cliché with a college audience that if the automobile had made the same exponential advances as the transistor, a car would get 100,000 miles to the gallon and cost only 50 cents. And then one of the students in the first row said, 'Sure, Mr Vice President, but it would be less than a millimetre long'.

These new advances are allowing us to explore new frontiers – from a galaxy 12 billion light years away to the smallest genetic switch inside a human cell. Within three weeks, the first of several brand new low earth orbiting satellite systems will make it possible to make a phone call from any point on the earth's surface to any other point. Within three years, we will have high-speed wireless Internet access from anywhere on Earth.

Just two short years ago, the United States was able to land a rover on Mars equipped with an off-the-shelf wireless remote modem – which prompted more than three-quarters of a billion hits on the Internet when those images were broadcast back to Earth. In the coming months, NASA will work with several of your governments to launch the new international space station, which is the size of two football fields.

At MIT in Boston, researchers are even busy adding a third sensation to virtual reality: not just sight and sound – but touch. By using an electronic thimble, you can touch an object on a computer screen, and it immediately appears as a hologram next to you. If you run your fingers over it, the object can become rough or smooth – whatever the computer commands.

It means that in a few short years, the blind will be able to feel a computer image, and armchair tourists will be able to run their hands over the rough sandstone of Stonehenge or the smooth marble of the Taj Mahal.

None of these stunning achievements would have been possible without telecommunications. Thanks to all of you, we know that today, we are at the dawn of a new technology and telecommunications renaissance, one that is still in its infancy.

But perhaps the greatest promise of this electronic and digital age lies not in what is new, but in the values that are renewed.

As each breathtaking new development brings us closer together in communication, and in common cause – building a true global electronic village – we have the chance to spread a new prosperity, a new literacy, a new love of freedom and democracy – and even a new sense of community to the farthest regions of the world.

That is why, four years ago, I set forth five principles that I believe are essential to reap the full harvest of the Global Information Infrastructure. Those five principles were: private investment, competition, open access, flexible regulatory framework, and universal service.

These are not just common principles, but common values we all need to strengthen. I am heartened to report enormous progress on all five.

First, we have encouraged private investment, because private investment is the lifeblood of innovation. Today, we see the results – over $600 billion of private capital has been invested in telecommunications since 1994. More than 48 telecom operators have been privatized. I invite any remaining doubters to go back to Buenos Aires and ask Argentina how well privatization works – just since we met there they have gone from 4 million telephone lines to more than 18 million. Not only is their privatized system more efficient and more profitable – it is bringing an entire generation of Argentinians closer together.

Second, we have promoted competition, because competition leads to innovation, better services, and better prices for consumers.

In 1994, only seven countries had competitive markets for basic voice service. Today, 47 countries either have full competition or are committed to it. One of those is South Africa, which last year decided to license a second cellular operator. And in just one year, the number of subscribers jumped from 40,000 to 340,000.

Here in the United States, we have also taken broad steps to promote competition.

Since 1996, when we signed a landmark telecommunications law that advances all five principles, the birth of dozens of new competitors has raised $20 billion to invest in advanced communications, and created over 50,000 jobs. Now, we need competition between fibre-optic cables around the globe, especially with the stunning expansion of broadband capacity. The bottom line is: competition works if we let it.

Third, we have made open access a priority, because open access guarantees that every user of the GII will be able to reach thousands of different sources of information from every country, in every language. Today, the Internet is turning that goal into a reality. Here in the United States, it took radio 38 years to reach 50 million people, personal computers 16 years, and television 13 years. The Internet took only four years.

Today, there are 100 million Internet users. By the year 2000, there will be 320 million. Maintaining open access means that we will speed up the day when every child in any village or city is able to reach across a keyboard and reach every book ever written, every song ever composed, and every painting ever painted.

We have seen the dramatic benefits of open access to the telephone network. Similarly, as new technologies emerge, open access will increase competition and deliver great benefits to users and service providers alike. The ITU's role in setting standards is crucial to this goal.

Experience has shown that competition among multiple standards is the best way to meet users' diverse needs – as long as each individual standard is designed to increase, and not reduce, the potential for interoperability.

Fourth, we have worked toward a flexible regulatory framework, because it promotes competition and investment while protecting consumers.

A growing list of nations agree: over the past four years, 18 independent regulatory agencies have been established in the Americas, 17 in Africa, and 11 in the Asia Pacific region. I was pleased to see 58 nations recently commit to the World Trade Organization's Reference Paper on Regulatory Principles.

I want to commend one of them – OSIPTEL of Peru – which recently moved to promote competition by ending Telefonica's monopoly one year ahead of schedule.

Fifth, we have promoted universal service to basic telecommunications services, because the ability to pick up a phone or hook up a computer and have instant access to your village, your nation, and your world is one of the most liberating and empowering forces in human history, and it should be available to all people.

Since 1994, the principle of universal access has led to more than 200 million phone lines being added. For example, China is installing 14.5 million lines per year – equal to half of Britain's entire network.

This isn't just a story of numbers and statistics, but families and faces. In Thailand, a group of students with disabilities use the Flying Wheelchair Bulletin Board to talk to other students with disabilities around the world. They have been amazed to learn about legislation passed in other countries to help the disabled become full members of society – and now they are trying to raise awareness at home. In Longbeach, Australia, a woman named Christine Chapel lives on a sheep ranch in the Australian outback. By telecommuting through the GII, she recently earned a bachelor's degree at a university more than 1500 kilometres from her home.

Thanks to the work we set in motion four years ago, the structure for the Global Information Infrastructure is largely in place. The Information Superhighways of many nations are beginning to take shape. Now more than ever before, we must all decide where they will lead.

My message to you is simple: today, on the eve of a new century and a new millennium, we have an unprecedented opportunity to use these powerful new forces of technology to advance our oldest and most cherished values.

We have a chance to extend knowledge and prosperity to our most isolated inner cities, to the barrios, the favelas, the colonias and our most remote rural villages; to bring twenty-first century learning and communication to places that don't even have phone service today; to share specialized medical technology where there are barely enough family doctors today; to strengthen democracy and freedom by putting it on-line, where it is so much harder for it to be suppressed or denied. Today, we are more connected than ever before. Now, let us use our new tools and technology to build on that interdependence – to build a stronger global community, and make real our common values.

Today, I want to pose five great challenges that still remain to be met. Together, they make up a Digital Declaration of Interdependence that can create a brighter world for us all.

First, we must improve access to technology so everyone on the planet is within walking distance of voice and data telecommunications services within the next decade.

Right now, 65 per cent of the world's households have no phone service. Half of the world's population has never made a phone call. Iceland has more Internet hosts than all of Africa. Today, I challenge the business community to create a global business plan – to put data and voice telecommunication within an hour's walk of everybody on the planet by the end of the next decade. This plan should include ways to stimulate demand. It should involve local business. It should allow for access to distance learning and telemedicine. It should provide hands-on training. We know it can be done – and it must be done.

Second, we must overcome our language barriers and develop technology with real-time digital translation so anyone on the planet can talk to anyone else.

Just imagine what it would be like to pick up a phone, call anywhere in the world, and have your voice translated instantly so you could have a conversation without language being a barrier. Just imagine if the translation many of you are receiving through your earphones here today could be accomplished digitally and instantly. I can see the day when we have a true digital dialogue around the world – when a universal translator can instantly shatter the language barriers that so often hold us back in this global and information age.

Imagine also a world where computers don't need keyboards, where you can simply speak into your PC, and have every word perfectly translated and typed. Imagine how much it could reduce the cost of doing business, and increase international co-operation. Imagine if there were no barriers between basic literacy and computer literacy – where any person who can speak can operate a computer and tap into the world's information simply by speaking into a small device.

Today, I want to challenge the research community: take these discoveries and develop new technology that allows people around the world to communicate with each other; that makes international co-operation easier; and that allows people to participate in our global community without losing their linguistic and cultural heritage.

Third, we must create a Global Knowledge Network of people who are working to improve the delivery of education, healthcare, agricultural resources, and sustainable development – and to ensure public safety.

Just imagine what it would be like if a sick child in rural Mongolia could be linked through videoconference to the Sydney Children's Hospital. A small sensor, like a mouse, could broadcast X-rays or an MRI back to Australia. A blood sample could be put on a slide and scanned for sickle cell anaemia. A leading doctor could prescribe treatment – and the tests would be waiting when the child arrived. Within a few short years, this technology can be in our hands.

In an age when information is everywhere, we should be able to find ways to group information by need.

Just think if every farmer in Africa could tap into a local weather channel that provides them with the information they need to plant and rotate their crops. And in natural disasters, we know that just an hour's advance warning can save thousands of lives.

Today, some of the most forward-thinking companies are using new 'knowledge management' techniques that share best practices and take advantage of accumulated knowledge. Today, I issue a challenge to the education community to use these same techniques to link practitioners, experts, and non-profit organizations that are working on our most pressing social and economic needs.

For example, in the world today, five billion people don't have access to secondary and higher education. If we can create a 'knowledge network' that extends distance learning around the globe, we can quadruple the number of people who have access to higher education and lifelong learning.

Fourth, we must use communications technology to ensure the free flow of ideas and support democracy and free speech.

Four years ago in Buenos Aires, I said that the GII would promote democracy and greatly increase people's participation in decision making, by making available the information they need to express their speech freely.

Self-government is built on the assumption that each citizen should have the power to control his or her own life.

More than five centuries ago, this concept was alive in Europe – but it didn't become functionally possible until the printing press helped to widely spread a large body of shared civic knowledge to an informed and engaged public.

Just as the printing press delivered that knowledge 500 years ago, I believe the GII can deliver a new wave of civic knowledge – comprehensive enough to strengthen the capacity for self-government everywhere. The continuing challenge to all of us – governmental and non-governmental organizations alike – is not to tell other nations what to do, or what values to pursue, but rather to empower people to recognize and act upon their own choices. We must continue to work to ensure that the GII promotes the free-flow of ideas and supports democracy around the globe.

Fifth, we must use communication technology to expand economic opportunity to all families and communities around the globe.

Everyone in every part of the world should have the opportunity to succeed if they are willing to work for it.

In a remote farming village near Chincehros, Peru, life has changed more in the past two years than in the previous half century. In 1996, an Internet service provider set up a Net-link for 50 peasant families. The village leaders formed an on-line partnership with an international export company, which arranged for its vegetables to be shipped and sold in New York. Before e-mail, the village's income was about $300 a month. Today, it has jumped to $1,500 a month.

Across the globe, micro-enterprise – which often starts with initial loans of as little as $50 – has been a path out of poverty for millions. Today, there are more than 500 million micro-entrepreneurs – like those Peruvian farmers who eke out an existence by selling their wares and service to their immediate communities.

There are countless micro-entrepreneurs whose quality of life and incomes would change dramatically overnight if they had access to the same tools.

Today, I challenge the non-profit community to work with development organizations to provide more of these opportunities. These networks will create jobs and enable micro-entrepreneurs to avoid a middle-man and keep more of their profits.

Some estimate that global electronic commerce will grow to more than $300 billion per year in just a few years. By the year 2010, we can triple the number of people who are able to support themselves and their families because they are able to reach world markets through the Internet. It will also help give consumers access to a whole new world of goods and services.

Today, I want to announce two additional steps our government will be taking to increase opportunity and empower micro-entrepreneurs across the globe. First, I am pleased to announce today that our Peace Corps has committed to make technology and communications an increasingly important strategic tool in the work of Peace Corps volunteers.

Before Peace Corps volunteers go into the field, the Peace Corps will make sure they have the know-how to enable people to use technology to gain information, improve education, and enhance economic development. Whenever possible, the Peace Corps will also help increase access to telecommunications in the communities it serves.

Second, I am proud to announce that USAID will lead a new initiative to promote Internet access and electronic commerce for development in eight countries. This initiative will go hand-in-hand with legal and regulatory reforms aimed at liberalization and universal access, to stimulate new businesses through electronic commerce, and demonstrate applications in democracy and governance, economic growth, environment, education, and medical assistance.

This initiative will build on the Leland initiative, a $15 million effort to provide 21 African countries with support for Internet connections.

This is our Digital Declaration of Interdependence – five challenges that can strengthen our global community for the twenty-first century.

Before I conclude, I want to say a special word about how we must work together to avoid the year 2000 computer problem – which could stall much of our progress in international telecommunications if we do not mount a major, worldwide, public and private crusade to fix it.

Today, we potentially have hundreds of millions of computers and devices that literally cannot read the year '2000'. This means that when the clock strikes midnight on 1 January 2000, everything from air traffic control to water systems, heart monitors to nuclear power plants could be affected.

Here in the United States, we have a major effort underway to cope with the challenge. Within the White House, we are pursuing a top-priority, high-level initiative to make sure our national government is prepared.

But in an era of global interdependence, there is a shared global responsibility to meet the challenge.

And I say to every single company, and every single nation, that has benefited from global trade, and global telecommunications: just as you have shared the benefits of this global and information age, you have an obligation to help shoulder this critical burden. All of our economies will be hurt if the year 2000 problem is not solved in time. One weak link in the system will weaken us all. I appreciate the work being done by our Federal Communication Commission and the ITU on this issue – but we have more work to do. Let us meet the year 2000 challenge together, so we can begin the twenty-first century with confidence, and without computer problems. Our ambassadors are ready to work with you and provide any technical assistance you need. Together, we must solve this problem.

Throughout this millennium, the story of human achievement has been a story of wonder, a story of discovery, a story of imagination, but also a story of courage – to try new things, to believe in what we can't see, and to boldly follow wherever the road may take us.

Today, that road of discovery is a highway of light and speed to connect the largest city to the smallest village across the globe. In a world once limited by borders and geography, the only limits we face today are the borders of our imagination. More than any other time in our history, the promise of new discovery and new technology has made it possible to renew and strengthen our oldest and most cherished values.

As we move into a new century and a new millennium, let us take that same sense of wonder, that same sense of discovery, and that same sense of courage to make real the values that centuries of human experience have aspired to create – to end suffering, to eradicate disease, to promote freedom, to educate our children, and to lift our families and our nations up.

We don't have a moment to waste. Because our children and our world are waiting. Thank you.

Select bibliography and further reading

Becker, L. (1980) 'The moral basis of property rights', in *Property,* Roland Penvork.

Bell, D. (1974) *The Coming of Post-industrial Society*, Heinemann Educational.

Brinson, J. D., and Radcliffe, M. (1997) *Multimedia: Law and business handbook: A practical guide for developers and publishers*, Ladera Press.

Brinson, J. D., and Radcliffe, M. (contributor) (1997) *Internet Legal Forms for Business*, Ladera Press.

Children's Partnership (1996) *Where We Stand*.

Cochrane, Dr P. (1998) *Tips for Time Travellers,* Orion.

Daniel, Sir J. (1996) *Mega-universities and Knowledge Media: Technology strategies for higher education*, Kogan Page.

De Sola Pool, I. (1983) *Technologies of Freedom*, MIT Press.

Drucker, P. (1969) *The Age of Discontinuity*, Heinemann.

Epper, K. (5 May 1995) 'A player goes after the big bucks in cyberspace', *American Banker,* clx (86).

Feeny, D., Islei, G. and Wilcocks, L. (1997) *Managing IT as a Strategic Resource*, McGraw-Hill.

Finley, M. (1995) *Why Teams Don't Work*, Peterson's.

Finley, M. (1996) *Why Change Doesn't Work*, Peterson's.

Finley, M. (1996) *Techno-Crazed*, Peterson's.

Finley, M., and Robbins, H. (1998) *Transcompetition*, McGraw-Hill.

Fukuyama, F. (1992) *The End of History*, Hamilton.

Gardner, H. (1993) *Frames of Mind: The theory of multiple intelligences*, Basic Books.

Gates, B., with Myhrcold, N., and Rinearson, P. (rev. edn, 1996) *The Road Ahead*, Penguin.

Goldstein, P. (1991) 'Copyright', *Journal of the Copyright Society of the USA*, 38 (3).

Gomes-Casseres, B. (July–August 1994) 'Group versus group: How alliance networks compete', *Harvard Business Review*, 72.

Gore, A. (1992) *Earth in the Balance*, Earthscan.

Hagel, J. III, and Armstrong, A. G. (1997) *Net Gain*, Harvard Business School Press.

Handy, C. (4th edn, 1993) *Understanding Organizations*, Penguin.

Handy, C. (1994) *The Empty Raincoat*, Hutchinson.

Handy, C. (1995) *The Age of Unreason*, Arrow.

Handy, C. (1995) *Gods of Management*, Arrow.

Handy, C. (1995) *Beyond Certainty*, Hutchinson.

Handy, C. (1995) *Waiting for the Mountain to Move*, Arrow.

Handy, C. (1998) *The Hungry Spirit*, Arrow.

Hughes, E. (March 1995) 'A long-term perspective on electronic commerce', newsletter Release 1.0, EDventure Holdings.

Jones, G. (1988) *Jones' Dictionary of Cable Television Terminology: Including related computer and satellite definitions*, Jones 21st Century.

Jones, G. (1991) *Make All America a School: Mind Extension University, the Education Network*, Jones 21st Century Inc.

Jones, G. (1997) *Cyberschools*, Jones Interactive Inc.

Jonscher, Dr C. J. (1999) *Wired Life*, Bantam.

Kahin, B. and Keller, J. (1997) *Co-ordinating the Internet*, MIT Press.

Katsh, E. (1995) *Law in a Digital World*, Oxford University Press.

Keet, E. E. (1985) *Preventing Piracy*, Addison Wesley.

Krol, E. (1994) *The Whole Internet*, O'Reilly & Associates.

Laurillard, D. (1993) *Rethinking University Teaching*, Routledge.

Leer, A. (1999) *Masters of the Wired World*, Financial Times Management.

Lindauer, Professor T. (1995) *The Trouble with Computers*, MIT Press.

McFarlane, G. (1989) *A Practical Introduction to Copyright*, Waterlow.

McLuhan, M. and E. (1988) *Laws of the Media*, University of Toronto Press.

McLuhan, H. M. (1994) *Understanding Media: The extensions of man*, MIT Press.

Martin, Dr J. (1995) *The Great Transition*, Amacom.

Martin, Dr J. (1996) *Cybercorp: The new business revolution*, Amacom.

Murphy, B. (1983) *The World Wired Up*, Comedia.

Murray, A. (1978) *Reason and Society in the Middle Ages*, Clarendon Press.

Negroponte, N. (1995) *Being Digital*, Hodder & Stoughton.

Patterson, L. R. and Lindberg, S. W. (1991) *The Nature of Copyright*, University of Georgia Press.

Patton, P. (July 1995) 'E-money', *Popular Science*.

Peppard, J. (1993) *IT Strategy for Business*, Longman.

Porter, M. (1985) *Competitive Advantage*, The Free Press.

Postman, N. (1993) *Technopoly*, Vintage Books.

Puttnam, D., CBE (1997) *The Undeclared War*, HarperCollins.

Schön, D. (1971) *Beyond the Stable State*, Temple Smith.

Standage, T. (1998) *The Victorian Internet*, Weidenfeld & Nicolson.

Stewart, B. (1988) *The Media Lab*, Penguin.

Stewart, T. (1997) *Intellectual Capital*, Nicholas Brealey.

Stoll, C. (1995) *Silicon Snake Oil: Second thoughts on the Information Highway*, Doubleday.

Tapscott, D. (1998) *Blueprint to the Digital Economy*, McGraw-Hill.

Toffler, A. (1981) *The Third Wave*, Collins.

Toffler, A. (1990) *Powershift*, Bantam.

Toffler, A. (1991) *Future Shock*, Macmillan.

Toffler, A. (1995) *War and Anti-war*, Warner.

Toffler, A. and H. (1995) *Creating a New Civilization*, Atlanta Turner.

Glossary

ADSL
Asymmetric Digital Subscriber Line. A system that boosts signals and reduces the noise in telecommunications traffic in existing copper wire networks, thereby increasing the capacity of telecommunications networks.

ATM
Asynchronous Transfer Mode. A packet-switching system and communication protocol for high-speed transfer of high volumes of data in telecommunication networks, making use of existing cables and network infrastructure.

Authoring tools
Computer software programs designed to help create interactive multimedia programs for use off-line and/or on-line.

Bandwidth
The amount of data that can be carried by an electronic (digital or analogue) communication network.

BBS
Bulletin Board System. Internet or other network services where users connect to exchange messages and files.

BIS
Business Information System.

Browser
A software program that enables users to work with information and files stored on the Internet or other networks. Popular Internet browsers include Netscape and Microsoft's Internet Explorer.

CASE
Computer-assisted software engineering.

CATV
Community Antenna Television.

CBT
Computer-based training.

CD-I
Compact Disc-Interactive.

CD-ROM
Compact Disc-Read-only Memory.

Clipper chip
On 16 April 1993, a US presidential initiative announced the introduction of a 'key escrow chip' that supposedly would provide secure telecommunications and networks without compromising law-enforcement interests and national security. It was envisaged that the chip would be implemented in all communication devices sold in the United States. The chip is based on a classified symmetrical algorithm called Skipjack, developed by the National Security Agency, that is many times more secure than DES or RSA. Government agencies have the ability to decrypt the data being encrypted by the clipper chip as they hold a decryption key for every chip sold, together with information on who the devices were sold to. The intention with the clipper chip was to resolve the tension between the government's need to protect national security and law-enforcement interests and the users' need for privacy and security. The proposed scheme has not been well received in the market. *See also* DES *and* RSA.

COI
Communities of interest.

CPM
Cost per million of impressions. A standard way of calculating the price and effectiveness of advertising.

Cryptography
The science of encrypting/decrypting data and information, including principles, methods and mechanisms.

DAB
Digital Audio Broadcasting.

DBS
Direct Broadcast Satellite.

Decryption
A method of decoding encrypted data, restoring it to its original form.

DECT
Digital Enhanced Cordless Telecommunication.

DES
Data Encryption Standard. A single-key algorithm adopted by the US National Institute of Standards and Technology (NIST) for public use. Widely used, but considered less secure than public key cryptography.

Digital signature
A string of encrypted digital values representing the identity of the sender and/or source of data, allowing the receiver to verify sender and/or data authenticity. The longer the encryption key, the more secure the signature. Most keys are 512-bit, but encryption experts recommend 1024-bit keys.

DNS
Domain Name System. *See also* Domain name.

Domain name
The part of an Internet address – such as '.com' or '.org' or '.net' or '.AC' – that classifies the kind of address it is, such as a web site or e-mail address, to help organize and manage Internet traffic.

DTH
Direct To Home. Satellite signals transmitted direct to individual receivers via their satellite dishes.

DTV
Digital Television.

DVB
Digital Video Broadcasting.

DVD
Digital Versatile Disc. A high-density optical digital compact disc that is available in a number of different formats based on internationally proposed standards' specifications, including the following:

DVD-ROM: Digital Versatile Disc-Read Only Memory. A high-density version of CD-ROM.

DVD-Video: Digital Versatile Disc-Video. Non-recordable video disc, intended for use with TV sets as a playback facility for films (comparable to video cassettes, except you cannot record on DVD-Video discs).

DVD-Audio: A better, high-density version of the digital audio compact disc.

DVD-WO: Digital Versatile Disc-Write Once. A version of the DVD-ROM that can be used for making recordings, but only once.

DVD-RAM: Digital Versatile Disc-Random Access Memory. A rewritable high-density optical disc, intended as an integral PC component for the purpose of using multimedia/high volumes of data – a high-capacity PC hard disk.

DVD-E: Digital Versatile Disc-Erasable. A fully recordable optical disc – the digital equivalent of a video cassette.

DVI
Digital Video Interactive. A version of the CD-ROM that has a limited capacity for storing video using compression techniques.

DWDM
Dense Wave Division Multiplexing. Increases the capacity of fibre-optic cables so they are even faster.

EC
European Commission.

EDI
Electronic data interchange encryption. A method of coding and transforming data into an unintelligible state so it cannot be accessed in its original form.

ESP
Enterprise service providers. IT departments run as ISPs. *See also* ISP.

EU
European Union.

FCC
Federal Communications Commission (United States).

GII
Global Information Infrastructure.

GIS
Global Information Society.

GLOBE
Global Learning and Observations to Benefit the Environment. Vice President Al Gore's initiative in the US for students and teachers from all over the US to work with research scientists to learn more about the world. Students report data via the Internet and can then download material that helps them understand their data in a global context.

GSM
Global System for Mobile. An international industry standard for digital mobile telephony that is widely adopted in Europe and, increasingly, worldwide, except in the United States.

HDTV
High-definition television.

HTML
Hypertext Mark-up Language. A standard format for hypertext files on the Internet/WWW developed by the Internet Engineering Task Force (IETF).

HTTP
Hypertext Transfer Protocol. A standard format for data transfers over the Internet/WWW developed by the Internet Engineering Task Force.

Hypertext
A method of structuring data, linking text to other related texts in a collection of material. For example, formatting an Internet address in text so that if you click on it, that site's home page appears on your screen.

ICT
Information and Communications Technology.

IDEA
International Data Encryption Algorithm.

IETF
Internet Engineering Task Force.

IGO
Intergovernmental Organizations. An example would be the United Nations.

Intelligent agent
A software program that works as an automated information-gathering tool. The program has the capability to process information about individual users and their specific information requirements. The program 'learns' about users' particular search patterns and subject interests and uses this information to adapt the tool to individual users, hence its name. The intelligent agent acts on your instructions – 'go and find this information for me' – and travels (surfs the Net) within and across databases and networks to get the information for you.

Internet
A global system of many open, interconnected computer networks.

IP
Internet Protocol. A communications protocol that lets packets of data traverse multiple networks on its way to its final destination. *See also* TCP.

ISBN
International Standard Book Number. A worldwide standard system for identifying and registering books that have been published. (ASBN in America.)

ISDN
Integrated Services Digital Network. Standard for digital delivery of telephony and data services.

ISDN
Integrated Subscriber Digital Network. An industry standard and a protocol for transferring voice and data over telecommunications networks.

ISO
International Organization for Standardization. The ISO's members are national standards organizations.

ISP
Internet service provider. A company that rents or owns a telecommunications infrastructure that connects to the Internet and offers customers dial-up or fixed access facilities.

ISSN
International Standard Serial Number. A worldwide standard system for identifying and registering journals.

ITS
Intelligent transport systems.

ITU
International Telecommunication Union. An organization under the administration of the United Nations that deals with telecommunications and standards.

I-TV
Interactive television.

JPEG
Joint Photographic Experts Group. A collaboration between the ITU and ISO to develop standards for the compression of continuous-tone still images.

Key
A series of computer instructions that controls the process of encryption and decryption.

LEO
Low Earth Orbit. Satellite communications system.

Metcalfe's Law
Named after Bob Metcalfe, inventor of the Ethernet and founder of 3Com. The law states that the value of a network grows exponentially – that is, the number of users squared gives the value of a network.

MHEG
Multimedia and Hypermedia information coding Experts Group. An ISO group that works on the development of standards for bit-stream specifications for multimedia and hypermedia applications.

MNE
Multinational enterprise.

Moore's Law
This states that around every 18 months, the speed of microprocessors doubles and their cost goes down proportionally.

MPEG
Motion Picture Experts Group. An ISO group working on the development of standards for the storage and retrieval of video and audio in digital media.

MSC
Multimedia Super Corridor.

MUD
Multi-user domain.

NASA
National Aeronautics and Space Administration (United States).

Net
Slang for the Internet, the Information Superhighway or the Global Information Infrastructure.

Newsgroups
A system allowing Internet users to join on-line communities for the purpose of accessing and sharing information on specific areas of interest, and possibly participating in debates and on-line discussions. Some newsgroups are open and others are closed. Some are very loosely organized and others are highly structured and moderated.

NGO
Non-governmental organization. For example, Greenpeace.

NII
National Information Infrastructure.

NTSC
National Television Systems Committee. One of the world's three incompatible analogue colour video standards used, for instance, in the United States, Canada and Japan. The other two are PAL and SECAM (used in France). The NTSC is the inferior standard, giving a poorer resolution of video images – a maximum of 525 lines per image as opposed to 625 lines available using PAL. *See also* PAL and SECAM.

OECD
Organization for Economic Co-operation and Development.

Oftel
Office of Telecommunications. UK telecommunications watchdog.

P3P
Platform for Privacy Preferences. Technology serving to protect privacy.

PAL
Phase Alteration Line. Analogue colour video standard, used in most of Europe, Australia, Africa and South America. *See also* NTSC and SECAM.

PARC
Palo Alto Research Center. Invented Windows, the mouse, icons and pull-down menus for PCs.

PDA
Personal Digital Assistant. Hand-held devices, such as electronic organizers or pocket-size computers.

PDF

Portable Document Format. A proprietary standard for formatting documents for digital distribution, developed by Adobe Systems.

PGP

Pretty Good Privacy. A software program developed by P. Zimmermann and available free in the public domain over the Internet. The program is used to encrypt and decrypt messages and data sent over the Internet.

PHS

Personal Handyphone System.

PICS

Platform for Internet Content Selection. A tool for filtering Internet material so the user defines what is accessed – for example, parents can limit children's access to unsuitable sites.

PPV

Pay per view.

RAM

Random Access Memory. The memory storage on computer chips.

RSA

Rivest-Shamir-Adleman cipher. A comprehensive set of public key-based cryptographic algorithms, named after the inventors, developed since 1977 at the Massachusetts Institute of Technology. Several RSA algorithms are protected (not in Europe) by US patents held by the Public Key Partners (PKP) company, formed jointly by MIT and Stanford.

SECAM

Système Electronique Couleur Avec Memoire. Analogue colour video standard, developed and used in France. *See also* NTSC and PAL.

SET

Standard Electronic Transaction. A standard developed by Mastercard and Visa to enable secure transactions on the Internet.

SGML

Standard Generalized Mark-up Language. An ISO standard for marking up content and structuring it for electronic use.

S-HTTP

Secure Hypertext Transfer Protocol. Security technology proposed as a standard for the Internet.

SME

Small and medium-sized enterprises.

SSL

Secure Socket Layer. Proprietary security technology developed by Netscape and proposed as a standard for the Internet.

STM
Scientific, technical and medical (publishing).

TCP
Transmission Control Protocol. It followed the Internet Protocol (IP).

TRIPS
Trade-Related aspects of Intellectual Property Rights. Sets minimum international standards for the protection of intellectual property.

URL
Uniform Resource Locator. The address of an Internet document or site.

VBI
Vertical blank interval. The blank lines in television images, invisible to the naked eye. These lines can be used to transmit data to anyone with access to a television set capable of decoding the signal, such as sets with Teletext or types of decoders.

VLSI
Very large scale integration.

VOD
Video on demand.

VR
Virtual reality.

VRML
Virtual Reality Mark-up Language.

W3C
Worldwide Web Consortium. Introduced the Platform for Privacy Preferences (P3P). *See also* P3P.

Web
Slang for the World Wide Web (WWW).

WIPO
World Intellectual Property Organization.

WTO
World Trade Organization (previously General Agreement on Tariffs and Trade, GATT).

WWW
The World Wide Web. A networked system for organizing information on the Internet, which uses hypertext links. *See also* hypertext.

xDMA
Division Multiple Access.

xDSL
Digital Subscriber Loop. A broadband delivery mechanism.

Index

Advertising,
   collaborative, 128
   direct marketing, 127
   interactive, 128
   network marketing, 127
   transforming, 126
Asia,
   India. *See* Developing world
   initiatives in, 22–4
   Japan. *See* Japan

Barriers,
   encryption systems,
      illegality of some, 104
   identification systems, 103
   information,
      intellectual property in, 102
      integrating money and, 102
   money, moving, 102
   regulatory frameworks, 104
   rights, establishing, 103
   transactional systems, 103

Cable companies,
   strength of, 15
Change,
   agents of, 6
   drivers of,
      political, 6
      socio-economic, 6
      technological, 6
   pace of, 1–2
Choice,
   loss of, 105
Computer technology,
   effect of, 3
   intelligent fridges, 7
   network developments, 9
   wearable computers, 7
Content,
   importance of, 50–1
   media, 112
   producers. *See* Publishing
   types of, 51
Convergence,
   meaning of, 46–7
Copyright. *See* Intellectual property
Credit and debit cards, 85–6,
   brokering, 90
   qualifying as merchant for, 87
   smart cards, 87–90
   third-party clearing, 90
Customer,
   ignoring the, 52

Deregulation, 106
Developing world,
 computing in, 24–5
 provision for, 25
Digital nervous system, 9
Digital television,
 BBC and, 125
 growth of, 16, 123–6

E-commerce,
 defining, 74–5
 future of, 93–4
 money, moving, 102
 predictions for, 72–3
 security, lack of, 86
 transactional systems for, 84
  costs of, 86
  credit and debit cards, 85–6, 87
  emerging, 84
  existing, 84
  financial transactions, 86
  subscription and licensing, 85
  time-consuming, 87
 value of, 75–6
Electronic cash, 90–1
Electronic cheques, 91
Electronic data interchange, 92–3
Encryption,
 role of, 79–80
 software for, 82
 standards for, 80–2
  DES, 81
  IDEA, 82
  RSA, 81
 systems, illegality of some, 104
European Union,
 Bangemann Report, 170–9
 European Information Society, 18
 five priorities of, 21

Film and television industry, 113
Financial transactions. *See* E-commerce
Future,
 commercial vision, 5
 corporate vision, 8
 developments, predicting, 107–8
 political vision of, 4
 social vision of, 5
 visions of,
  importance of, 6
  need for, 9

Global Information Infrastructure, 11
 agenda for co-operation, 21
 architectures of, 12
 economic impact of, 25–6
 five principles of, 20–21
 progress towards, 37–8
 rise of, 17
Global Information Market,
 growth of, stages in the, 44–5
Global Information Society,
 emergence of, 3–6
 information city states and, 168–9
 perceptions of, 11
 political visions of, 7
 social reform and, 138
 society, impact on, 169
Government,
 rationalization in, 139
 reinventing, 139–41
Guru,
 definition of, 8
 hype of, 8
 nature of, 10

Human capital, 97–9

ICT initiatives in education, 145–9
 See also Life-long learning
Identification systems, 103

Individual,
  control and, 158
  digital divide, 166–8
  impact on, 155, 157–8
  life-long learning and, 158
  on-line shopping, 156
  teleworking, impact of, 159–64
    cyberspace side-effects, 164–6
    management of, 164
    net addiction, 164
Information,
  access to, loss of, 106–7
  assets, 53–4
  barriers to exploiting,
    intellectual property in, 102
    integrating money and, 102
  economic values of, 55
  encoding and identifiers, 82–3
  formats for disseminating, 114
  knowledge age, towards the, 96–7
  market, efficiency in, 105
  transactions, 76–7
  world market for, 95
Innovation,
  rate of change and, 32–3
Intellectual property, 56–7
  Anglo-American rights, 68–9
  Berne Convention, 61
  collecting societies, role of, 70–1
  copyright,
    administration of, 67–8
    application of, 66
    defining, 64–5
    international environment, in, 60–4
    origin of, 58–60
    perspectives on, 64
    trade mechanism, as, 64
    trading in, 67
  Dutch model, 69
  German–Spanish model, 69
  legislation, proposed, 61–4
  Nordic model, 69–70
  protection, duration of, 63
  Universal Copyright Convention, 61
Intercast,
  birth of, 16
Internet,
  connections, growth in, 15
  history of 12–13
  hosts, 14
  social phenomenon of, 12

Japan,
  OFL-21, 19

Knowledge management, 97–102

Libraries,
  role of, 153–4
Life-long learning, 141–2
  educational content, 144
  grid for learning, 146–7
  individual and, 158
  individual learning accounts, 147
  networks for learning, 142–3
  skills shortage, 144–5
  technology, costs of, 143

Market,
  data on the, interpreting, 41–3
  evolving structure of, 47–8
  layers within the, 47–8
  redefining the, 48–9
  searching for the, 39
  sizing the, 40–1
Media technology,
  types of, 28–9
Money. *See* E-commerce
  See also Credit and debit cards

National borders,
    looking beyond, 2

Organizations,
    adapt, need to, 9
    business models, 110
    challenges, 109–11
    information and communications
        technology, 111
    knowledge management systems, 110

Poverty, 148
Printing press,
    established status of, 30
    invention of, 28
Privacy, infringement of, 106
Public services,
    government,
        rationalization in, 139
        reinventing, 139–41
    libraries, role of, 153–4
    life-long learning, 141–2
        educational content, 144
        educational initiatives, 145–6
        grid for learning, 146–7
        individual learning accounts, 147
        networks for learning, 142–3
        skills shortage, 144–5
        technology, costs of, 143
    poverty, 148
    public-private sector partnerships,
        149–54
        educational publishing, 150
        roles and responsibilities, 152
        World Learning Network, 151–2
    World Links for Development
        programme, 148–9
Publishers,
    bulk products, future of, 118–21
    challenges for, 115–18
    convergence, understanding, 116

    copyrights, exploiting, 115
    customers, treatment of, 116
    digital technology, impact of, 118
    hybrid products, 119, 120
    information technology, impact
        of, 114
    intellectual property rights,
        managing, 122
    mixed media environment, in, 112
    personalized newspapers, 120
    product portfolios, 120

Regulatory frameworks, 105

Satellite broadcasting,
    emergence of, 16
Security,
    challenge of, 78–9
    encryption. *See* Encryption
    identification systems, 103
    lack of, 106
Software,
    sales of, 76
    worldwide market for, 35

Technologies,
    convergence between, 34
    killer application, quest for, 35
    investment in,
        managing, 36
        timing of, 37
Telecommunications industry
    cable. *See* Cable companies
    position of, 14
    satellite. *See* Satellite broadcasting
    voice services, reduction in, 15
    work of, 13
Telegraph,
    invention of, 27
    Victorian Internet, impact of, 28
Teleworking, impact of, 159–64

cyberspace side-effects, 164–6
  management of, 164
  net addiction, 164
Transactional systems, 84, 103
  costs of, 87
  credit and debit cards, 85–6, 87
  emerging, 84
  existing, 84
  financial transactions, 86
  subscription and licensing, 85
  time-consuming, 87

United States,
  information infrastructure task
      force, 19
    committees of, 19–20
  International Telecommunications
      Union,
    Conference, address to, 192–201

Vice President Al Gore's
    address to, 180–91
  national information infrastructure, 18
  trading advantage of, 34

Value creation, 129–37
  communities of interest, 134–6
    clusters of, 135
  Internet portals, 134–5
  strategic alliances, 136–7

World,
  shrinking, 1

World Wide Web,
  growth of, 13

Writing,
  impact of, 31

Also by Anne Leer

Masters of the Wired World

Provocative and prescient, illuminating and agenda-setting: today's masters of our wired world speak about their visions of work and life in our digital age.

ISBN: 0273 63559 X

ft.com - books for the future minded

The revolution has happened, no one has died, there have been no barricades, but clearly it has happened. Driven by technology business has been freed. No longer tied by the old ways, the forces of imagination have driven a massive transformation in the way we do business at every level; overturning the way we work and the way we manage.

For just abut every discipline in business – from marketing to motivation – this is ground zero.

ft.com

ft.com titles include:

Funky Business

Generation Entrepreneur

Net-Trading — Alpesh Patel

Trading on Line — Alpesh Patel

for more information contact your local bookseller.